T0174704

Online@AsiaPacific

Media across the Asia-Pacific region are at once mobile, social and locative. Mobile in that the media is ever-present, social in that these media facilitate public and interpersonal interaction and locative in that this social communication is geographically placed. The Asia-Pacific region has been pivotal in the production, shaping and consumption of personal new media technologies, and through mobile and social media we can see emerging certain types of personal politics that are inflected by the local.

The six case studies that inform this book – Seoul, Tokyo, Shanghai, Manila, Singapore and Melbourne – offer a range of economic, socio-cultural and linguistic differences, enabling the authors to provide new insights into specific issues pertaining to mobile media in each city. These include mobile, social and locative media as a form of crisis management in post-3/11 Tokyo; generational shifts in Shanghai; political discussion and the shifting social fabric in Singapore; and the erosion of public and private, and work and leisure paradigms in Melbourne. Through its striking case studies, this book sheds new light on how the region and its contested and multiple identities are evolving, and concludes by revealing the impact of mobile media on how place is shaped, as well as shaping, practices of mobility, intimacy and a sense of belonging.

Employing comprehensive, cross-disciplinary frameworks from theoretical approaches such as media sociology, ethnography, cultural studies, and media and communication studies, *Online@AsiaPacific* will be of great interest to students and scholars of Asian culture and society, cybercultures, new media studies, communication studies and internet studies.

Larissa Hjorth is Associate Professor in Games at RMIT University, Australia.

Michael Arnold is Senior Lecturer at the University of Melbourne, Australia.

Asia's Transformations

Edited by Mark Selden, Cornell University, USA

The books in this series explore the political, social, economic and cultural consequences of Asia's transformations in the twentieth and twenty-first centuries. The series emphasizes the tumultuous interplay of local, national, regional and global forces as Asia bids to become the hub of the world economy. While focusing on the contemporary, it also looks back to analyse the antecedents of Asia's contested rise.

This series comprises several strands:

Asia's Transformations

Titles include:

Asia's Great Cities

Each volume aims to capture the heartbeat of the contemporary city from multiple perspectives emblematic of the authors' own deep familiarity with the distinctive faces of the city, its history, society, culture, politics and economics, and its evolving position in national, regional and global frameworks. While most volumes emphasize urban developments since the Second World War, some pay close attention to the legacy of the longue durée in shaping the contemporary. Thematic and comparative volumes address such themes as urbanization, economic and financial linkages, architecture and space, wealth and power, gendered relationships, planning and anarchy, and ethnographies in national and regional perspective. Titles include:

1 **Bangkok***
   Place, practice and representation
   Marc Askew

2 **Representing Calcutta***
   Modernity, nationalism and the
   colonial uncanny
   Swati Chattopadhyay

3 **Singapore***
   Wealth, power and the culture
   of control
   Carl A. Trocki

4 **The City in South Asia**
   James Heitzman

5 **Global Shanghai, 1850–2010***
   A history in fragments
   Jeffrey N. Wasserstrom

6 **Hong Kong***
   Becoming a global city
   Stephen Chiu and Tai-Lok Lui

Asia.com is a series which focuses on the ways in which new information and communication technologies are influencing politics, society and culture in Asia. Titles include:

1 **Japanese Cybercultures***
   Edited by Mark McLelland and
   Nanette Gottlieb

2 **Asia.com***
   Asia encounters the Internet
   Edited by K. C. Ho, Randolph
   Kluver and Kenneth C. C. Yang

3 **The Internet in Indonesia's**
   New Democracy*
   David T. Hill and Krishna Sen

4 **Chinese Cyberspaces***
   Technological changes and
   political effects
   Edited by Jens Damm and
   Simona Thomas

5 **Mobile Media in the Asia-Pacific**
   Gender and the art of being
   mobile
   Larissa Hjorth

6 **Online@AsiaPacific**
   Mobile, social and locative
   media in the Asia-Pacific
   Larissa Hjorth and
   Michael Arnold

Literature and Society

Literature and Society is a series that seeks to demonstrate the ways in which Asian literature is influenced by the politics, society and culture in which it is produced. Titles include:

Routledge Studies in Asia's Transformations

Routledge Studies in Asia's Transformations is a forum for innovative new research intended for a high-level specialist readership.

Titles include:

Critical Asian Scholarship

Critical Asian Scholarship is a series intended to showcase the most important individual contributions to scholarship in Asian Studies. Each of the volumes presents a leading Asian scholar addressing themes that are central to his or her most significant and lasting contribution to Asian studies. The series is committed to the rich variety of research and writing on Asia, and is not restricted to any particular discipline, theoretical approach or geographical expertise.

* Available in paperback

Online@AsiaPacific

Mobile, social and locative media
in the Asia-Pacific

**Larissa Hjorth and
Michael Arnold**

LONDON AND NEW YORK

First published 2013
by Routledge
2 Park Square, Milton Park, Abingdon, Oxon OX14 4RN

Simultaneously published in the USA and Canada
by Routledge
711 Third Avenue, New York, NY 10017

Routledge is an imprint of the Taylor & Francis Group, an informa business

British Library Cataloguing in Publication Data
A catalogue record for this book is available from the British Library

Library of Congress Cataloging in Publication Data
Hjorth, Larissa.
Online@AsiaPacific : mobile, social and locative media in the Asia-Pacific /
[Larissa Hjorth and Michael Arnold].
    p. cm. – (Asia.com ; 7)
  Includes bibliographical references and index.
  1. Social media–Asia–Case studies. 2. Social media–Pacific Area–Case
studies. 3. Smartphones–Asia–Case studies. 4. Smartphones–Pacific Area–
Case studies. I. Arnold, Michael, 1952- II. Title. III. Title:
Online@AsiaPacific. IV. Title: Online at Asia Pacific. V. Series: Asia.com ;
7.
  HM851.H59 2013
  302.23'1–dc23
                        2012034590

ISBN: 978-0-415-67216-0 (hbk)
ISBN: 978-0-203-58433-0 (ebk)

Typeset in Times New Roman
by Taylor & Francis Books

Contents

Figures

Acknowledgements

First, the authors would like to thank the Australian Research Council for the Discovery and APD fellowship (DP0986998), entitled *Online@AsiaPacific*, that allowed this study to be fully realised.

We would also like to thank series editor Mark Selden for his help and wisdom in the conception of this book. Also, we would like to thank Stephanie Rogers, Ed Needle and Hannah Mack at Routledge for their help throughout the publication process.

Second, we would like to thank the wonderful community of researchers who are exploring social and mobile media for all your insights and general inspiration. We would also like to acknowledge the support of RMIT University and the University of Melbourne. We would like to thank the research assistant in each location who helped with recruitment, humour and general fieldwork logistics: Shobha Vadrevu, Susan Jo, Ng Li Ting, Yuewen Chu, Bora Na, Jungyoun Moon, 'Yonnie' Kyoung-Hwa Kim and Airah Cadiogan.

Larissa would like to thank her family (special thanks to Mum) and friends, and dedicates this book to her son, Jesper, and brother, Greg.

Michael would particularly like to thank Tess and Andrew for putting up with him during much of the drafting.

All names used in examples are pseudonyms.

Abbreviations

apps	applications
GPS	Global Positioning System
IM	instant message/messaging/messenger
LBS	location-based services
MMS	multimedia messaging service
PC	personal computer
SMS	short message service
SNS	social network site/s
UCC	user-created content
UGC	user-generated content

1   Introduction

Mobile, social and locative media @ Asia-Pacific

Sitting in a Shinchon café in the busy neighbourhood of Seoul, Hyunjin uses her iPhone to log onto the Korean social network site (SNS) Cyworld mini-hompy while waiting for her friend, Soohyun. Remembering that Soohyun now prefers Facebook, she quickly migrates there to see that Soohyun, according to Facebook Places, has just arrived at Shinchon station. Hyunjin quickly takes a camera phone picture of her coffee and uploads it onto Facebook with the title 'waiting'. The next minute, a laughing Soohyun is in front of Hyunjin holding her phone with Facebook open on it, showing the reply 'Not anymore'.

Meanwhile, in Tokyo, Machiko is reading a *keitai shōsetsu* (mobile novel) as she rides the train from work. She is happy to see that her favourite author has released a new novel. She wants to share the excitement and quickly sends the link to her best friend, Mariko, using the Japanese SNS, Mixi. Mariko immediately replies with a smiley face and both girls read the story simultaneously while occupying two different spaces. In an ambiguity common to mobile, social and locative media, they are both together and apart. Alternatively, in post-3/11 Japan, young adult Toshi has taken to using the locative media game *Foursquare* so that he and his friends might always know where each other are.

In Manila, José misses his cousin Xavier, who has just moved to Hong Kong with a scholarship to study at the City University. On his PC he sees that Xavier has just changed his relationship status on Facebook to 'it's complicated'. Burning with curiosity, José pokes Xavier who then appears online and the boys immediately start to instant message (IM) about Xavier's new (imaginary or real) girlfriend.

Over in Shanghai, Jia misses her daughter, Yuewen, who has just moved away for university work placement. Before she left, Yuewen thoughtfully installed the most up-to-date software on her mum's 'pirate' smartphone (*shanzhai*) – that is, a less expensive, unlicensed copy of a branded smartphone. As instructed by her mum, Yuewen registered her for all the most popular games, especially social media games like the farm simulation *Happy Farm* – for even though the game had its hey-day in 2009, it is still played by millions. Each day Jia logs onto China's version of Facebook, Renren, and signs onto *Happy Farm*. Seeing that Yuewen is not online protecting her crops, Jia uses the most popular IM, QQ, to send a message to Yuewen to see if she has time for a quick play in *Happy Farm*. Yuewen is typical of China's Generation Y (*ba ling hou*) in that location-based service (LBS) mobile games like *Jiepang*, along with microblog Weibo, are her favourite media. However, reading her mum's message she quickly signed into *Happy Farm* to catch up on gossip with her mum.

Sitting in Starbucks in Singapore, Jenny is looking at Facebook on her Samsung Galaxy when she comes across an unflattering picture of herself taken at a party on Saturday. She then takes a moment to look at her reflection in her Galaxy tablet and puffs up her hair. Jenny then holds the tablet above her head, a known strategy for making 'flattering' pictures, puckers up her lips and takes a picture. Happy with the image she then uploads to it to Facebook making it her new profile picture.

These are but a few of the millions of intimate vignettes deploying media across the Asia-Pacific region that are at once mobile, social and locative – mobile in so much as the media is ever-present, social in that these media facilitate public and interpersonal interaction and locative in that this social communication is geographically placed. With the uneven but increasing rise of smartphones across the region, mobile media are increasingly becoming sites for growing social media use through SNS like Facebook and locative services like Google Maps and *Foursquare*. In this phenomenon, what constitutes the mobile, social and locative are determined by the local as multiple modes of presence (net-presence, co-presence, tele-presence) move across platforms, contexts and media. Across numerous technical platforms, personal and cultural contexts, and through a wide variety of social media, people young and old are using mobile, social and locative media to rehearse earlier forms of ritual and, at the same time, create new forms of intimacy and different contexts for the expression of sociality. Regional cities such as Seoul and Tokyo have long been centres of innovation in the invention and popularisation of mobile media – the transistor radio of the 1960s and the Walkman of the 1980s being early examples. In these locations, the relationship between personal, mobile, social and locative media is quotidian and, for the most part, tacit in its familiarity. In other locations like Australia, China or India, convergence through smartphones is more novel. Mobile social media are a global phenomenon, but they are also local at every point.

While our work has been located in the Asia-Pacific, much of the Anglophone literature on SNS to date has focused upon its use by young people in Western contexts (boyd and Ellison 2008; McLelland and Goggin 2009). As SNS are becoming globally quotidian sites for emerging forms of familial interaction, socialising, relationship management and identity construction (Bennett 2008; Bennett et al. 2009; Ito et al. 2008; Madianou and Miller 2012; Rheingold 2008), we need to attend to difference as well as commonality and, in particular, to the difference that place makes. We must then, in turn, pay attention to the way in which place, as one of the most contested notions in this field (Wilken and Goggin 2012a), is being redefined by the multiple and micro politics of presence and co-presence afforded by social and mobile media.

With the Arab Spring uprisings in the Middle East, we have seen ways in which social and mobile media can be used to help mobilise new forms of politics at the same time as amplifying paradoxes around media effects and affects. For example, the control/freedom paradox of the online that has been addressed by Wendy Chun (2006) can be seen in the recent 'liberation technology' (Christensen 2011; Diamond and Plattner 2012) rhetoric of the Arab Spring in which media can both be a site for emancipation (in the case of Egypt and Tunisia) and the reinforcement of the authoritarian state (Iran). This paradoxical dynamic around the role of new media and emerging forms of politics is most evident in the 'ambivalent' and yet 'situated' context of the Asia-Pacific. From demonstrations against the government in post-3/11 Japan, to the political deployment of Facebook in Singapore, to the use of locative media for corporate surveillance in South Korea (Lee 2011), we are seeing social and mobile media being utilised to both reinforce older forms of politics while also creating more intimate and micro politics. While older forms of demonstration have attracted focus through the use of social and mobile media, it is the social, the private, the intimate that we seek to explore in *Online@AsiaPacific*. We argue that in the ambivalent but situated (Wilson and Dirlik 1995) context of the Asia-Pacific region we can find various micro and intimate social and political formations that are played out through social mobile media practices. Specifically, we reflect upon how mobile media practices are affording new types of personal and political performativity, as well as how they amplify existing social and political nuances. We see these emergent practices as best understood through the collisions between intimate, mobile and social publics.

In particular, we differentiate 'intimate publics' (that are tightly bound and share common emotional ground), from 'social publics' (that also share emotional affinities but are broader and less tightly bound by those affinities), and 'social networks' (that are not constituted in common affect but are instrumentally related in interconnected and ramified ego-based formations). By deploying the notion of intimate publics and social publics as distinct from social networks, we argue that performances of affective interpersonal intimacy reflect an emerging approach to identity and collectivity, and the management of the social labour required to engage with others in this new public sphere.

In all of the examples we explore throughout the book, we see a variety of socialities, mobilities and immobilities across technological, geographic and psychological spaces. Each vignette highlights the importance that place – both lived and imagined – takes in informing mobile media practices. In each scenario we see that media that are at once mobile, social and locative are mediating a different experience of each of these phenomena, as well as producing a new meaning of what it is to be intimate.

Accordingly, we argue that these mobile media practices are defined first by their relationship to, and redefinition of, sociality, intimacy and place. In these practices, that entail various and sometimes conflicting forms of presence, (co, tele, net), we find an array of engagements and distractions that are shaped by the social, the mobile and the intimate in relation to place. Drawing on our own empirical work and calling on the work of Lauren Berlant (1998), danah boyd (2010), Anne Galloway (2010), Mimi Sheller (2004), Michael Warner (2002) and others, we see that being social, being intimate and being public are not straightforward, mutually exclusive social binaries, and we see that being mobile and being in a place can be complementary. This requires us to revisit definitions of sociality, intimacy, mobility and public in relation to place, context and presence. This phenomenon suggests a need for conceptualising emergent and minute forms of politics through mobile, social and locative media as being anything but trivial.

While social media might in a sense encourage collapsing contexts (boyd 2010) and presence bleed (Gregg 2011), mobile media also amplifies the various dimensions of place as lived and imagined, as geographic, social and psychological (Hjorth 2005; Ito 2002). Increasingly, mobile media highlight the multiple forms of presence that form, inform and transform places into a series of entanglements (Ingold 2008). The 'collapsed context' – in the sense of a novel combination of publics – is situated in any particular example of mobile social media use. *It is its own context*, and in that sense its own space, inward facing and constituted by the actions of the occupants of the space, and, at the same time, outwardly linked in its connection to other contexts – through media and through culture. In being so connected, presence does 'bleed' from one context to another – but is this not always the case? What presence in context is hermetically sealed? In this temporal-spatial 'piano accordion dynamic', place, mobility, publics and intimates become new sites for different social performances and provide new resources for different social performances in the Asia-Pacific region. These performances hinge upon the emotional and social labour required to make social connection with people, to generate and distribute user-created content (UCC) and all of the attendant 'vernacular creativity' (Burgess 2008) that goes into these emergent forms of immaterial labour. From *keitai shōsetsu* and camera phone images to 'check ins' and 'pokes', mobile media is providing new ways to make and share various forms of sociality.

However, in an age of data-mining and ever more sophisticated methods of deriving surplus value from immaterial labour, the cartographies of personalisation can take a darker, more exploitative route, and the 'technological sublime' (Nye 1994) continues to elude us. As Mark Andrejevic (2011) has eloquently argued (drawing on the work by Tiziana Terranova 2000), the 'social factory' of capitalism renders users' expressions and gestures into a series of profiles that are then sold to marketers. It has become commonplace for companies to use cookies in order to pass on all information gathered about users to advertisers.

For critics such as philosopher Edward Casey (2012), psychologist and sociologist Sherry Turkle (2011), and media theorist and activist Geert Lovink (2012), social media have flattened the rich tapestry of the social into a mere media activity. Lovink, for example, pleads for a more historically and politically nuanced notion of the social whereby social media are channelled for 'cause' (2012). As Lovink notes, 'the networks without cause are time eaters, and we're only being sucked deeper into the social cave without knowing what to look for' (2012: 6). Lovink, Andrejevic, Terranova, Turkle and many other critical commentators are not impressed by the flickering shadows on the analogical cave wall and are searching for non-trivial causes for social networks. In the case of the Asia-Pacific, we see emergent forms of social and political causes around mobile media that both define the social and political as they do the media. Specifically, this takes the forms of intimate, mobile and social publics.

Understanding the emergent mobile, social and locative media convergence requires us to move beyond binaries and paradoxes such as empowerment versus exploitation, control versus freedom, place and no-place, liberation and authoritarian, intimate and public, and instead to focus upon localised notions of intimacy and place situated in contexts that include mobile social media as 'social actors' (Latour 2005).

Studies of new media owe a great debt to studies of technology more generally, which in turn are indebted to studies of science. To reach back and draw upon science studies we see that modernity's epistemological project of 'purification' has always involved the production of 'hybrids' (Latour 1993). Purification attempted to separate people from things, nature from society, facts from politics, culture from science, and so on, but it is through this effort rather than despite it that hybrids proliferate. Throughout this work we acknowledge the futility of purification and accept the hybridity of our analytic constructs. As Ingrid Richardson puts it ' … it is obvious, therefore, that in the teleculture of the twenty-first century, it is no longer possible to consider space in terms of dichotomized categories of here/there, near/far, personal/private, inner/outer or presence/absence' (2011: 41). In this model, intimacy is not 'pure' but is conceptualised as something that has always been mediated – if not by media technologies then by language, personal objects, gestures, memories and place.

In a similar vein we argue that the politics of social media is not 'pure' either – that is, 'politics' is not a distinct category of activity that one takes up in particular times and particular places but, rather, is a particular sensibility or a perspective that one might bring to bear on all aspects of daily life. In this sense all of our social performances, our subjectivities and inter-subjectivities, our public lives and our private lives are political. In the same way, our politics are also social, and personal, and public, and private. Politics is thus played out in important ways around the kitchen table and through routine SNS use as well as in the streets and through the ballot box. Now, this claim for what might be called 'the politics of the prosaic' is not radical, and it has been made many times before, but is often missing from recent public and academic commentary on the contemporary political role of social media (Colman 2010).

A key factor in this has been the focus on the use of social media in political activity that is anything but prosaic (Christensen 2011; Diamond and

Plattner 2012). In recent years, revolutionary movements in Libya, Tunisia, Egypt, Yemen, Morocco, Syria, Bahrain, and other countries in North Africa and the Middle East, have attempted (and in several cases succeeded) in nothing less than the overthrow of the state (Segerberg and Lance Bennett 2011). In the same time period, the 'Occupy' movement has been a local and international political phenomenon, first in North America, but then, according to Wikipedia, has spread across some 95 cities in 82 countries. This is clearly politics on a grand scale, and for those with an interest in the political implications and the political potential of social media, this was clearly the place to be looking. However, even here, where the stated objectives are as far-reaching as the overthrow of dictatorship and reformation of capitalism, the political is also personal. To the extent that the social media used by the Arab Spring and Occupy movements were effective in mobilising, coordinating, motivating and informing people, they were effective because they were personal, prosaic, inter-subjective and everyday. They were effective – that is, efficient, fast, cheap, and easily configured and reconfigured for various purposes, but they were also *affective* – that is, their functionality was structured on what we call social and intimate publics, and had the credibility derived from the social capital accumulated by those publics.

In *Online@AsiaPacific* we do not focus on the politics of social media through these grand movements, but we do attend to the politics of social media in everyday life. We do so because the politics of family life that is split between Manila and Singapore is important in its own right (Chapters 5, 6), because the multifarious mobility of a new Chinese generation is important in its own right (Chapter 4), because the regulation of social media in Seoul is important in its own right (Chapter 2), because the trend towards 'power-blogging' and the alternative it poses to party-political blogging is important in its own right (Chapter 11), and because the personal responses to the Fukushima disaster are important in their own right (Chapter 3). Of course, in all of this, everyday life is as political as it is personal, private, subjective and intersubjective. There is no purity here; grand politics is built on the everyday, and the everyday is grand politics, and where these and many other hybrids proliferate, we need nuanced studies of places where the 'interior is the new exterior' (Sukhder Sandhi cited in Margaroni and Yiannopoulou 2005: 222), studies of public-intimacy, present-absences, personal-politics and all manner of other 'monsters' (Law 1991). In order to understand the complex, political, social, cultural, technical and above all dynamic nature of mobile social media in the Asia-Pacific, we suggest two key concepts: mobile intimacy and intimate (and social) publics.

Mobile intimacy

One way to understand the tensions around salient and transitory modes of intimacy is in terms of 'mobile intimacy'. By 'mobile', we are not only referring to technologies that move with us and enable us to move, but also the various ways in which non-geographic mobilities play out through mobile media practices. In considering the forms mobility takes beyond mobility in geographic space we might first do well to remember that as a notion, mobility qua 'being moved' has long been attached to emotion (Lasén 2004), particularly labile or volatile emotion, but also its more sanguine forms. Second, mobility is also closely connected to the properties of fluidity, and we argue that fluidity (and its close cousin, instability) is important in understanding the structural conditions of mobile intimacy. Fluids have moving surfaces (inner and outer), moving boundaries (private and public), often caused by moving currents (flows of communication). In addition to these two spatial referents of the trope, mobility may also be put in a temporal context, in which case it refers to transience, time-shifting, speed and moving in time. We argue in forthcoming chapters that all these forms of mobility bear upon our experience of intimacy and our understanding of intimacy in conditions of mobile intimacy.

In regard to the various forms of large-scale global mobility that characterise our era – mobile people, mobile ideas, mobile resources, mobile markets, mobile labour and mobile capital – the computer and the internet are clearly implicated (Castells 1996). In regard to various forms of smaller-scale mobility – the daily mobility of family members, the mobility of a given work force, the mobility of our personal arrangements in time and place, the mobile phone, the smartphone and their various social applications are also implicated. As technologies of propinquity (temporal and spatial proximity), they are both instrumental in, and symbolic of, new erosions of the boundary between family and profession, public and private, work and leisure (Wajcman et al. 2009). While the movement of intimacy towards the public was happening long before social and mobile media (Berlant 1998), the ways of mapping mobile, social and locative media require explanation.

The widespread appropriation of LBS and Global Positioning System (GPS) as part of the everyday mobile media experience has shifted the manner in which we imagine and navigate the online in conjunction with physical spaces. One way of conceptualising this straddling between co-present worlds is identifying the localised and vernacular versions of intimate publics in an age of mobile intimacy: that is, the ways in which *intimacy* and our various forms of *mobility* (across technological, geographic, psychological, physical and temporal differences) infuse public and private spaces through mobile media's simultaneous mediation of both intimacy and space. Personal mobile media present us with boundaries between online and offline worlds, public and private spaces, an inner life and a social performance, and at the same time enable us to skip back and forth across those boundaries at will. This sociotechnical configuration has constructed a hybrid in which our geographic position and our location in place are overlaid with an electronic position. This technology can both draw attention to position and place (through LBS for example), and can elide position and place (through communications at a distance). At the same time relational presence is achieved, which is both emotional and social. *This overlaying of the material-geographic and electronic-social sets the conditions for what we call mobile intimacy.*

Not that this phenomenon is entirely new. A case could be made to use the historical continuity and discontinuity of mobile intimacy as a rubric for understanding and marking particular epochs as the overlay between mobility and intimacy changes forms, contexts, platforms and affects. As Timo Kopomaa (2000) observes, today's personalised mobile media can be seen as an extension of nineteenth- and twentieth-century mobile media such as the pocket watch and the wristwatch, which both personalised and mobilised time-telling. Similarly, technologies such as mobile media reconstruct earlier co-present practices and interstitials of intimacy: for example, the metaphor of 'posting' SMS (short message service) both reflects and subverts earlier epistolary traditions like nineteenth-century letter writing (Hjorth 2005). As Esther Milne (2004) observes, new forms of telepresence such as email are linked into earlier practices of intimacy through presence-in-absence achieved via media such as visiting cards. In this way, the intimate presence-in-absence and co-presence enacted by mobile technologies should be viewed as part of a lineage of technologies of propinquity. However, there are some striking differences too. Mobile media can been considered as a part of shifts in conceptualising and practising intimacy from no longer being a 'private' activity but instead being a pivotal component of public sphere performativity. Intimacy has taken on new geo-imaginaries, most notably as a kind of 'publicness' that is epitomised by the mobile phone (Fortunati 2002: 48).

The development and local deployment of mobile and social media has been accompanied by, and is contingent on, the rise of UCC and UGC (user-generated content). One way of understanding the mobile media phenomenon is through the difference between UCC and UGC and their attendant forms of immaterial labour – creative, affective, emotional and social. While the former denotes the user's agency in the creation process – that is, the user becomes a producer, or 'produser' (Bruns 2005) – the latter is marked by the user's role in connecting up the circulation process. In short, UCC is *made* by the user, while UGC is *circulated* by the user. UCC and UGC are linked to notions of the personal – especially through the selection of content, but also through the further amplification of the user's context, subjectivities and locality through personal technologies such as social and mobile media.

The Asia-Pacific region has been pivotal in the production, shaping and consumption of personal new media technologies (Hjorth 2009a; ILO 2008), and through social and mobile media we can see emerging certain types of personal politics that are inflected by the local. In Manila, Seoul, Shanghai, Tokyo and Melbourne, the practices of personalisation differ, highlighting the growing importance of place in shaping networked and mobile media. Through these personalisation practices we can gain a sense of how users and their communities are engaging in emerging forms of intimacy, and also creativity, literacy and politics. In each location, what constitutes UCC differs. In Manila, Seoul, Shanghai, Tokyo and Melbourne, UCC reflects and enhances the vernacular (Burgess 2008). Factors such as techno-cultural infrastructure, governmental media literacy programmes, politics and socio-cultural conditions play a key role in determining the types of UCC. As Gibson et al. observe:

> physical geography is an active agent in the 'new' landscapes made possible by mobiles – just as it was in earlier attempts to build railways or telegraphs across continents. In terms of physical infrastructure, the experience of Internet and phone service varies greatly across space.
>
> (2012: 125)

UCC reflects place as well as geography, and shows how place has multiple and ever-changing emotional, social, political and psychological dimensions that are both lived and imagined. Place is inflected by a sense of locality (Massey 1993a, 1993b) such as that offered by a community. It is both intimate and public in that it can be both social and mobile.

Intimate publics and social publics

Although there have been attempts to totalise intimacy through a retreat to biological drives (e.g. Fisher 2004) or through the determinism of evolutionary psychology (e.g. Buss 1994), it seems clear that our experience of intimacy as a lived existential reality, and the way we conceive of intimacy and define it as an abstraction, have changed markedly through time and place. Intimacy is not a fixed state, but is both fluid and contingent on circumstances – personal, historic, cultural and sociotechnical (Jamieson 1999; Sexton and Sexton 1982). We argue in this book that among these circumstances are recent sociotechnical changes associated with the rise of social media and 'affective' technologies such as mobile phones, providing yet another of the many contingencies that shape the conception and performance of intimacy.

Past changes in sociotechnologies have had profound influences on intimacy, just as intimacy has motivated profound developments in socio-technologies. Changes in Western home architecture for example, has for centuries materialised in bricks and wood different concepts of what a family is and what a family does, what privacy is and what intimacy is, and in turn, these bricks shaped the performance of family life, privacy and intimacy over centuries (Rybczynski 1986; Sexton and Sexton 1982). Changes in socio-technologies deployed for contraception and, more recently, for conception, have obvious implications for the expression of intimacy and the role intimacy itself plays in constituting relationships, as opposed to economics, or family politics for example (Giddens 1992). Communication is clearly relevant to a consideration of intimacy and of the hundreds of definitions of intimacy, most include reference to the significance of communication – definitional formulations such as *the reciprocal exchange of privileged information, reciprocal self-disclosure*, or *a privileged perspective on another's depth and on another's wholeness* being typical of many (see, for example, Jamieson 1999).

Given the central place of interpersonal communication in our understanding and experience of intimacy, it is clear that any technologies we might use to mediate interpersonal communication warrant a consideration of their implications for intimacy. If we laid this out in a longitudinal fashion we could say that communicative sociotechnologies shape communication which in turn shapes intimacy, which shapes the appropriation and deployment of communicative technologies, which shapes communication, and so on and on. Alternatively, we might construct a vertical model and say that communicative technology overlay communications, which, in turn, overlay the experience and concept of intimacy. And yet again, we might say that our communications technologies, our interpersonal communication, and our concept and performance of intimacy come together in daily life in a performance that hybridises technology, communication and intimacy.

One of the key properties of this hybrid is its position in relation to privacy and publicness. Whereas the etymological roots of 'intimacy' – from the Latin *intimus*, innermost, inward – might imply privacy as a pre-condition, we argue that intimacy's fluidity enables it to flourish in conditions where the private–public binary has not been purified, but is messy, breached, porous and shifting. And perhaps this is not so new either. The purity of intimacy as strictly personal and interpersonal, private and not public, emotional and not strategic, has long been sullied by the establishment of home, family, marriage and all the other institutionalised relationships that are at once private in the relation, and public in the institutionalisation of the relation.

Writing before the onset of social media, Berlant (1998: 281) observed that intimacy has taken on new geographies and forms of mobility, most notably as a kind of 'publicness'. Social media constitutes a new sociotechnical instantiation of public intimacy. Indeed, as intimacy is negotiated within networked social media, the publicness – along with the continuous, multitasking full-timeness – becomes increasingly palpable. Intimate relations are not simply performed both in pairs and in the self-defined and bounded groups we call 'intimate publics', they are also performed in geographic public but electronic privacy, and in electronic public but geographic private. The moves across the boundaries of the interpersonal-group, geographic public–private, and electronic public–private are quick and frequent. The very existence of a boundary to move across is also compromised, as within the same social performance we attend to, as we traverse the interpersonal and the group, the geographic public and our private interlocutor (who might be here, or at a distance), and/or our electronic public and private interlocutor (who also might be here, or at a distance).

Intimate publics and their deployment of media that are at once personal, mobile and social, are thus situating intimacy in a fluid interpersonal and conceptual space in which binaries and boundaries are problematic. As mobile, social and locative media become more pervasive, different modes of using these media mean that increasingly publics are defined by *intimate*, rather than *networked*, relationships. Describing these relationships and tracing the contours of these faint and shifting boundaries is of course one of the tasks of this book.

And just as intimacy can no longer rely on pure binaries to underpin it, so too the notion of the 'public' – and its foundational binaries – become subject to the same fluidity, the same hybridity. As referenced in the above discussion of intimacy, the notion of mutually exclusive private spaces and public spaces is problematised by sociotechnologies that enable public interaction from a position of privacy; private interaction from a public position; to switch rapidly between the two, and to conduct both private and public interactions in the same performance. As Sheller puts it, 'there are new modes of public-in-private and private-in-public that disrupt commonly held spatial models of these as two separate "spheres"' (2004: 39). Social media also offer affordances for how they facilitate the construction of multiple publics, and multiple modes of addressing those publics and their members, either as a group sharing personal intimacies, or as interpersonal dyads, or in a mode in which we alternate between group and dyad in the same performance. This too is a phenomenon that pre-dates mobile social media (see Goffman 1969 on everyday performativity), but is materialised in different ways as it is mediated electronically. Through social media, multiple publics are formed around multiple personas, sometimes constructed by the same person, and the membership of these publics shifts and overlaps.

Unstable and fluid though it is, there are, however, some more stable properties of the concept of 'public' that allow for a social formation in the performance of intimacy. First, a public is a group, and as such it situates us as members of a collective, not as individuals. The common ground shared by the collective – the sense of collective self that derives from intersubjective interests, the interpersonal exchanges and an investment in the history and the future of these interests and exchanges – is important in relation to intimacy. Second, publics are self-formed entities emergent in the actions of their members, and the volunteerism and agency implicit in this is important for the construction and expression of intimacy, as is the capacity to rapidly gel together and just as rapidly dissolve. Third, publics are bounded, albeit with boundaries that are fluid and permeable, but nonetheless enable each public to draw together and, at the same time, stand in relation to individuals and other publics. A public's boundary is in this way similar to a horizon, what Jeff Malpas calls 'the marker of an internal unity that is also outwardly integrated' (2012: 33).

Important too is that a public lacks institutional being (Warner 2002: 61): that is, like a community, it is not an arm of the state, but stands between individuals and the state. These properties of collectivity, self-formation, boundedness and non-institutionality give publics the prerequisites for political agency that Habermas sees as important in a public but lacking in an 'audience'. These 'mobile publics' (Galloway 2010: 69), like intimate publics, afford a space for political play. This political play is often characterised by the intimate, fleeting and micro gestures within social and mobile media.

We recognise, though, that not all publics that gel around an emotional affinity via social media can be described as intimate. The coming together of loosely defined friends and acquaintances forms a public that shares collective ground, is self-forming, shares a horizon and is not institutionalised, and it does this through a shared social affect. However the nature of this affect is not strong enough nor tightly bound enough to warrant the term 'intimate'. They are, after all, just friends. It is however a 'social public' in so much as the common ground, the motivating dynamic for a coming-together, is a collective emotional or affective horizon, albeit more loosely defined and more fluid than is the case with an intimate public.

These characteristics are, we think, significantly different from the characteristics of a 'network', a model which privileges ramified dyadic relationships, and fails to signify collectivity, emotional affect and a shared horizon. By emphasising hybrids of sociality, intimacy, mobility and publics rather than focusing on networks, we are trying to bring back a more nuanced relationship between sociality, politics, multiple publics and media practice. Social media sites that are 'networked publics' (boyd 2011), as contrasted to social or intimate publics, are formations that are structured by the logic and reality of computer networks – a privileging of the technical, and by the logic and reality of networked individualism – a privileging of the instrumental. As technical-social networks the model is structural rather than procedural, and elides emotion, politics, commonality and other ill-disciplined properties. A social public as we present it here is not *structured* in this way. It is emergent in the collective performance of its constituents, and in the collective experience of this performance by its constituents, performances and experiences which are shared in parallel (not serially), and which are social, (not individual). It is a fluid and messy coming-together, rather than one cleanly structured around the node and the link.

As will be seen in the case studies throughout the book, and as is argued specifically in Chapter 8, conjoining sociality, intimacy and public – and thus qualifying each with the conjunction of the other – creates a hybrid category of relation that we think useful in grasping the conditions for intersubjectivity created by mobile social media. Through these probes – social publics, mobile publics and intimate publics – we seek to add to the ever ambivalent and yet situated place of the Asia-Pacific. We will argue that through the micronarrative lens of mobile, social and locative media we can find new maps for understanding the region and its 'affect' as a cartography that is perpetually being challenged and redefined.

Social publics, mobile publics and intimate publics will be used as conceptual probes that will allow us to move into more culturally nuanced understandings of what it means to be online in the Asia-Pacific. Although China has been the main focus of researchers interested in the politics of Internet regulation and democracy (Bruns and Jacobs 2006; Damm and Thomas 2006; Hughes and Wacker 2003; Lovink 2007; Tai 2012 [2006]; Yu 2007), and seemingly more democratic places like South Korea have been heralded through UCC netizens media like *OhmyNews*, the politics of intimate publics and their social media use has slipped under the radar (Koch et al. 2009; Yu 2007). In *Online@AsiaPacific* we seek to reignite the relationship between the political and personal through media practices, especially as the online increasingly and unevenly migrates to locative, social and mobile media contexts.

For some of our informants, social media is about making a humorous video and uploading to YouTube; for others, the video is an intimate, emotion-charged family gathering via Skype. Acts of creativity such as taking a camera phone picture and uploading to share with a defined group of friends gathers together a social public, while for others, the personalisation of mobile and social media provides social and political tools to disseminate information and help in times of disaster, crisis or grief, as was witnessed in the devastating earthquake and subsequent tsunami and nuclear plant crisis in Japan (Hjorth and Kim 2011). These micronarratives are as creative as they are political, are often intimate as well as social, and demonstrate the ways in which users have agency for expression. In short, UCC connects the personal to vernacular politics in a way that affirms and expands upon the Habermasian politics of a public.

While the deployment of social mobile media expands earlier modes of civic engagement and media – as evidenced by the role of SMS in the 'people power' revolution in the Philippines (Rafael 2003), Korea at the turn of the century (Rheingold 2002) and subsequently in the 2011–12 'Arab Spring' (Christensen 2011; Segerberg and Lance Bennett 2011) – social media in the context of intimate publics also departs from previous media by providing various modes of visual and aural communication with greater *affective* personalisation. Within the highly connected and personalised worlds of social and mobile media, the capacity for political engagement and its relationship to the personal takes on new forms. Much of the earlier discussion of mobile media use for political agency was evoked by Rheingold's (2002) 'smart mobs' notion. Although extending notion of smart mobs, social mobile media also provide new spaces for networked, *effective* civic responses and connected, *affective* interpersonal responses. Whilst the notion of socially networked political action existed prior to media such as mobile phones and social media, these conduits allow for a new sense of collective affective power that makes us *feel* more 'connected'. It is at this affective, interpersonal level that we would like to consider the role of mobile intimacy and intimate publics in connecting a *political vernacular* that reflects the personal, the public and a situated sense of place.

Although much work has been conducted into the role of social and mobile media in socialising, relationship management and identity construction (boyd 2007; Ito et al. 2008) or, more overtly, political examples of civic engagement (Bennett 2008; Bennett et al. 2009; Rheingold 2008), there have been few investigations of the affective interpersonal sociality and intimacy that is part and parcel of political and civic participation in this new public sphere. Through the lens of social publics and intimate publics we propose some ways in which to think about how mobile, social and locative media are deployed in the Asia-Pacific.

Why the Asia-Pacific?

A social media cartography of the Asia-Pacific not only signposts the movement towards locative media and the overlaying of the electronic and the geographic, but also operates as a metaphor for reimagining the region. For some, the rubric of 'Asia-Pacific' is too problematic to be useful, with its vexed geo-political histories and significant internal variations, and instead they opt for viewing the region as part of a broader twenty-first-century notion of the 'global South' (Dirlik 2007; Ling and Horst 2011). However, part of our interest in continuing to use 'Asia-Pacific' is that it is a marker of a particular time and politics that informed the particularities of mobile, social and locative media. By exploring the region through notions such as 'mobile intimacy' and 'intimate publics' we seek to expose some of the multiple and contested identities and localities. As symbolic of broader media ecologies and cultural practice, mobile, social and locative media can provide insight into the micro, messo and macro levels of intimacy and publics at play today.

As noted in a previous study by Hjorth (2009a), through the lens of new technologies – specifically mobile technologies – the region is not only noted for its rapid economic and technological growth, but also for becoming a powerful cultural index globally. This rise in the global currency of 'Asia', and the resurgence of new forms of regionalism and cultural proximity are, as Taiwanese cultural theorist Kuan-Hsing Chen (1998: 27) warns, a phenomenon to be wary of, especially since they may signify the re-emergence of old colonial and imperialist agendas. This image and practice of 'consuming Asia' (Chua 2000) reflects not only the divergent models for consumption in the region but also the way the Asia-Pacific is imagined globally. The intensification of transnational capital in the region is concisely diagnosed by Leo Ching (2000) as a conflation between consumerism and emerging forms of Asian modernity. As Ching surmises, 'Asia has become a market, and Asianness has become a commodity circulating globally through late capitalism' (2000: 257). The concept of the region as an imperial compression of various cultural identities and histories has come under much scrutiny particularly in the case of the 'shrinking of the Pacific' (Wilson 2000: 565) connoted by the Asia-Pacific.

Once a discursive geopolitical rubric, the Asia-Pacific – as a site for contesting local identities and transnational flows of people, media, goods and capital – has come under much radical revision and reconceptualisation (Arrighi 1994; Arrighi, Hamashita and Selden 2003; Dirlik 2007; Wilson 2000). This has led theorists such as Robert Wilson and Arif Dirlik to utilise 'Asia/Pacific' as 'not just an ideological recuperated term' (Wilson and Dirlik

1995), but as an imagined geo-political space that has a double reading as both 'situated yet ambivalent' (Wilson 2000: 567). Specifically, the diverse and perpetually changing interstitials constituting the Asia-Pacific have been repositioned as a contested space for multiple forms of identity. Far from the view widely held in the 1970s, of the region as being a bloc of satellite 'newly industrialised countries' (such as Taiwan and South Korea) oscillating around the region's first industrial nation, Japan, we now see a profoundly different picture. In particular, the phone was instrumental (at both a symbolic and material level) in the uneven economic and cultural capital in the region.

In this formation of shifting peripheries and emerging centres such as China (Arrighi 1994; Dirlik 2007), the mobile phone takes on particular significance. This scenario is presciently depicted in Robison and Goodman's *The New Rich in Asia* (1996), which identifies the mobile phone as an index for increasingly common transnational consumption and new narratives of modernity in the region. With the arrival of the mobile phone coinciding with the rise of the Asia-Pacific, the mobile phone became a poignant and 'rich' signifier for analysing local and transnational formations. However, behind the powerful symbol of the mobile phone lies a story about the emergence of localised practices enacted by actual users.

Despite the region encompassing some of the key consumers of social and mobile media, it has only recently gained focus (McLelland and Goggin 2009; Hjorth 2009a; McLelland 2007). Accounts of Indonesia being the second largest market for Facebook and the third largest for Twitter (Nugroho 2011), coupled with the tremendous growth of China's mobile-phone internet – whereby hundreds of millions of rural workers are getting online (CNNIC 2011) – attract little analysis as to what these types of practices reflect about culture, sociality and the differences place makes. Behind Facebook's popularity in the US and in much of the West, a different picture appears, in which Facebook is yet to gain the stranglehold that the 'network effect' provides. The Asia-Pacific boasts some of the oldest models of social and mobile media, such as South Korea's Cyworld minihompy and China's QQ. In 2009, when Twitter was blocked by Chinese authorities, Chinese in their millions adopted the rich media equivalent, Weibo. While official news is organised by the state, Weibo plays a key role in presenting multiple unofficial stories that are often more true than what has been 'reported'. In China, three-quarters of its 485 million online users do so via mobile media (318 million, CNNIC 2011). While mobile media provides a bridge for cross-generational intimacy, it is LBS that distinguish generational media usage as a practice only for China's Generation Y (Hjorth and Arnold 2011a). Alternatively, in Singapore and Seoul, parents are using locative media to keep a 'friendly eye' on their children.

Examples of SNS active in the region include Facebook, MySpace, Flikr, YouTube, LinkedIn, Cyworld, mixi and 2ch (*ni channeru*). Once a preoccupation of youth cultures, and associated with geeks, students and teenagers, SNS over the last couple of years have now been taken up by children, politicians, artists, business people and professionals as a vehicle for self-representation and self-contextualisation (boyd and Ellison 2008). Social media in a wide variety of forms have become an integral part of urban everyday life. It seems that anyone and everyone is signing up and that in some circles in the region, as in the West, *not* to have an online presence is *not* to have a social presence. Thus, a study of the use of SNS today is therefore a study of people engaged in everyday life – and is more likely to give access to cultural mainstreams across the region than sub-cultural tributaries.

Across the plethora of different SNS, modes of access (via PC or mobile), and online communities in the region, there are commonalities as well as distinctions that mark the Asia-Pacific's uneven embrace of social media. For youth across the region, mobile social media is not only a fundamental part of everyday life, but also a space that allows them to maintain intergenerational contact in the face of geographic distance. It is no longer just 'youth' that are using social media as adult-to-adult and intergenerational forms of dialogue expand with the increased net accessibility and technical literacy. As we will discuss in our case study chapters, mobile and social media are providing ways for families to stay in contact either when geographically distant or in the same locality. Through the use of these media, cross-generational mobile intimacy is maintained. Moreover, the demographics are shifting too as Internet access becomes not only a middle-class prerogative but also an integral part of the new mobile working class (Qiu 2008). For example, in China, it is the working class that is growing exponentially as the main users of the mobile internet (CNNIC 2011).

By taking six case studies of the region, *Online@AsiaPacific* seeks to reflect upon the politics of mobile intimacy and intimate publics in the convergence between mobile, social and locative media. As we discuss in the various chapters – especially in the second part of the book – we see mobile media providing new ways in which to imagine the complexity of place in the face of various mobilities. Drawing from Ingrid Richardson and Rowan Wilken (2012) we see place as a perpetual process of 'placing' across a variety of presences (co-presence, absent-presence, tele-presence) that involves what Tim Ingold sees as entanglements (2008). In this way, the focus turns away from viewing the region as a series of networked cultures and instead reflecting upon the nodes of mobile intimacy as they oscillate across placing, 'emplaced' (Pink 2011) and entanglements.

Summaries of the chapters

One of the most difficult parts of this study was the size and scale of the project. How can one capture the various contesting practices and cultures of this region? We wanted to capture the uneven development of the media across the multiple and opposing identities. We wanted to capture it over time in order to put the mobile, social and locative media convergence into context. We wanted to take all the rhetoric about media revolutions and transform it into a dialogue about media evolution that acknowledges the saliency of intimacy as an act that has always been mediated and co-present. We wanted to connect the discussions about political agency to the realities of banalities and intimacies at the level of everyday. We wanted to take divergent examples of locations in the region in order to highlight its contestations and multiplicities that are highlighted by intimate politics and publics.

This study evolved over three years. We were fortunate enough to receive an Australian Research Council discovery grant to conduct the study – without the funding, a study of this nature would still be just a dream. As a small team of two, we managed to conduct longitudinal case studies of six locations – Seoul, Tokyo, Shanghai, Manila, Singapore and Melbourne – over three years. By no means exhaustive in their depiction of the region, these six locations were chosen for the economic, socio-cultural, linguistic and religious differences. Each year fieldwork was conducted in each of the six locations. The fieldwork consisted of focus groups, surveys and in-depth interviews. After each initial focus group, the survey and interview questions were revised to reflect the concerns and interests of the participants.

Rather than arriving at this study with preconceptions about media use we wanted to allow for naturally occurring data; we wanted to be guided by our experts: the respondents. For example, in Shanghai, the use of social and mobile media to maintain intimacy between the generations became a key issue, leading us to interview both students and their parents to discuss this phenomenon. In Melbourne and Singapore, the adoption of social media via smartphones by older generations was prevalent and so we interviewed both younger and older participants. With an age demographic between 18 and 60 years we sought to undermine the conflation between youth and new media. For example, in Melbourne and Singapore we found many examples where older participants were using Facebook via an iPhone. In each location we had wonderful research assistants who also operated as informants. Overall, we interviewed, surveyed and conducted focus groups with about 50 respondents in each location each year. This resulted in over 900 respondents. Rather than summarise all these responses, we have chosen particular individual micronarratives that we believe reflect the specifics of each place.

During the three years (2009–12) we witnessed the rise of locative media into mainstream practice. Concurrently, we also saw the growing ubiquity of smartphones and their copies (*shanzhai*) that afforded new demographics access to emergent locative and social media. We also watched as the cartographies of mobile, social and locative media became more pervasive across various 'divides': generational, locational and socio-economic. Initially this study focused upon understanding the relationship between online notions and localised of community with offline practices. However, as smartphones seemingly eroded online–offline divisions, our understanding of co-presence changed. We soon began to realise we were studying cases of intimacy, mobility and place. In 2009, only locations like Tokyo and Seoul boasted mobile, social and locative media convergence. But by 2012, each location had its own rendition. *Online@AsiaPacific* is about those renditions.

The architecture of this book is two-fold. First, it consists of case studies from each of the six locations. These case studies are not meant to be representative of the totality of the location, but rather to provide insight into some of the specific, localised stories of mobile intimacy in each place. This is followed by the second section, which provides a more conceptual frame for reading the case studies and how they reflect some of the book's key themes around intimacy and place.

In Part I we visit the six locations. Chapter 2 explores cartographies of the mobile intimacy in the context of Seoul (South Korea). Once a location lauded for its democracy via media (Kim 2003), South Korea's reputation has more recently been challenged by events such as the arrest of the blogger 'Minerva'. In this chapter we reflect how close intimate relations (*ilchon*) are shaped by, and through localised notions of place (*bang*). In Chapter 3, we move to Tokyo (Japan) to reflect upon the performance of mobile intimacy post-3/11. Here we consider the role of mobile, social and locative media as a form of crisis management. Is current media providing new avenues for affective response? How much does this reflects older media tropes?

In Chapter 4 we then consider how locative media games like *Jiepang* are predominantly the preoccupation of Generation Y (*ba ling hou*) in Shanghai (China) and how examining this locative media practice might say something about generational shifts to understanding mobile intimacy. Moreover, we explore how locative media practice is impacting upon intimate, ambient and co-present visualities of camera phone – taking and sharing, and what this says about intimacy and place in Shanghai. This study on the changing visualities of place is further extended in Chapter 10. Chapter 5 migrates to Manila (the Philippines) to contemplate how social and mobile media is reflecting types of intimate distance. With a high percentage of females leaving the country for care work aboard, we consider how this diaspora is reflected in the media practices across generations, time zones and countries.

We then move to Singapore in Chapter 6 to contemplate the role of mobile intimacy and political affect. Can the growing sense of political discussion in social media spaces be demonstrative of Singapore's shifting social fabric? Lastly, in Chapter 7, we consider the relationship of the public to the intimate through a case study of mobile, social and locative media in Melbourne (Australia) through the iPhone. As one of the most popular smartphones, the iPhone has ushered Australians into a fast-track mobile, social and locative media convergence. Many older people who had never used social media are suddenly embracing a mobile version. Writing during the initial roll out the National Broadband Network (NBN) we see some tensions playing out between erosions around public and private, work and leisure paradigms.

We then move onto Part II where we revisit our key rubric such as intimate publics and mobile intimacy. In Chapter 8 we reconceptualise the debates around metaphors about the online as a network or community in light of mobile, social and locative media convergence. In Chapter 9 we then consider how the new types of mobile intimacy are creating new topographies for reimaging the region. In Chapter 10 we consider the impact locative media is having on camera phone practices. We argue that rather than conceptualising camera phone practices as 'networked' visuality, like the first-generation studies pioneered by Ito and Okabe (2003, 2005), we see visual cultures moving towards a type of embodied intimacy that we call 'emplaced' (Pink 2011) cartographies. In the concluding chapter, Chapter 11, we summarise the book's journey and possible future destinations for intimacy across mobile, social and locative media terrains.

By situating the rise of locative, social and mobile media in the region, we hope to provide new insights into how the region and its contested and multiple identities are evolving. Whilst many of our examples are informed by the various social, cultural, linguistic, economic and technological factors in each context, they are also adding to the global emergent body of research around this phenomenon. Place, in all its complexity, has always mattered to mobile media. And through mobile media we see the ways place is shaped, and is shaping, practices of mobility, intimacy and a sense of belonging. As mobile media evolves to include locative and social media we see new and multiple maps for understanding the emotional, social and psychological dimensions of place (and placing) at a local, regional and global level.

Part I
Locating the mobile

2 Locating intimacies of place and gender (Seoul)

Hyun-kim had been dating Sang-hee for under a week when one day at University Sang-hee started to decorate her new boyfriend's mobile phone (both inside and outside the device) with cute characters. Within a month, Sang-hee had updated the camera phone's pictures on Hyun-kim's phone, making sure there were plenty of pictures of them together as well as flattering self-portraits (*sel-ca*). This move was then followed by Sang-hee's colonialisation of Hyun-kim's social media – his SNS Cyworld minihompy and Facebook soon overflowed with a plethora of images of them together. As is often the case with social media, this new content spoke to multiple publics. It is Sang-hee speaking to Hyun-kim, reminding him of their relationship, and it is Sang-hee and Hyun-kim together, speaking to their other intimates of their relationship. Much like an engagement ring on the finger, which is always present and tacitly tells people that the owner is 'taken', Hyun-kim's mobile media highlighted and documented Sang-hee's intimate relationship. The *piéce de résistance* was when Sang-hee took a picture of her eye and saved it as a screen saver on Hyun-kim's mobile phone. Wherever he went she was always present and omnipresent. Watching. Listening. Waiting.

Soo-kyung is a popular young Korean woman with many friends. Like many 18-year-old girls she spends a lot of her time socialising, including meeting up with friends in internet cafés, called *PC bangs* (PC rooms). Some of her friends are present *in* the PC *bang*, while at the same time and in the same place others are made to be present *through* the PC *bang*. In addition, with her iPhone perpetually in her hand, Soo-kyung is typical of young mobile adults who concurrently socialise online, while also hanging out with friends offline, wherever they may be. A third place for Soo-kyung to socialise is her minihompy – an online graphical 'apartment' in which Soo-kyung and her friends might to talk, listen to music and exchange gifts. Soo-kyung also uses Facebook and, as is the case with many younger users, minihompy and Facebook are used for gatherings of different intimate publics.

When her parents asked to 'friend' her on social media, Soo-kyung felt she had little choice, and now Soo-kyung and her parents communicate at her minihompy, as well as on the phone and at home. Since its beginning in the late 1990s, Cyworld minihompy has increasingly become a cross-generational social media with many parents and grandparents being active users (Hjorth 2009a). And while Soo-kyung is mindful of the need to perpetually edit her privacy settings in light of this fact, sometimes things happen too quickly online, and oftentimes the boundaries around intimate publics begin to overlap. In Chapter 1 we spoke of the fluidity of the publics that assemble around social media, of their uncertain boundaries and of the speed with which currents of communications move. Such fluidity was evident when Soo-kyung's best friend, He-ran, became depressed after her boyfriend dumped her for another girl. He-ran's messages on minihompy and Facebook became increasingly desperate and strange as she tried to stalk her boyfriend via social media. Soo-kyung tried to console her best friend, via social media, along with frequent visits to her house, to continue to comfort her and to prevent her from self-harm. Soo-kyung's parents also became aware of He-ran's distress via the minihompy postings and confronted their daughter with their concerns. Soo-kyung explained the situation and then all three met with He-ran's parents. Together, the intimate public that assembled around these events was able to intervene and persuade He-ran to consult a counsellor.

These two vivid examples illustrate the way gender, mobility, place, social media and intimacy are practicsd in Seoul, South Korea (henceforth Korea). Each story reflects the different ways that offline corporeal places ('cutified' handsets, worried people, lounge-room meetings and distressed bodies) intersect with social media to constitute hybrid places (*bangs*, colonised profiles, sites for social-media stalking, minihompy confessionals). Both stories are concerned with the performance of gendered relations among young lovers, the first a story of falling in love, the second a story of falling out of love, each using social media and the intimate publics that gather around social media as crucial elements in the performance. Each story is concerned with the fluid boundaries, or the horizon, that is established around intimate publics through social action and social media. In the first story, the attempt to mark off an intimate 'world of two' is clear, though it is equally clear that this world was designed to announce itself to wider publics.

In the second story we see that the boundaries of intimate publics overlap and move across generations and across families. These intimate publics are brought together by common ground that is emotional, not instrumental; each is performative rather than structured or institutionalised; each intertwines the performance of social media with the corporeal worlds of decorated handsets and hurt emotions. We suggest that these characteristics are not captured by the concept of a 'network', nor a 'community', but are better represented as an intimate public. And so we see hybrids emerging, intertwining intimate publics bounded in different but overlapping ways, social media of various kinds, and emotions of various kinds, all played out in places where online and offline performances intersect. To unpack the issues introduced in these stories, we begin with the wider context and remind the reader of some of Seoul's characteristic features. As we hope will become clear, we argue that place matters.

Korea's capital, Seoul, is no stranger to mobile, social and locative media convergence (Yoon 2006). Korea has 50.2 million registered mobile phones (Korean Communications Commission 2010), which is greater than the number of people; as early as 2005, 96.8 per cent of South Korean mobile phones had internet access (Ahonen and O'Reilly 2007: 242) and in 2012 it has more than 20 million smartphone users out of a population of 48.6 million (PhysOrg 2011). In 2006 Korea became the first country to achieve over 50 per cent broadband penetration per capita (Ahonen and O'Reilly 2007: 173). It currently has the fastest broadband network in the world (100 Mbit/s), accessed by 34.4 per cent of the population (Seoul Metropolitan Government 2012). By 2015 residents will have free Wi Fi internet access at 10,430 public places (PhysOrg 2011) and Seoul was the world's first city to introduce mobile TV DMB and wireless broadband, both available in all subway lines, buses and taxis, along with 4G LTE and Wi Fi (Kim 2005; PhysOrg 2011). Against this backdrop it is not surprising that electronics is important to the Seoul economy, the world's sixth most powerful according to Forbes (Zumbrun 2008), and home to global high-tech companies like Samsung and LG. There are tens of thousands of PC *bangs* in Seoul, despite the fact that everyone has a computer at home, and multiplayer games like *World of WarCraft* are national sports (Huhh 2008).

The importance of community both online and offline is palpable in Seoul, and the metaphor of the family is key to the South Korean nation-state (Cho 2000). This translates to online worlds with nearly 70 per cent of users having some form of online community, often based around games, fashion or food (eMarketer 2012). Despite Facebook just surpassing Cyworld minihompy in 2012 as the market leading SNS in South Korea (Nielsen KoreanClick 2012), minihompy is still used by nearly 70 per cent of the population. Part of the rise of Facebook has been its mobile media app with nearly 67 per cent of social media users accessing Facebook via the mobile phone (KISA 2012). Nearly 90 per cent of 20–29-year-olds are regular users of social media (KISA 2012).

Advanced technical infrastructure is obviously part of the reason Seoul has such high rates of social media use, including locative social media, and this in turn is part of the reason it has the infrastructure it does. However, the digital infrastructure is but one layer of the built environment, stretched out over other material, social and cultural layers that also constitute Seoul as a place. Population density is very high in Seoul and most people live in relatively small high-rise apartments in very large apartment blocks, increasing the efficiency with which infrastructure is installed, and perhaps increasing the social proclivity for more expansive digital worlds. Young people typically live with their parents until they marry, no doubt increasing the social significance of third places, including the *bang* and minihompy, to be discussed later in this chapter. Korea also has one of the longest working

Figure 2.1 Cyworld minihompy by artist Emil Goh

weeks (2,357 hours per year) and the shortest number of holidays in the OECD (Olson 2008), reducing opportunities for offline recreation and sociality and increasing the significance of online recreation and sociality.

Korean politics also plays into the mix of material and immaterial elements that makes Seoul 'a place'. In Korea, online, social and mobile media spaces were once viewed as helping progress Korean forms of democracy (Kim 2003: 325). For Korean sociologist Shin Dong Kim (2003) and anthropologist Haejoang Cho (2004), the development of a specific type of democracy in Korea has been supported in part by technologies such as mobile phones. However, more recently, the link between technology and democracy on the one hand, and technology and government (that is, 'technonationalism', see West 2006), on the other, has come under question.

For technophiles the link between the internet and democracy is self-evident. In this techno-utopian discourse the internet is, in and of itself, a powerful force for liberty and democracy – usually understood in terms of a neo-liberal, free-market political economy, underpinned by a hyper-individualistic culture. As a force for democracy the internet would erase the power of the mass media, treat censorship as a bad-link and route around it, decentralise decision making and diminish the power of government, erase national boundaries, undermine the power of institutions, erode racism and sexism, and so on, and on, and on – see for example Barlow (1996).

Anti-democratic forces have, of course, not found the internet to be an irresistible force, and social media continues to be politically contested ground in Korea, as in other places. In April 2009 blogger Park Dae-sung (known as 'Minerva') was arrested, jailed, but subsequently acquitted for posts that presciently commented on global and Korean economics in general, and President Myung-Bak Lee's financial administration in particular (Abell 2009; Hjorth 2011a; Wallace 2012). The correlation between online and off-line identity has long been an issue in Korea with regulation requiring citizen identification numbers to establish online accounts with Cyworld and online games, and legislation proposed to extend this to other online activity. In the face of interventions such as the eradication of online anonymity (Pfanner 2011), the proposed 'Cyber Defamation Law' and heavy-handed policing of online media by the Korean Communications Commission, the view that many younger Koreans had of social media, as providing a relatively safe place for self-expression, and perhaps a place that they could lay claim to as their own, has been severely shaken. Instead of providing safe havens and alternative spaces, many of our respondents saw that it could also be shaped to serve government agendas, and expressed a growing sense of distrust with the online.

Further fuelling this distrust, or rather this new sense of realism, was the co-option of social media by Korean corporations for their own purposes. One such purpose was to advertise directly but surreptitiously to young people, who are cynical about advertising, but might be persuaded by advertising pretending to be UCC (Hjorth 2011a). In a second widely publicised example, Samsung also made surreptitious use of mobile media. Korean mobile-phone services enable handsets associated with any given number to be tracked through geographic space in real time (O 2004), in effect providing an automated 24/7 stalking service. Samsung were alleged to have used this service surreptitiously to track the movements of six employees as they attempted to establish a labour union (Hjorth 2011a; Lee 2011), another move that drew attention to the vulnerability of people in the online world.

In addition to the online incursions of government and commercial corporations, the Korean military have also made strategic use of online resources, an important move given the significance of the military in Korean life – a country that is still technically at war with the North, and that conscripts all young men into military service. Young conscripts were once banned from using mobile and social media, but social media are now seen by the authorities to play a support role in military life. Similarly, massively multiplayer military games have been taken in from the 'nerd-culture' and have been harnessed by the military, which has come to recognise the significant role games can play in imparting ideologies, and skills in strategic and tactical decision making, leadership and team work. Rather than new media and gaming interrupting or distracting their military education, they are now seen as consistent with and integral to the training regime.

The use of social media we discuss in this chapter is thus embedded in an interesting and quite particular place. It is a place with arguably the best technical infrastructure in the world, made widely available across all demographics. It is a place whose residents have embraced mobile and social media with enthusiasm. And it is also a place where the institutions and publics assembling around social media have the capacity for political as well as interpersonal action, all of which makes social media and their publics contested ground. In this chapter we suggest that the Korean context presents very particular ways of overlaying social media and sociality, mobile media and place, and intimacy and publics.

In the particular context of Seoul, this overlay is best understood through Korean notions of place (*bang* or room 방) and intimacy (*ilchon* or first relation 일촌), a familial relationship based on one degree of separation. Our respondents clearly demonstrated how their motivations for and usage of various types of social media were linked by these two key concepts – the *bang* and the *ilchon*. This localised version of sociality and space shows how social media in general, and LBS more particularly, reinforce, extend and reinterpret traditional notions of family, culture, space and place.

In Korea, one can find various forms of the *bang*, some being physical places – *jjimjilbang* (hot room or bath house) PC *bang* (computer room), DVD *bang* and *noraebang* (music), and others being online, exemplified in the minihompy. In each case, space in Korea is rendered a 'place' through sociality. Notions of public and private do not translate so well into the *bang*, which is neither entirely public nor private, but rather a vehicle for its occupants' will, or, to borrow a line of thinking from Doel, in a *bang* 'there is no space, only spacing, no place, only placing' (2000: 125). In other words, the *bang* does not have a predetermined purpose that exists prior to its occupation – instead the occupants sharing the space actively determine the use.

In Florence Chee's (2005) ethnography on PC *bang* and the politics of online multiplayer games, it is argued that these spaces are 'third spaces' between home and work. For Korean youth, most of whom still live at home before getting married, these third spaces, in particular the minihompy, operate as private spaces in which groups of intimates – intimate publics – might assemble. As Jun-Sok Huhh (2008) observes, PC *bang* ensured the success of online games in Korea by nurturing both the culture and the business side of the industry; thus the online game as a digital place is seen as synonymous with the PC *bang* as a physical place. According to Hee-jeong Choi, in each case the *bang* is an independent space for the sharing of ideas that is 'static in form, yet flexible in functionality' (2009: 93).

Like the *bang* (social space), *ilchon* (intimacy) has also been repurposed by new media. In the peculiarly Korean SNS, Cyworld minihompy, friends are called *ilchon*, a concept traditionally used to denote one degree of distance from family members in a Korean kinship (i.e. one's mother is one chon) (Hjorth 2011a; Hjorth and Kim 2005). As a form of emplacement, the overlapping relationship between *bangs* and *ilchon* also foregrounds the motivations of locative media use and LBS games in Korea. Far from a 'phoneur' dystopia where users of commercial location-based games become nodes in the commercial information circuits (Luke 2006), many LBS gamers spoke about the play outside the official game – that is, the unofficial forms of play through overlaying the *ilchon* and *bang* in novel and, as we shall see, gendered ways.

In particular, the relationship between *bangs* and *ilchon* clearly foregrounds the use of locative media in Korea. From *flags* – which is part of Cyworld and neatly links into and extends the *ilchon* network of minihompy – to another locative game, *IN*, LBS in Korea are used to overlap the *ilchon* onto the *bang*. Users transform *bangs* into meaningful spaces by overlaying the *ilchon*. Friends, family and associates become part of the co-present journey as they render *bangs* into places through increasingly popular mobile platforms. The redeployment of the *bang* and *ilchon* through LBS also reflects the increasing pressure for the young to be part of *Chalnajok* (Cho 2009), with '*Chal-na*' meaning 'instant' and '*jok*' refering to a 'tribe' (INNOCEAN report as found in D.K. Lee 2009). In a country long familiar with the deployment of GPS via mobile phones and cars, locative media provides a natural extension of the mobile and social. In Cyworld *flags* we see a connection between *mobility* and *immobility* through *creative and situated sociality*.

One way in which the *bang* is being overlaid with the *ilchon* in new ways is through LBS camera phone practices. In particular, LBS are providing new ways for visualising 'intimacy' and 'publics' in different ways. Earlier studies of camera phones focused upon images as part of a 'network of connections' (Ito and Okabe 2005), whereas they could, as Sarah Pink suggests, have more appropriately been seen as an intensity of entangled lines in understanding of contemporary visual cultures, not as 'an intersection of nodes in networks, but in terms of a meshwork of moving things' (2011: 8).

Just as the second generation of locative media demonstrates a more nuanced, and yet paradoxically private–public, located-free floating practice, so too are we witnessing a second generation of camera phone images that move away from *networked* to *emplaced* practices, a discussion that will also be followed up in Chapter 4's Shanghai case study and again in Chapter 10.

These locative media practices shift experiences from context to context, and, at the same time, generate new ways in which images can be placed and *emplaced*. In this movement away from *networked* and towards *emplaced visuality*, LBS provide a co-present cartography whereby contemporary and traditional notions of place and intimacy are overlaid. In the context of Korea, LBS camera phone practices are overlaying traditional notions of place (*bang*) and intimacy (*ilchon*) through *emplacement*. That is, rather than images being about place as a networked geography, LBS camera phone images evoke a complex, multisensory experience of place and intimacy. We will discuss this more in Chapter 10.

This deployment of technological spaces is not about substituting the virtual for the actual but rather about supplementing actual relationships and actual places. In Korea, face-to-face interactions have always been pivotal to intimacy and to social capital, and the relevance of the technology is linked intrinsically to face-to-face interaction (Hjorth and Kim 2005). The *ilchon* and the *bang* link place to intimacy, and are concepts that reflect a traditional Korean sense of relationship and reflect a sense of relationship in contemporary technocultures. So, for example, in the context of Korea's oldest and most popular social media application, Cyworld minihompy, regularly used by 48 million Koreans (Hjorth 2009a), *ilchon* is both an analogy reaching back through traditional culture, and also a contemporary technocultural practice. Cyworld has adopted the term *ilchon* to describe its cyber-relations.

Mobile intimacy in Seoul also takes a particular route – one that both reflects and subverts traditional notions of the intimate (*ilchon*) and place *(bang)*. As mobile phones increasingly become the platform for social and locative media practices, questions about the changing relationship between intimacy and public/private spaces come to the forefront. Far from eroding the importance of place, mobile media further reinforce its significance in the maintenance of intimacy (Ito 2002). However, the ways in which place, intimacy and location are visualised is changing with the increasing popularity of locative media and the growing use of smartphones. In particular, some LBS such as Facebook Places and *Foursquare* are creating social media game cartographies that overlay the electronic, emotional and social onto localities in new ways. Drawing on the histories of urban mobile gaming (de Souza e Silva and Hjorth 2009), LBS games like *Foursquare*, *Jiepang* (China see Chapter 4), *flags*, *SeeOn* and *IN* (South Korea), not only transform urban spaces into play places but also provide new ways for co-presence, intimacy and the social to converge across increasingly blurred online and offline spaces.

Let us return to the opening vignette in which the mobile phone played a pivotal symbolic role in the passage of coupledom, when the female partner colonised her boyfriend's phone, tagging it with cute 'feminine' customisation characters. In this case, the mobile phone reminds us of Igor Kopytoff's (1986) notion of objects as having biographies. Mobile phone customisation – or 'cartographies of personalization' (Hjorth 2009a) – reflects a user's grappling between their own experiences and memories and the increasing role of the mobile phone as a repository for and of the user's intimacy. Things such as the cute decals that might be fixed to a mobile phone provide us with semiotic points of reference that are ontological markers of identity for constructing oneself and one's world (Arnold et al. 2006).

Following Elaine Lally's (2002) excellent advice that material culture may act in an anchoring mode, as a scaffolding for the self, or as a placeholder which has a role for individuals in maintaining a sense of self in everyday life, Arnold et al. (2006) suggest that things constitute reference points around which identity, inter-subjectivity and memory are articulated, constructed, negotiated and contested. Our things are selected, collected and assembled in acts of self-selection and self-assembly, and world assembly. The way the process takes place is described informally as externalising the internal (as we express the psyche's agency and build our environment) and internalising the external (as our environment shapes our psyche). More formally, externalisation is described as self-alienation, and internalisation as sublation, reabsorption or reincorporation (Bourdieu 1984 [1979]; Lally 2002).

As Leopoldina Fortunati (2002) has noted, the mobile phone is an intimate thing. In such an argument, the mobile phone becomes a symbol of older rituals, i.e. the engagement ring. As an object that is always close and frequently visible, in the hand or on the table, the highly feminised customisation of the phone clearly signposted to others that the boy was engaged. And if there was any doubt, the message was reinforced by the picture of her all-watching, omnipresent eye as a screen saver on his phone. Reminding him to call. Always co-present. Also reminding him to behave!

The mobile phone has long been a repository for ambient intimate co-presence. However, as we move unevenly towards mobile, social and locative media convergence, the cartographies of mobile intimacy – and the types of co-presence they express – are evolving. As Manuel Castells et al. observe, 'communication can be both instrumental and expressive' (2007: 153), and with tools such as texting, emailing, camera phone imagery, video and sound, the mobile phone provides many vehicles for self-expression. These forms of expression play across various levels – individual, social and cultural. Practices such as texting can 'express social inequalities' (Pertierra 2006: 100) concurrent to creating 'an amplification of inner subjectivity' (Pertierra 2006: 101). For 35-year-old Kahyun, LBS were equal parts communication with co-present friends as they were expressions of her inner subjectivities – especially through camera phone pictures. As Kahyun notes, LBS were changing the frequency and the ways in which she photographed a place. Not only did LBS encourage users to take and share more pictures but also these images needed to be 'unique' responses to the experience of place, a need which results in

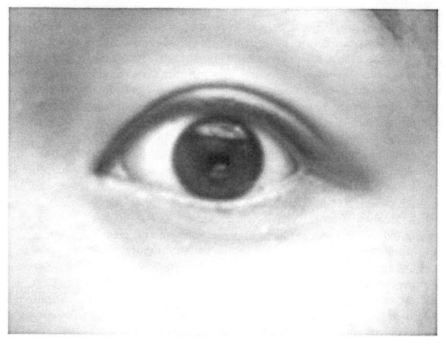

Figure 2.2 Mobile girlfriend (girlfriend's eye as mobile phone screen saver)

respondents using more smartphone filter apps to create more professional and ambient pictures.

The popularity of the camera phone in Korea has thus been pivotal in both changing and documenting shifts in everyday life in Seoul (D.H Lee 2009), and is a dominant and vibrant example of the use of UCC *bang* and *ilchon* in Korea. Given that the Korean company Samsung was the first to pioneer high-resolution camera phones that could be used to take images to send to online sites such as minihompy, it is not surprising that Korea has an active networked visual culture (Hjorth 2009a; Lee 2005, 2009a, 2009b). The camera phone is always there, 'on hand' (both literally and metaphorically), to capture the trivialities of everyday (Hjorth 2007b), and to move representations of this (material) place to this (online) *bang*, reinforcing (our) *ilchon*.

Camera phones further infuse the private with the public under the ubiquitous trope of the personal. As Ilpo Koskinen (2007) has noted, camera phones partake in 'the aesthetic of banality'; in other words, by taking images of the everyday, camera phone images represent a 'common banality' (Mørk Petersen 2009) that is ordered by 'vernacular creativity' (Burgess 2008). But in its 'banality', camera phone imagery is also about power. As feminist scholars such as Meagham Morris (1988) have noted, banality is the naturalisation and normalisation of power. From the plethora of *sel-ca* (self portraits) to the images of food, sharing images through networked contexts like minihompy have become an integral component in Korean everyday life.

While camera phone self-portraiture is a globally popular genre, we are also witnessing the flourishing of vernacular visualities that reflect a localised notion of place, social and identity making practices (Hjorth 2007b; Lee 2009a). With the addition of locative media to the social and mobile media equation, the social and personal is overlaid onto place in new ways. Specifically, by sharing an image and comment about a place through LBS, users can create different ways to experience and record journeys and, in turn, impact upon how place is recorded, experienced and thus remembered. This is especially the case with the overlaying of ambient images within moving narratives of place as afforded by LBS. Far from banal and boring, these images were often unique and creative. These images are not only about the vernacular qualities of UCC, they signal new types of emplaced visualities. While the first generation of camera phone studies emphasised the three 'Ss' – sharing, storing and saving – of the 'networked' images (Ito and Okabe 2005), the second generation, with the added element of locative media, sees an embrace of Pink's notion of 'emplaced images' (2011). Rather than the three 'Ss' operating to contextualise the image, LBS camera phones are clearly overlaid electronically onto geographic locations. However, through a variety of visual techniques as well as subject matter, they tend to evoke a more multiple and contested notion of place as something that is an interplay between intimacy and sociality.

By emplaced, we are suggesting a complex mapping of localised notions of place, sociality and visuality. Here place is multi-dimensional and multi-faceted space that is imagined and experienced, geographic and psychological. As Rowan Wilken and Gerard Goggin note in *Mobile Technologies and Place*, place is one of the most contested, ambiguous and complex terms today (2012b: 5). Wilken and Goggin view place as unbounded and relational, and observe that it 'can be understood as all-pervasive in the way that it informs and shapes everyday lived experience – including how it is filtered and experienced via the use of mobile technologies' (2012b: 6). As social geographer Doreen Massey notes, maps provide little understanding of the complex elusiveness of place as a collection of 'stories-so-far':

> One way of seeing 'places' is as on the surface of maps ... But to escape from an imagination of space as surface is to abandon also that view of place. If space is rather a simultaneity of stories-so-far, then places are collections of those stories, articulations within the wider power-geometries of space. Their character will be a product of these intersections within that wider setting, and of what is made of them ... And, too, of the non-meetings-up, the disconnections and the relations not established, the exclusions. All this contributes to the specificity of place.
>
> (2005: 130)

The use of camera phone images by LBS is indicative of Massey's notion of place as a series of 'stories-so-far' that reflect disjuncture as much as presence. In LBS camera phone images we see that place is a notion that is tied as much to intimacy as it is co-presence; just as intimacy is always mediated so too are notions of place. The rise of 'emplaced' rather than 'networked' visuality in LBS camera phone practices is a response to the changing cartography of co-presence whereby binaries between online and offline experiences don't hold. Moreover, given that these images are so much bound to a specific experience of place, they reflect an intersection of senses that are not just visual. For example, our respondents noted that they often took pictures of shared food in order to create a sense of taste or smell that would be evoked by their images. This multisensory evocation was in response to the need to create multi-dimensional and ambient experiences of place that were overlaid by intimacy, or the need to convey a sense of *bang* with the *ilchon*.

Along with the capacity to emplace images, LBS also provide a capacity for surveillance, as we saw in our opening vignette. For Chang-hee, father of Soo-kyung, social and locative media allowed for the surveillance of his daughter and the potential for intervention in her life. In a version of what Misa Matsuda (2009) noted in her study of Japanese mother and children relationships, in which the mobile phone functioned as a 'mum in the pocket', Chang-hee spoke of how he and his wife were able to be a 'friendly, caring eye' in monitoring their daughter via minihompy conversation and locational *flags*. As we saw, this parental 'überveillence' became important in the performance of *ilchon* and in bringing together an intimate public around emotional health issues. Here the 'dark' surveillance evident in the aforementioned Minerva scandal, and in the Samsung SDI mobile tracking scandal, can also provide ways for familial benevolence.

LBS is also used by friends to track one another. For example, a male respondent, Ki-Sang, aged 20, frequently uses LBS to find friends in physical proximity, in which case he would call to catch up. However, Ki-Sang noted that his female friends seemed much more LBS active than he did, through by taking pictures and participating in LBS based games (i.e. getting badges). As Ki-Sang observed: '... many of my girlfriends seem to be so visible on flags. They always seem to be uploading pretty pictures of themselves with friends at cool places. I feel lazy in comparison.' The *ilchon* notion is extended into the geosocial cartographies of *flags*. One needs to be an *ilchon* to see another's flag postings, reinforcing the point that *mobile intimacy* can be understood as an overlaying of the geospatial with the emotional and the social. Through overlaying text and images via social media *ilchon*-type groups, users not only created their own forms of mobile intimacy but also did so to their own 'intimate publics'. The public performativity of *Chalnajok* ('instant tribe') also constructs divisions between those who are active versus those who are 'lazy'. Female respondents seemed less happy to be viewed as lazy and thus more active in maintaining the *Chalnajok* so prevalent with Korean contemporary culture. For Hyunjin, a female respondent aged 28, place is clearly a shared experience, reflecting the Korean *bang*. She stated:

I use it [LBS] to share my feeling or beautiful photos with others when-
ever I visit new places. Or sometimes I use it [LBS] when I'm curious who
is in the same place with me. … I think using it [LBS] changes the way
I record a place rather than the way I experience a place. Getting points
or stickers makes me think about the places more meaningfully.

What is especially pertinent in Hyunjin's comments is the fact that she
believed LBS 'changes the way I *record* a place rather than the way I *experience*
a place'. This is a curious point of differentiation. Does not the recording of
the place then affect the way in which it is relived and re-experienced as part
of mnemonic narrations? These sentiments were also echoed by Soohyun. It
would seem that the *experience* of a place is located geographically and in
time, but the *recording* of that place enables a time-shift, as the experience is
recalled and shared. In this way, recording brings together the social and
spatial, or in the case of Korea, the *ilchon* and the *bang*. As Soohyun
notes:

I have always liked to take pictures of a place to share with friends. I used
to use my minihompy to share but now it's easier to place pictures in the
location they occurred. This makes a different type of archive … an
archive that links to place and does not float free.

Although locative media have attracted much critical attention of late as a
convergence between urban, gaming and mobile media studies (de Souza e
Silva and Frith 2012; Gordon and de Souza e Silva 2011), little attention has
been paid to the ways these locative media practices are gendered. This is
despite the fact that gender informs fundamental questions about locative
media, such as questions concerning intimacy, privacy and surveillance (Cincotta
et al. 2011). Although both mobile media (Fortunati 2009; Hjorth 2009a;
Wajcman et al. 2009) and gaming (Hjorth 2009a; Kennedy 2002; Pearce
2009) have recognised the importance of gender, at the crossroads of these
two areas the pivotal role of gender is missing.

Through various forms of media practice associated with games (Hjorth
2009a; Hjorth, Na and Huhh 2009) and camera phone sharing (Lee 2005),
one can see numerous modes of localised gender performativity; the 'regu-
lated iterations' that Judith Butler (1991) associates with gender. This gendered
culture plays out in Korean LBS use in numerous ways, with female users
taking and sharing more photos, as our informant Ki-Sang observed. Indeed,
for some women, the pressure to be part of the *Chalnajok* means that they
feel compelled to take and share pictures despite feeling apprehensive. One
female, Nara Ara, aged 27, noted: 'Sometimes I don't want to take endless
pictures and share them. I may be feeling sad or be having a bad hair day. But
then when I get pictures from my friends this makes me want to return the
feelings.' For others, the gesture of creating and sharing visual cultures
through LBS is about a type of 'girl culture' that expresses itself through both

the quantity of images taken and shared, through the types of images women take (ones without people), and through the contexts in which they share or 'emplace' them. In these ways female respondents spoke of camera phone pictures as enhancing the geosocial co-present experience. For female Soohyun, aged 30, the narrating of place by overlaying images and comments onto place, is perceived as highly gendered. She notes:

> Usually, female users view it as a game to be played. For example, they record comments or put photos of the places where they've been before. Or they use LBS so that they can get points and coupons to use … But, male users use LBS to leave their footprints so they can find out how they moved in certain situations. I think they don't have big interests about getting coupons or recording histories through posting photos or comments.

For Kahyun, LBS are 'girls' games' and she uses various kinds as a way to play with place and friends. However, she was concerned about privacy issues, something that wasn't an issue for male respondents. As Kahyun notes:

> I use Daum Map, Four season, and ittime. I'm using it [LBS] like playing game. I let people check where I am or get points. Also I can see where I have visited and how many times I've been there. I find it [LBS] makes me take more pictures. I also find that the types of pictures I am taking is changing. I used to take more *sel-ca* but now I like to take pictures of objects and food that are in some way unique to the place.

In this chapter we have attempted to situate social and locative media as it is experienced in the particular social and cultural conditions that occur in Seoul. While debate in the West tends to focus on the implications of LBS for privacy and security, locative media are also providing us with new geosocial visualities and spatial narratives for reimaging a sense of place. Through the lens of Korean LBS, we can see that there is an overlaying of emotional, electronic and geographic territories with forms of sociality that straddle online and offline, game and non-game, mobile and immobile spaces. Korean LBS use illustrates that mobile intimacy is a locational and mnemonic cartography. Locational memories are recorded, narrated and overlaid onto other cartographies and, in particular, the emotional, psychological and geo-spatial *ilchon* and *bang*.

   Through the coordination of camera phone images and text, female respondents in Seoul were enacting and narrating a sense of place in new ways that also rehearsed older practices of co-present intimacy. Rather than first-generation camera phone studies that reflected 'networked visuality', LBS camera phone practices are highlighting the significance of 'emplaced visualities'. By interweaving the social with place through co-present cartographies, Korean LBS users are reinventing the context and content for camera phone studies.

Through locative media, respondents can overlay the mobile and social with the electronic and geographic for their *ilchon*. Their located UCC is not made public, but is presented through the minihompy, visited by a select intimate public – symbolic *ilchons* – who have access to their locative media assemblages. That is, locative media was being used as an integral part of everyday Korean life to reinforce the significant relationship among the *ilchon*, and between the *ilchon* and *bang*. As LBS media plays out, these types of narrations of place will no doubt impact upon how one remembers, experiences and records. Whilst how these micronarratives move from the private and intimate into a semi-public space is yet to be determined, one thing remains clear – LBS are as much informed by as they are transforming, a localised and socialised notion of place in which gendered performativity is a necessary everyday practice.

In the next chapter we will turn to another location known for its mobile media innovation and convergence: Tokyo, Japan. In light of the earthquake, tsunami and Fukushima nuclear meltdown called '3/11' (11 March 2011), we reflect upon how mobile media both rehearses traditional forms and creates new modes of intimate co-presence. Specifically, we consider how mobile media operated in crisis and grief management in the aftermath of 3/11. Here we see the significance of the locative media dropped away and instead respondents found themselves resorting to older methods of media practice.

3 Spectres of mobile intimacy

Mobile media in crisis management of 3/11 (Tokyo)

When the 3/11 Tōhoku earthquake hit Tokyo on 11 March 2011 at 2.46 p.m., 20-year-old Toshi mistook it for the haptic features of his PlayStation Portable (PSP) game. Toshi and a friend were at home playing a PSP 'monster hunter' game that, as it happens, involved simulated earthquakes as part of gameplay. Toshi was momentarily caught between the offline world and the online world, where the properties of one world occupy the other, and the sensing of the offline quake was attributed to the online game.

When his fish tank overflowed and his books began falling to the floor, the game moved from the foreground to the background of his experience, and Toshi and his friend realised a real quake had occurred. Toshi's first move was to try to contact his parents, to ascertain their wellbeing and to reassure them of his, and the mobile phone, or *keitai*, was used for this purpose. Toshi's parents were elderly and only used to *keitai* for voice-call and email, but on this occasion, they did not pick up. Toshi then moved from a voice-call, which afforded real-time conversation with his mother or father in particular, to asynchronous media, and sent an email to his parents, followed by a posting on Twitter – 'I'm ok, hope family and friends are too' – which afforded asynchronous communication with his public of Twitter followers. One can see here a move through the social media Toshi deployed, from synchronous interpersonal communication, to asynchronous interpersonal communication, to asynchronous communication with a bounded public, that parallels a move in Toshi's affective relations, from the more intimate to the less intimate.

Of course Toshi was only one of millions going through a similar experience and soon the social-media feeds were ballooning with comments, reports of events, pleas and calls of distress, all streaming across the screen in real time as Toshi and his friend watched together on their *keitai*. A plethora of stories emerged about the earthquake, surreal and terrifying camera phone footage of the tsunami that would kill tens of thousands began to appear, followed by the unfolding of a crisis at the Fukushima nuclear plant. Immersed in this seemingly never-ending stream of catastrophe piled on catastrophe, Toshi and his friend felt overwhelmed, helpless and besieged. Those of us who watched the events in Japan from a safe distance in space and time found the images horrifying and harrowing, and it was no doubt infinitely more so for those watching proximate events in real time, captured and disseminated by compatriots and friends directly experiencing the events. Toshi and his friend sat in his room and watched, transfixed by the terrible kaleidoscope of stories unfolding across social media such as Twitter, 2ch and mixi, until it all became too much to take in and deal with, and shock, sadness and confusion overcame them. Unable to cope with any more, they turned back to their game and to the safety and comfort of the game world. But the game was no longer engaging.

Hyun-suk is a male international student from Korea who was on campus when the quake happened and, like Toshi, the first thing he and his friends did was contact family to reassure them of his safety, followed by quickly posting a message on his Korean SNS Cyworld minihompy saying 'I'm alive and ok'. Hyun-suk and his Korean student friends then congregated in one campus room for the next four days, stunned by the horror of it all. For Hyun-suk, the comfort of face-to-face discussion of the events as they unfolded was essential in emotionally surviving the event.

During this time, Hyun-suk's view of social media also changed. Once upon a time he had viewed it as a conversation; as a mode of communication that was multi-directional and reciprocal. However, during the course of the events of 3/11, he saw it as being more like a conference than a conversation. Communications were not interpersonal, multi-directional or reciprocal, and he felt bombarded with often-conflicting reports, interpretations and stories. Through this experience of social media in time of disaster, he also felt more acutely Korean. Far from being a space for expressing emotion and comforting others, as it would be in Korea, Hyun-suk felt that the Japanese Twitter community regarded emotional outbursts as 'uncivilised'. Place matters to social media, and UCC reflects place in particular ways – in this case reflecting a sense of Japanese stoicism, that from a Korean perspective is interpreted as a form of emotional repression. This perceived absence of conversation and sense of emotional repression left Hyun-suk feeling burdened by social media, and yearning for more face-to-face conversations with his friends.

The earthquake hit Yuki, a young Japanese woman, as she waited in the Shibuya subway station to catch her train home. Being underground, Yuki was protected from the worst effects and, once the tremors ceased, she and her fellow passengers made their way to the street to be met by a confused and crowded chaos. Her *keitai's* battery was very nearly flat, so rather than use it, she saved it in case of an immediate emergency. To gather news of just what had happened and what was still happening, she relied on the oldest methods, and listened to nearby conversations as she moved through the street from group to group. As a relatively shy person, and as someone who had normalised Japanese reserve, Yuki was amazed to see strangers gathering and talking, and she listened and watched intently. With subway services suspended, Yuki had a long walk home and, as she moved out of the city, people

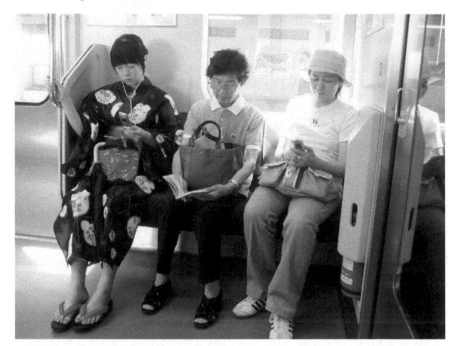

Figure 3.1 Three generations of the mobile

on the street thinned out. For five hours she walked the surreal streets feeling alone and afraid. But hugging her *keitai* made her feel slightly less alone, as if the object itself was full of all her friends and family. She checked her Twitter a few times quickly.

Inherent in the theme of the book is the observation that social media is both mobile and situated. To give a sense of the way social media is situated in the particular milieu and times of Tokyo, we begin with exemplary cases of Japanese social media – the *keitai* and the *keitai shōsetsu*. We then move to discuss these Japanese social media in the particular context of the disasters of 2011, using historical examples of Japanese media, and using our focus group to illustrate the significance of mobile social media in this very particular sociotechnical, cultural and historical context.

Keitai shōsetsu

At the time of Japan's 2011 earthquake, the tsunami that quickly followed and the subsequent Fukushima nuclear disaster, the social media device of choice was the *keitai*, an internet-enabled, 'smart' mobile phone, bristling with personalised applications, media and UCC. While the *keitai* does create particular affordances in terms of the intimate and omnipresent relationship with the online, it also amplifies a relationship to the offline and a sense of mapping and moving through a place. As Mizuko Ito and Daisuke Okabe (2003) observed in the case of camera phone practices, the relationship between context and content is coordinated by ambient and intimate co-presence. In most places in the West the 'smartphone' is a relatively recent innovation, but in Japan the *keitai* has for over a decade been *the* vehicle of choice for the online. As an ideal vehicle for and of 'the personal', the *keitai* highlights Japan's position as a global centre for innovation around personal technologies (Ito 2005) – including the Walkman, the Game Boy, the Discman and NTT DoCoMo's i-mode (which provided an early form of mobile access to selected internet services).

The Kindle, Samsung tablet, iPad, Kobo and a variety of other mobile media devices are now well-known products for distributing and consuming works of literature, but perhaps the first of all was the mobile-phone novel (*keitai shōsetsu*). Initiated in Japan around 2000, *keitai shōsetsu* have become a national phenomenon. Yourgrau describes *keitai shōsetsu* thus:

> Most *keitai shōsetsu* auteurs hail from Japan's vast demographic of teenage girls and twentysomething young women, who thumb out lurid, mawkish romances on their keypads in scraps of manga-like dialogue, skimpy action, texting slang and *emoji* (emoticons). They post these skeletal pseudo-confessions in installments, under cute pseudonyms, on dedicated websites such as Magic i-land and Wild Strawberry.
>
> Astronomically popular, 'thumb novels' are much decried as trash for yahori ('slow learners'). But over the past few years this trashy subculture has stormed Japanese commercial book publishing. In 2007 – *keitai shōsetsu*'s annus mirabilis – half of the top 10 fiction bestsellers in the shrinking Japanese book market originated on cellphones.
>
> (2009 n.p)

The success of *keitai shōsetsu* can be attributed to a variety of factors: Japan's *keitai* market where screens are big enough to allow for relatively easy reading; the ubiquity of long commutes on public transport; the specific characteristics of the Japanese language and its characters; and the long tradition of the 'personal, pedestrian and portable' (Ito et al. 2005) as part of everyday life. Perhaps most significant about devices such as the *keitai shōsetsu,* the Walkman and the Game Boy is the capacity they have to cocoon the user from geographic presence, and in a sense relocate the user to a personalised space – an aural space, a game space or, in the case of the *keitai shōsetsu*, a story space. As a medium for cultural production and consumption, the content of *keitai shōsetsu* has mainly been embraced by young women, as both readers and writers, as a forum that provides new avenues and contexts for expression around gendered and previously tacit practices, particularly domestic ones (Hjorth 2009b).

The *keitai shōsetsu* phenomenon began in 1999 with the founding of one of Japan's most pivotal UCC sites for mobile internet, Maho No Airando (*maho* meaning 'magic'). Although *keitai shōsetsu* were initially written by professionals, by the mid-2000s everyday users had begun to be inspired to write and disseminate their own *keitai shōsetsu*, and now millions of titles are produced each year. Predominantly written *by* women *for* women, this mode of new media also highlights the significance of remediation (Bolter and Grusin 1999), and many of the successful *keitai shōsetsu* are adapted back into older media such as film, *manga* and *anime*. *Keitai shōsetsu* can also be seen as an extension of earlier gendered tropes of Japanese new media that were dubbed in the 1980s the 'Anomalous Female Teenage Handwriting' phenomenon (Kinsella 1995). Characterised by *'kawaii'* (cute) transformations of the Japanese alphabet – *hiragana* – which has a history as a 'women's language' – this emerging genre of new media writing soon dominated mobile communication. The earliest occurrence of this was in a phenomenon called the 'highschool girl pager revolution' whereby female UCC hijacked (through personalisation techniques) a technology that industry had aimed at businessmen ('salarymen') (Fujimoto 2005; Hjorth 2003; Matsuda 2005).

For Yonnie Kyoung-Hwa Kim, *keitai shōsetsu* needs to be understood as 'refashioning emails rather than literature' (2012: 9). Often young people move between emails and *keitai shōsetsu* as both genres and modes of address evoke a similar type of intimacy. Here, it is important to remember that in Japan the *keitai* has long been the dominant mode for accessing the internet and thus mobile internet emails are akin to SMS in other cultural contexts. In addition, *keitai shōsetsu* can also been seen as an extension of literary traditions evoked by arguably one of the most famous novels in the world (written in AD 1000), *The Tale of Genji*. Drawing on *haiku*, letters and love sonnets, 'Murasaki Shikibu's' (not her real name, thought to be Fujiwara Takako) *The Tale of Genji* deployed *hiragana* to tell both the male and female side of the numerous lovers of a playboy, 'Genji' (Hjorth 2009a).

The *keitai shōsetsu* phenomenon in Tokyo is indicative of the significant and multi-faceted role the *keitai* plays in everyday life. As long ago as 1999, when people in many countries were still using the mobile phone for voice calls and SMS, Japan had used i-mode to leap-frog into the mobile internet. It was not long before *keitai* UCC developed – of which the *keitai shōsetsu* is exemplary.

Like the *keitai*, *shōsetsu* plays on the significance of the *personal* within Japanese tradition (Fujimoto 2005); a fact that can be evidenced in Japan's successful role in 'electronic individualism' (Kogawa 1984) from the Sony Walkman to the Nintendo Game Boy. The *keitai shōsetsu* epitomises the specific role the personal has played in Japan upon both micro (individual) and macro (national) levels (McVeigh 2003). Through the *keitai shōsetsu* and its emerging modes of creative, social, affective and emotional labour (i.e. UCC), we can see the pivotal role of the *keitai* in extending the notion of the 'personal' (Ito et al. 2005). While these 'personal' and 'intimate' elements of the *keitai* are remediated in that they rehearse

Figure 3.2 Keitai customisation

and revise older media/rituals and vice versa, they are also shaped by socio-cultural events. This is particularly amplified in the case of crisis management.

Mobile media and disaster in Japan

New media didn't make revolutions happen in the Middle East and North Africa, and it didn't make the consequences of disaster go away in Japan, but for many who were directly involved or were keen observers, it did frame how these consequential events were conceptualised and experienced. It might also be said that events such as disasters and revolutions frame how new media are perceived and experienced, and if there was ever any doubt, recent revolutions and disasters have politicised the affordances of social media. Old media too have been framed by war, revolution and disaster, some being popularised, for example ship's radio after the sinking of the *Titanic* (Sconce 2000), others weaponised, for example mass media as propaganda during the First World War (Lasswell 1971).

In the case of Japan, one of the most notorious regions in the world for frequent earthquakes, many historical examples of then contemporary new media framing crisis can be found. While each new media form comes with its novel affective culture, each is also a remediation of previous modes of emotional interpellation. Each medium partakes in its own economy of co-presence, presence-at-a-distance (see discussion of the various modalities in Chapter 11; also see Richardson and Wilken 2012), forms of intimacy and forms of public action. So, the death of a celebrity such as Princess Diana can provoke an outpouring of public grief that is at once distant and yet intimately frenzied, while the death of a hitherto unknown person, such as the Tunisian street vendor Mohamed Bouazizi, can provoke an outpouring of grief that translates his public into a powerful political actor. In Chapter 10 we will discuss how that one might be described as the actions of a Mob, and the other the actions of a Public. In both cases intimacy and publics have been invoked and mediated, it's just *how* the affective forms of labour are harnessed, and to what collective end, that have changed. In each case twenty-first century 'participatory' media creates its own types of affective cultures that can arrest the public and their emotional labour in new ways.

An early Japanese example of the role participatory media play in a disastrous situation is the case of the production and dissemination of picture postcards after the Great Kantō Earthquake in Taishō era (1912–1926). As discussed elsewhere (Hjorth and Kim 2011a, 2011b), picture postcards emerged during Japan's high industrialisation as a phenomenon to depict various types of modernisation practices. Postcards, especially with real photo images, were immensely popular before the era of visual mass media. According to Sato (1994), the postcard played a key role in creating and demonstrating new modes of visuality around modern everyday life, a role now being played by camera phone practices.

In September 1923 a 7.9 magnitude earthquake hit Tokyo and its environs. Devastated cityscapes were quickly rendered into snapshots, printed onto a picture postcard and mass produced for immediate sale. Picture postcards became the 'hottest' medium to inform various publics of what happened in the city, using actual images of the city. Most sold out as soon as they were released, while in an early precedent for current controversies, others were banned due to their sensational or inhumane subject content. Picture postcards used photo-realism to capture a place, and used industrial techniques for rapid printing and distribution, thus preserving a sense of the time. These mass-produced but highly situated images, combined with the personalisation of the senders' words on the back, combined powerful media affordances still present in today's social media. The postcard said, 'share this experience with me'. And while the postcard was ostensibly a dyadic medium, sent from one person to one other person, it was also unsealed, and both image and message were immediately available to anyone handling the card, and postcards were of course passed from hand to hand and put on display among social and intimate publics.

Another Japanese example of the historical deployment of new media during times of crisis was the use of (pre-web internet) PC networks in the times following the Kobe earthquake of 1995. From the outset, PC networks have been used not just for data sharing and file sharing, but have also been used as 'technologies for cooperation' or to support 'communities for mutual aid' (Rheingold 1993, 2002; Takano 1995). The Kobe experience provided one of the first examples of the potential of PC networks as 'technologies for journalism' (Hjorth and Kim 2011a, 2011b). In the face of what was perceived as the failure of the mass media to adequately cover the Kobe disaster, grass-root journalism grew in response. It was a moment of social awakening for PC networks as they became an alternative vehicle for mass communication as well as a context for the distribution of the social. PC network activism around the Kobe earthquake was celebrated in terms of its vividness and ability to harness both an informational and social function, and for its pragmatic work in coordinating help and recovery from the disaster.

According to Takano (1995), the Kobe earthquake and its associated forms of networked UCC highlighted the debut of a new social medium in the public sphere – the Internet. In Kobe the internet functioned as both a social and informational media that was collaborative, user-driven and participatory in nature, and if these features sound familiar it is because they are often viewed as characteristic of contemporary Web 2.0 media, rather than Web 1.0 static publishing. However, as the old saying goes, the future is always here, it's just unevenly distributed, and in times of crisis, we see that flashes of future media are apparent while at the same time older media is tested and often re-assigned.

Having set out the broader sociotechnical and historical context, we will now move to explore the role of mobile, social and locative media in Tokyo around the time of 3/11. Here, we are investigating the affects and effects, the uses and the limits, of social media during this crisis by drawing on fieldwork conducted by Kim and Hjorth in the aftermath of 3/11. This comprised a focus group of five graduate students (three females, two males, all in their twenties) as well as diaries completed by over 50 students, aged between 20 and 30 years old. Given Tokyo's long history of mobile media innovation, this case study provided a way to reflect upon the boundaries and possibilities of the media in times of grief and trauma. Did it alleviate or amplify feelings of sadness or fear? Did it bring people together or make people more aware of the distances and differences? How can we map the types of affective cultures produced by, and through, social mobile media?

While there is a body of literature around crisis and public trauma through older media discourses (Bernard Donals 2001; Caruth 1995; Lacapra 2001; Wolfreys 2002), much social media discussion has been around civic engagement or identity management (Bennett 2008; boyd 2007; Rheingold 2008). Moreover, given the way in which grief has many layers and levels that take various arbitrary forms subject to both the individual and collective situation, it is a messy phenomenon to map. Grief, like most emotions, doesn't function when it should. Emotions take awry and undulating contours and shapes that are as vivid as they are painfully visceral. So how are media used in different ways to reflect the internal emotions and affect of the user?

Case study: the 'mourning' after

Kim and Hjorth's fieldwork was conducted in Tokyo in May 2011, when the horrendous experiences of 3/11 were still fresh in everyone's memory, but enough time had passed for experiences to be discussed in a composed manner. Rather than steering with leading questions, the conversations took shape organically, occasionally led by rudimentary questions.

Although our informants were all acquaintances in the same faculty, their personal stories clearly reflect five very different experiences of the events of 3/11 and its aftermath. As will be seen, these five different reactions are evident in their diverse use of old and new media, and their attitudes to the effects and affects of old and new media. Importantly, the focus group was made up of Tokyo residents of both Japanese and non-Japanese backgrounds. This cultural diversity together with geographic distance (from family and friends) had important implications for the different uses of social media, and expectation formed around social media use at a point of crisis.

We began the conversation about the role of social media in both helping and perhaps hindering people's management of a crisis and the attendant affective culture. As mentioned in the opening vignette of this chapter, for Korean student Hyun-suk, social media functioned as 'a conference rather than a conversation'. Here, the liberatory, participatory and 'conversational' elements often ascribed to social media were clearly not present, and he expressed both distrust and feelings of being 'bombarded'. It was the events of 3/11 that clearly shifted his feelings on the media. As Hyun-suk elaborated:

> Before 3/11, I thought Twitter is a tool for information delivery. It still is, but I feel now more burden doing activities like tweeting or re-tweeting information. I now would rather choose to tweet very trivial matters with no relation with social situation. It might be a self-discipline or self-controlling but I don't think it's the right context for expressing emotion around important matters. If a person who resides in Tokyo says critical matters, people may consider the person uncivilised grumbler. I actually gave up saying what I wanted to say because of this judgmental atmosphere. Now the atmosphere has been distantly changed. Everybody started to criticised government and TEPCO [Tokyo Electric Power Company] with the Fukushima nuclear disaster.

Hyun-suk's reaction above illustrates how disappointed he became in the affective nature of Twitter and its community in response to the crisis. Here we see that mobile intimacy, and its relationship to intimate publics, is informed by various factors – especially socio-cultural. Hyun-suk's expectations, and thus disappointment, about the intimate and consoling nature of mobile media like Twitter was undeniably informed by his media experiences in Korea. However, in Japan, the way mobile intimacy plays out is much more reserved, discreet and subtle. Alternatively, for Chinese female student Jie, the *keitai* was informative, useful and comforting:

> I was working in my part-time job in e-book publishers close to campus when it happened. When I first felt the first big shake, I hid myself under the desk with other people in the office. As soon as I knew the hypocenter was close to Sendai – one staff told me after checking her *keitai* – I tried to call to my friend living in Sendai. It was a miracle that I was able to connect to her; and I was relieved to hear she was safe. I was lucky as my boss gave me a ride home [public transport was in turmoil].

Yuki, the Japanese woman described in the opening vignette, was also comforted by her *keitai*, which played a role at a metaphoric level as a repository for all her intimates, as well as in a literal way, allowing her access to Twitter and other social media. For Toshi, however, mobile media in the form of the PSP played an important role by providing him and his friend a space to escape from the horror and confusion of the events as they unfolded. Toshi's reaction to the aftermath was to deploy older media to escape from the disaster. The image Toshi paints is one in which social media was overwhelming in its bombardment, to which he responded by switching to older media that provided the comfort of familiarity and had no relationship to the current events. As he said:

> I intentionally avoided information on the earthquake. There were so many discussions about the earthquake. I was fed up with it so that I decided not to be disturbed. I actually kept searching for animation channel on cable TV instead of news. I looked at Mixi once, but found all the 'tsubuyaki' was about the earthquake and its aftershocks. Then, I gave up logging onto Mixi. I went back to my game but felt distracted.

Meanwhile, much of Yuki's anxiety was couched around her usage of the *keitai* and its limited battery life, as the *keitai* played a significant role in how the events of the crisis unfolded. Drawing her information from newer 'conversational' media like Twitter rather than TV, the new media also provided a form of counselling. She, like so many of the informants, deployed a mosaic of different media – both old and new – to try to make sense of the event. As Yuki noted:

> On the first day, while I was walked home, the *keitai* was the only medium and form of comfort I had. As soon as I got home, I turned on TV to find such a shocking video. I didn't feel like watching it as I was alone. I needed to talk to people, gauge how other people were feeling. I preferred media like Twitter or Internet BBS ... I liked Twitter because it informed me of my close people's news: whether they are safe, how they are doing, and so on. Once a friend came to visit me then I felt strong enough to watch the TV with her.

Yuki clearly deployed a patchwork of media practices and mobile intimacy affects – from participatory media conversations to older, 'packaged' media. Interestingly, it was the older media that frightened Yuki the most. Partly this was because of the visual and aural economies of TV which made her feel helpless, and, partly this was because in comparison to media like Twitter, TV does not mediate a discursive intimate or social public. Yuki's response strongly contrasts to that of Toshi who escaped into the older media as a reprieve from the relentless dialogue of new media. Indeed, given the awry nature of grief with its layers of shock and sadness overlaid with moments of disbelief, it is not surprising to see these textures playing out through new and older media practices. As cartographies of personalisation (mobile phone customisation via users; see Hjorth 2009a), media practices reflect inner subjectivities as they also express social currencies. Although the role of social media in times of crisis has attracted some interesting research of late (Bruns et al. 2012), it is important to explore how people are feeling during their participation in such media. While thousands may tweet, retweet and follow tweets, Twitter's function in the grieving process is not universally applauded, as evidenced by contrasting views of Toshi, Yuki and Hyun-suk. Data-mining and visualisations may paint pictures of media phenomenon during these times but, as anyone who has lost an intimate will attest, they are abstract in the reality of grief's texture. Instead, there needs to be more ethnographies of media affect and mobile intimacy to understand the micro, messo and macro levels of intimate publics in times of trauma.

For Yue, social media brought her great relief as she was able to almost immediately contact friends and family throughout China. She deployed both old and new media to 'figure out what was happening'. This coordination of both old and new, push and pull media was reflected in other informants' responses. As Yue stated:

> At first, I tried to talk to family and friends in China through email. After I went to campus, I met a few friends staying night there. There I could access to Internet as well as watch a small TV to figure out what was happening. I got back to my room next day. Then I tried to report in several websites that I was safe – Renren, Weibo, Twitter, and Facebook.

Here we see how Yue is attuned to her how her different media practices speak to numerous intimate publics. It was not enough to post on Twitter or Facebook, which are not accessible to her Chinese friends and family in China. So too, for Yue's non-Chinese friends it was important to post to English sites like Facebook and not just to Renren or Weibo. For another Chinese student living in Tokyo, Jie, it was the *keitai* that first gave her news about the event. She then used both international (Twitter and Facebook) and Chinese social media (Renren and Weibo) to make contact with her friends and family, as well as finding information to help during the emergency:

When the earthquake occurred I was in the office and we had no TV there. When I got back to my room, I soon turned on TV and accessed to internet. I Skyped with my parents, then checked Twitter, Facebook, and a Chinese social media site. I messaged to friends that I was safe and everything was all right. I could get some information about what I should take in this emergency.

Through the deployment of both old and new media, across online and offline spaces, we see some of the ways in which media is used in coping, or not, with a crisis situation. From Toshi (who used media such as games to shield and hide from the event) and Jie (who used a variety of old and new media to both contact friends and family), we can see how emotions are played through and by the media, as well as it being a method of accessing information. Far from new media replacing older forms of media and mediated intimacy, we see how various modes of subjectivity and affect play out in their own coordinated media practices across the various intimate publics.

In these cases mobile media is heading in two different directions. First, more than one decade on from the 'people power' or 'smart mob' (Rheingold 2002) mobile-phone civic engagement examples, in the Philippines (Pertierra 2006; Rafael 2003), in South Korea (Kim 2003), and now in Tokyo, mobile media is providing new *effective* and *affective* models for capturing, sharing and commemorating events that encapsulate both collective and individual experiences. These conduits allow for a new sense of collective affective power that makes us *feel* more 'connected', and the 'perpetual contact' (Katz and Aakhus 2002) of mobile media affords new types of co-presence. It is the mobile phone's mobility that, dialectically, makes place even more important (Ito 2002), particularly one's place in the midst of a disaster. Grief can take new technocultural routes for connecting intimate publics as well as creating new modes of mobile intimate affects, and in this context new types of intimate citizen journalism have emerged.

But the *keitai* was not only a collector, transcriber, translator and disseminator of these horrific events; it also shaped the *affective* nature of the event. It fused the real with the reel. Here we see how digital media both creates new types of affective economies at the same time as rehearsing older media (Hjorth 2007b). In the UCC images of the 3/11 disaster, mobile media devices appear against the backdrop of human voices gasping in terror. Here, the devices became a way for the user to move identity, from one experiencing the terror of the moment, into the recorder of events; an ability to migrate momentarily from the overwhelming shock and horror of it all, to the narrator of the reel. One decade on from the first generation of camera phone studies, new networked and emplaced visualities are producing different types of affective micronarratives.

The other view of mobile media became evident through its limits. As millions panicked and attempted to call family and friends to see if they were okay, the phone lines jammed. The only other time this happened in Japan was in the 1990s when high-school girls jammed the pagers meant for businessmen with their cacophony of text messages (Hjorth 2003; Matsuda 2005). As we saw, for some, the perpetual contact with the deluge of horrific events via social and mobile media was overwhelming. They instead deflected from the media in favour of face-to-face consoling, or even gaming. For others, like Yuki, even the symbol of the *keitai* as a repository for all her intimates gave her solace in the face of her fears. Hugging her *keitai* was akin to being close to her intimates.

These two directions signal both the possibilities and limits of mobile media in negotiating the online and offline worlds. This is but one example of the cartographies mapped by mobile media – as a communicative, creative and political expressive tool – as it moves across online and offline worlds into geosocial terrain. While the deployment of social mobile media expands earlier modes of civic engagement and media, it also departs from the previous media by providing various modes of visual, textual and aural communication with *greater affective personalisation*. Within the highly networked and personalised worlds of social and mobile media, the capacity for public engagement and its relationship to the personal takes on unique forms. Social mobile media provide new spaces for networked, *effective* civic responses and *affective* interpersonal responses.

Conclusion: postcards from intimate publics

In an age where the 'interior is the new exterior' (Sukhder Sandhi cited in Margaroni and Yiannopoulou 2005: 222) and intimacy has gone public (Berlant 1998), how do we begin to conceptualise the role social mobile media plays in our lives? Does it help ease the pain in times of crisis? Does it provide new avenues for networked counselling and helping coordinate and disseminate information? Or does it bombard us with too many events and too much affect, to the point where, like Toshi, we retreat from participation entirely? Not only is the quantity of UCC flowing through mobile media a problem to be dealt with; Hyun-suk also pointed out that the 'tone' struck by the mix of effective and affective communication is problematic. For many reserved Japanese, the quake related UCC was no doubt too emotive, but for Hyun-suk it was not emotive enough. Far from new media displacing older media, we see that the assemblage of old and new, online and offline media practice is deployed to reflect the user's emotional space in times of crisis. In the case of crisis management, we can see that various types of mobile intimacy are played out through old and new, online and offline media.

Affective and personal technologies like social and mobile media make us rethink old psychological models of emotion that see emotions as coming from inside an individual or group (Lasén 2004). As Sara Ahmed (2004: 8) argues in *The Cultural Politics of Emotion*, the way in which we understand emotions has been inverted – 'the "inside out" model has become an "outside in" model'. In the case of social mobile media, we are requiring new models and methods in order to examine the types of affective cultures and surfaces produced through, and by, the media. By exploring case studies of social media usage during points of crisis and the attendant deluge of grief, we can begin to understand some of the textures of affect around the participation in twenty-first century media. While personal technologies like the *keitai* are rewriting the relationship between mobility and intimacy, it is important to remember that sociotechnologies like the *keitai* are part of a lineage of technologies of propinquity (Hjorth 2005; Milne 2004).

These debates about the emotional affects of social media are not new: such issues were also pivotal in the debates surrounding the advent of the postcard. For Milne (2011), the postcard 'reveals that intimacy is a culturally constructed system of signification rather than an empirically verifiable, naturally occurring state'. As Milne (2012) observes, the affect of media content on intimacy is signified, but is not empirically verifiable. Twitter, like the postcard, does not 'necessarily foreclose the production of intimacy and presence' but creates different affects around types of public intimacy. So, too, our attempts to manage our various intimate public and private emotions both online and offline are amplified in moments of crisis and grief.

Through the lens of social media we see that the media are affording some new types of public action and public 'counselling' at the same time as they are highlighting the need for older forms of public action and mediated intimacy, including face-to-face forms. Like the montage of grief that leaves its textures on an emotional terrain for ever, social media deploy both new and old forms of intimacy and affective cultures.

In the next chapter we explore the changing fabric of image-making processes as camera phones undergo re-contextualisation through locative media. Through the case study of locative media camera phone practices in Shanghai, we explore how these new visualities are reflecting emerging tapestries of mobile intimacy and place.

4 The place of intimate visualities

Ba ling hou, LBS and camera phones (Shanghai)

Like many of her mobile compatriots, Ai lives in a different province to her mother and father, and relies upon her mobile phone to maintain contact. Typical of her generation of students, (those born after 1980, or the *ba ling hou*), Ai has grown up immersed in digital technologies both inside and outside of the classroom. Also typical of her 'one child per family' generation, Ai is transferring her new media skills to her parents, so that they might keep in constant contact despite geographic distance. Casual, social games like *Happy Farm* suit this purpose, but Ai could never have predicted that her mother would become such a keen player. In its heyday around 2009 *Happy Farm* captured tens of millions of players in Shanghai alone, though by late 2010 many younger people in particular had moved on to other games. But not Ai's mother. At least once a day Ai would receive an instant message from her mother on the free mobile internet service, QQ, requesting her to come to the fields (of *Happy Farm*). If Ai was very busy with work she would suggest another time, but given that she was adept at moving between the various applications, windows and platforms at university, she would often play with her mum on the fields of *Happy Farm*, and joke about stealing each other's vegetables. For Ai, these fleeting moments of play with her mother helped alleviate her longing to see her parents.

For male student Bao, social media games had lost much of their appeal since they hit the mainstream in 2009. They became games that his uncle or parents played, not him. Instead, Bao enjoyed location-based mobile games like *Jiepang*, which involves 'checking-in' online when he visits various offline places, to notify others of his presence, to comment on the place and to win prizes. He especially liked the game as many female students also played it, and he saw it as a fun way to play with them. He noticed that female users tended to take more photos and that often the photos were really interesting. Bao had started to take photos with his iPhone but still wasn't confident enough to upload them to *Jiepang*. He also liked the location-based affordances of Renren (China's equivalent to Facebook), and loved when he could see that a friend was nearby, offering the chance to catch up with them face-to-face. Bao wondered how his parents ever met without a phone and location-based services (LBS).

Fang, a female teacher, was amazed at her parents' and grandparents' adoption of social and mobile media. Often her father would tell her about some interesting feature on China's oldest social media, QQ, that she didn't know. For Fang, the whole idea of young people being 'digital natives' who have a natural affinity for high technology is a misreading of the situation. Fang's uncle, for example, was 45 years old and yet played online games and social media more than any teenager she knew. With her busy teaching schedule Fang found that the only social media she had time for was Weibo (China's equivalent to Twitter, but with rich media capacities). The intimate, immediate and compressed nature of Weibo allowed her to quickly pick up current debates in bite-sized pieces, and feel connected without being overwhelmed.

For Zhong, QQ was a quintessential part of everyday life. His grandparents in a rural village used it. His parents in a peri-urban town used it. For many of the older generation, QQ had guided them into the world of the online through free and easy services accessed by the mobile phone. Zhong liked QQ's egalitarian qualities that enabled three-quarters – 318 million – of China's 485 million online users (CNNIC 2011) to go online via mobile media. Zhong remarked that if he were a fish then QQ would be his water.

In China, the mobile phone has been the key device for the uneven development of online media – providing new platforms, avenues and contexts for social and locative media engagement. While this phenomenon has been associated with cross-generational developments in media practices – especially around games – there are still marked, though often tacit differences between each generation's usage. In particular, while social media games are loved by the young and old, locative media games like *Jiepang* are much more likely to be played by the *ba ling hou* than by others. For the *ba ling hou* LBS games provide new ways to document, illustrate and narrate a sense of identity, sociality and place. Specifically, through LBS like *Jiepang*, the *ba ling hou* are providing new visualities of their journey as they migrate through various forms of mobility (physical and socio-economic). Just as the *ba ling hou* are part of the new social and economic mobilities of China today, they are also marked by particular relationships between technology, place, and intimacy.

As a consequence of educational reforms and China's booming but uneven economy, the *ba ling hou* are a generation for whom studying and working away from home is becoming the norm. Often from one-child families, they deploy mobile, social and locative media in particular ways to negotiate home and away co-presence (Hjorth and Arnold 2012). As the first generation to grow up in China's emerging net culture, the *ba ling hou* are a product of a significant 'IT in education' initiative that began in 1994, and the installation of the first national educational IT network, called CERNET (Chinese Education Research Network).

The *ba ling hou* were also the first group of students to be affected by the EISS policies (an acronym for 'Electronic Information Service System' or in

Figure 4.1 Shanghai and modernity

Chinese 'xiaoxiaotong') in which the government orchestrated the imple-
mentation of computers and online education within primary and secondary
schools. In November 2000, the EISS was initiated as a ten-year project to
enable 90 per cent of the independent middle schools and primary schools
throughout the country to have access to the internet, including the deployment of online resources to be shared amongst teachers and students. The *ba
ling hou* students are the CERNET and EISS generation, growing up with the
benefits of these policies giving them high media literacy, and positioning the
internet as a pivotal part of everyday life. The EISS, along with the proliferation
of Chinese electronics and software manufacturers, and global developments
in Web 2.0 participatory entertainment industries, has ensured that for most
university students in China today, the internet and mobile technologies are
an integral part of their daily life.

In China, there are three very different but interrelated phenomena evolving around online gaming communities – one highly political, another locative, and the other exceeding social. First, phenomena such as in-game
protesting (Chan 2009) have highlighted the role of the internet as a form of
public sphere for political agency (especially apparent in the microblogging
culture like Weibo). Second, the widespread use of locative-based games such
as China's *Foursquare* equivalent, *Jiepang*, in which electronic and co-present
social spaces like SNS are overlaid onto the geographic and physical, has

created different modes of locale, and different ways to be located. Third, the widespread use of casual social games like *Happy Farm*, played through SNS such as Renren and Kaixin, have resulted in millions of users, both young and old, socialising in intimate publics.

According to iResearch, a consulting group specialising in internet research, around 50 per cent of the 26 million daily users of renren.com, one of the main SNS, play online games (Cheng 2010). These games generate around half of the website's yearly income. 'In terms of user groups, SNS games are totally different from traditional network games,' says iResearch senior analyst Zhao Xufeng (cited in Cheng 2010). While the number of traditional network games (like massively multiplayer online games, or MMOGs) has remained relatively constant at 50 million, casual SNS gamers have grown in number from nothing to tens of millions in a few years (Cheng 2010). One of the key priorities for SNS gamers is communication, especially more novel and innovative ways of communicating – something that SNS games provide. Unlike the other dominant gaming genre, characterised as 'intense' or 'hardcore', SNS games are much more casual in their demands on engagement. However, behind this casualness is a play architecture that is often just as time-consuming – but takes the form of distracted, micro-engagement, and often users have the game open on their desktop behind other screens, such as word documents, email and IM.

Interestingly, the growing population of users migrating to these types of online games aren't the obvious demographic – young students. Rather, it is their parents and even grandparents of children living away from home who are being taught to use the internet. This cross-generational new media literacy emerging in China's increasingly mobile population casts social media such as QQ and online games such as *Happy Farm* in the role of maintaining kinship relations and helping to alleviate the negative effects of cross-generational class mobility.

Part of the reason for the cross-generational embrace of social media games in China has been the important role played by mobile media as, for many, it provides the context for accessing the online. In China, three-quarters of its 485 million online users do so via mobile media (318 million, CNNIC 2011). So too, the influence of a *shanzhai* (copy) culture, and widespread availability of 'copy' phones through the 'grey market' has ensured that smartphones are not just a privilege of the rich.

This chapter examines emergent smartphone visualities in relation to the Chinese LBS, *Jiepang*. As the vignette featuring Bao illustrated, *Jiepang* users scan 'check-in' to mark their visits to offline places, and consequently win prizes. However, *Jiepang* also allows users to use text and images to notify their friends about their movements and experiences, and it is this secondary, social motivation that we focus upon in this chapter. Specifically, *Jiepang* is becoming a space where *ba ling hou* users are toying around with various forms of visuality that both reflect and expand upon earlier photographic genres.

Figure 4.2 Multiple mobilities and immobilities

According to our respondents, unlike the dominant microblogs Sina and Weibo, which are used predominantly for self-portraiture, or Renren, which is deployed to express inner feelings, *Jiepang* visuality is more about new types of place-making. These place-making exercises are in a sense like diaries (Ito and Okabe 2005), recording daily journeys, but with their active use of filters and perspectives, *Jiepang* is also a medium for emergent forms of creative practice for the *ba ling hou*.

In order to explore the emergent locative visualities, this chapter first explores China's particular media and mobile cultures. We then move onto a case study of *Jiepang* users and their relationship to camera phone practices. This discussion of the emergent locative media visualities as 'emplaced cartographies' will be discussed further in Chapter 10.

China's media and mobile cultures

> But without censorship, I think I would be much less interesting. Trying to find possibilities through the difficulties can make life more interesting. I often see my cats put their toys in an area littered with obstacles, and their play becomes interesting and dramatic.
>
> (Ai Weiwei 2012: n.p.)

The paradox of control and freedom hardwired into the performance of the online (Chun 2006) is most apparent in China. As the quote by Chinese artist and dissident Ai Weiwei suggests, state control helps to make him a more interesting artist. Against the backdrop of regulation and restriction, Ai Weiwei's work flourishes in its political play with notions of freedom and control. In China, the freedom and control paradox is also intrinsic to the performance of class. Class shapes, and is shaped by, the media cultures that are characteristic of China's rapid economic growth and dramatically shifting cultural landscape of the twenty-first century (Donald, Keane and Hong 2002; Qiu 2008).

Through media cultures materialised in the *shanzhai*, we can see representations of socio-economic, geographic, generational, technological and psychological mobility, each of which complicates notions of age, class, place and identity. The *shanzhai* mobile phone in particular has provided a symbol for, and of, the growing migrant working class (Law and Peng 2006; Qiu 2008, 2009; Wallis 2011). Once upon a time, the *shanzhai*'s loud ringtone unambiguously signalled that it was a cheap and less desirable copy, and that its owner was a member of the 'have-less' class; however, more recently, the divide between copy and original has been further complicated by the abundance of high-quality *shanzhai* smartphones. Moreover, for older users, the loud ringtone and larger screen of the *shanzhai* smartphone is preferred. In providing for mobile media for all classes, and in providing a vivid example of technonationalism, the *shanzhai* occupies an important place in China's ICT industries, highlighting a culturally specific relationship between consumption, copying, creativity and new media.

In July 2011, three examples of *shanzhai* Apple stores were identified by an American blogger in China. Within 72 hours of the post she had received over one million hits and global news media companies avidly picked up the story (BBC 2011). The story seemed to spearhead a tension between two very different technocultures – the *shanzhai* culture of China, on the one hand, and the Apple culture of the US, on the other. Whereas the *shanzhai* culture makes a virtue of proliferation, the Apple culture makes a virtue of proprietary rights, a clash of cultures exacerbated by the ongoing friction and controversy associated with the working conditions enforced by Apple's manufacturer Foxconn, which have been described by some as barbaric (Qiu 2012).

However, this confrontation between the *shanzhai* and the Apple original, playing out globally as China confronts the economic power of the US, also highlights the complex localised nature of media practice. In addition to handsets, *shanzhai* culture is also evident in the replication of the photo and image editing apps that have become synonymous with iPhones. The types of visuality produced with these *shanzhai* phones and apps are not just 'networked' visuality, as reported by the first generation of camera phone studies (i.e. Ito and Okabe 2005) but, rather, as Sarah Pink has identified, are also part of the movement from 'networked visual events to emplaced images' (2011: 7). Rather than being 'snapshots' suspended in a placeless and timeless void, location-based camera phone practices become entangled within a sense of place, time and intimate publics. Here the node or the journey is emphasised, rather than being a means to an end.

Although a high-quality technological infrastructure and universal access to the internet are still very much an urban phenomenon, significant changes have occurred in rural areas, with the number of rural internet users nearly reaching 100 million (CNNIC 2011), and a rural usage growth rate that far exceeds the urban growth rate. While in urban city areas the internet is mainly accessed by the middle and upper class via personal computer, the rest of China's predominantly working class demography deploys GPRS (General Packet Radio Service) for internet access via the mobile phone. An increased uptake of social media is also notable along with the increase in internet access that accompanies economic and geographic movements.

Within China's net-scape, numerous types of SNS – representing different classes, communities and lifestyle clusters – can be observed. These SNS predominantly fall into two types – sites such as Renren, Kaixin (which is used by female 'white-collars') and MSN which are often simultaneously open on someone's desktop; whereas Fetion and the aforementioned QQ can be accessed both via mobile phones and computers. More recently, the colossal rise of China's version of Twitter, Weibo, has seen tens of millions making the most of its compressed, punchy and rich media context.

Having set out this background, we will move now to a discussion of emergent locative media practices.

Jiepang and the camera phone: a case study

The widespread availability of high-quality camera phones, accompanied by their in-phone editing applications and social and locative distribution services, has resulted in the production of new types of co-present visuality. In the first studies of camera phones, Ito and Okabe (2003, 2005, 2006) noted the pivotal role played by the three 'Ss' – sharing, storing and saving – in informing the context of what was predominantly 'banal' everyday content (Koskinen 2007). As camera phones became more commonplace – as did new contexts for image distribution, such as microblogging (i.e. Weibo) and LBS – emergent types of visual overlays become commonplace. In these located social practices, images are recording ambient, localised contexts in which the geographic is overlaid with the social and emotional.

While globally camera phone genres like self-portraiture have blossomed, we are also witnessing the flourishing of vernacular visualities that reflect a localised notion of place, social and identity-making practices (Hjorth 2007a; D.H Lee 2009a). With LBS such as Facebook Places, *Foursquare* and *Jiepang,* the superimposition of electronics and geography also overlays place with the social and personal. Specifically, by sharing an image and comment about a place through LBS, users create social ways to experience and record journeys and, in turn, make an impact upon how place is recorded, experienced and thus remembered. This is especially the case with the overlaying of ambient images within moving narratives of place as afforded by LBS.

Today's smartphones enable new forms of distribution and provide a plethora of apps, filters and lenses to help users create 'unique' and artistic camera phone images. Although the iPhone and other smartphone versions like Google Android were innovators in this space, through applications such as Hipstamatic, the *shanzhai* phones were not far behind, and in some instances were in front, by providing in-built FM radio, video cameras and better-quality digital cameras than the iPhone in particular. So too, social media like microblogs and LBS have acknowledged the growing power of camera phone photography by not only affording easy uploading and sharing but also providing filters and lenses to further enhance the 'professional' and 'artistic' dimensions of the photographic experience (Mørk Petersen 2009). In our respondents' photo albums we noted that while respondents used traditional genres like food and places, they did so by using filters and lenses in order to create highly aesthetic images. Far from being banal and boring, these images were often unique and creative. These images are not only about the vernacular qualities of UCC; they also represent new types of emplaced visualities.

Jiepang is a relatively new Chinese game that combines location-based mobility with social distribution of UCC. Although the first epoch of urban mobile gaming, played by groups such as Blast Theory, reconfigured the urban social fabric by transforming it into a play space (de Souza e Silva and Hjorth 2009), the latest is marked by a 'gamification' of social media, and the 'placing' of social media, through gameplay that involves visiting the 'newest', 'coolest' places and showing these places to friends. Moreover, *Jiepang* plays into the growing phenomenon of mobile microblogging in China, in which the camera phone plays an important role, and shapes how place is experienced and shared co-presently, a phenomenon sometimes called 'networked visualities' (Lee 2009; Villi 2010).

As a Chinese version of *Foursquare*, *Jiepang* renders places and movement into part of its gameplay architecture. The key motivation for users is both to see where their friends are, as well as to find and report on new 'cool' places. While discussions in Western contexts about *Foursquare* have been concerned with ideas of privacy and surveillance (epitomised by the 'please rob me' website), such notions about the individual and its relationship to the social don't translate well in the Chinese context. Part of the reason why *Jiepang* doesn't attract the same types of debates about privacy can be found in culturally specific notions like *guanxi*. For Cara Wallis, *guanxi* is a 'widely used yet ambiguous' (2011: 67) term that can mean many things: relationships, personal connections and social networks. As Wallis (2011) observes, in the case of Beijing, the deployment of social media is closely bounded by the notion of *guanxi*. She notes:

> In contrast to the individual-orientated nature of western cultures, where the autonomy of the individual is presupposed, Chinese social

organization has been described as relationship-orientated. In traditional Chinese culture ... there is no unique 'self' outside of social relationships and the personal obligations that inhere in those relationships ... despite the influences of communism, industrialization, urbanization, and westernisation, many have still found utility in conceptualising the Chinese sense of self as predominantly relationally focused.

(2011: 67)

The notion of *guanxi* has been significant in the rapid uptake of *Jiepang*. An early adopter will often persuade friends to join the new media network with the promise that it isn't for everyone but, rather, just for them (aka reflecting *guanxi* intimate relations). Here we see that *guanxi* fosters a tightening of the close social ties around an intimate public that often exclude other, less close contacts – a phenomenon Ichiyo Habuchi (2005) calls 'telecocooning'. By deploying new media like *Jiepang*, the *guanxi* associated with users of this service can be tightened by singling those out with similar lifestyles, socio-economic and technological backgrounds.

Jiepang is a geosocial game almost exclusively the preserve of the *ba ling hou*. *Jiepang* epitomises their relationship to the internet as a space that is public and also almost compulsory. Indeed, for this generation, there is a need to be 'always on' and omnipresent through media, and services like *Jiepang* facilitate this. That is to say, the *ba ling hou* use *Jiepang* to be part of the intimate publics in which the personal practices of the everyday become, on the one hand, commodified and, on the other, a further tethering of a sense of place (which is as much emotional and social as it is geographic and physical) with personal politics. The connection with place and location sharing is closing, linked to not only narrating their travels for themselves, but, more importantly, as a way to share co-present intimacy with friends. What emerged from discussions with our respondents was that, for many, the main motivation for *Jiepang* use was to record the places they went to, for both themselves (i.e. as an *aide-mémoire*) and also in order to share this information with their friends to extend the relationship between *guanxi* and place-making. Here we see that the personal is political insofar as the domestic and personal practices around these geosocial games are played out in public domains. But this public domain is a space of multiple localised communities that see their usage of *Jiepang* as not rendering them a *phoneur* – to recap, Luke's (2006) notion to describe the user as a mere node in information and commercialisation circuits – but rather, as forming a meaningful way to further enhance mobile intimacy.

While the ramifications of *Jiepang*'s darker side – that is, the way in which LBS weakens privacy and even invites stalking (Gazzard 2011) – are yet to fully play out, its deployment does illustrate the ways in which the *ba ling hou* are part of new generations in a culture in which Western notions of privacy may not apply. Moreover, *Jiepang* use highlights the way in which participation, as with privacy, is viewed differently in China. Such notions as watching – what we call 'lurking' in the West (Crawford 2009) – are seen as an *active* and *positive* part of online 'participation' (Goggin and Hjorth 2009).

Through the overlaying of highly edited camera phone images and comments, respondents narrated place in new ways. Often the visuals were deployed to present a unique image of the place, whether through the image genre, or, more often, using filters and lenses to create a mood. According to Ai (female, aged 25), *Jiepang* use was in order 'to record where I go to everyday. It's like a diary with location.' The other respondents shared Ai's sentiment – many viewed recording locational information via *Jiepang* as both for their own and other's benefit. For Bai (male, aged 27), *Jiepang* was primarily used to 'record where I had been' and having this information 'synchronised with social networks such as Weibo help to share with my followers'. Others didn't record everywhere they went, but, rather, used *Jiepang* only for those occasions when they went to new places.

For Bai, *Jiepang* was important in recording and archiving his activities and journeys. Unlike Ai, Bai didn't record each place he went to everyday, just a few highlights. Here we see the way in which gender inflects the ways in which *Jiepang* relates to ongoing endeavours to narrate the everyday. Bai viewed *Jiepang* as a tool for showing where he was when he wanted people to know. Sometimes checking in on *Jiepang* was accompanied by taking pictures of the place, an activity Bai definitely viewed as gendered, stating, 'usually females would spend more time on it than men, and take more photos'. Both these informants noted that recently there has been a growth in different LBS on smartphone and PC platforms, and that groups of friends would use similar ones – in short, the deployment of an LBS reflected the *guanxi*. With the additional dimension of camera phones interwoven with locative media, *guanxi* and place can take on more complex cartographies that place, emplace and embody visualities.

Camera phones and their image applications have mediated the 'professionalisation' of the amateur through an overabundance of photo filters and lenses, have vastly increased the number of images taken and shared, and perform as 'poetic' interventions that situate images within a place. In particular, through LBS like *Jiepang*, users are taking, editing and designing camera phone images as part of representing a place in a unique way that is then shared to reinforce *guanxi*. Unlike Sina and Weibo microblogs or Renren, which are about personal journeys and feelings that are accompanied (especially by female users) with self-portraits, *Jiepang* images not only demonstrate different photographic genres to reinforce the social elements of place, but also they tend to be much more 'artful' images.

Just as *Jiepang* is 'more about the journey', the accompanying images are not only akin to what Ito and Okabe (2005) identified as visual diaries, but are also indicative of an 'individual' experience that is then emplaced. Through images of mainly food and scenery, users try to give hints about a place while also trying to be more poetic in their images to indicate a sense of subjectivity.

While respondents noted that they used Renren for albums and archiving, *Jiepang* visual narratives were more about micronarratives about '*where* I am and doing/feeling what'. All respondents noted that *Jiepang* inspired them to take more camera phone pictures; and thanks to smartphones it was easier to take, edit and share images. Moreover, with *Jiepang*, respondents progressively felt the need to make visual and textual comments about places, especially through the idea that images were part of an event or movement. Thus *Jiepang* images are part of what Pink identifies as the multi-sensorality of images, whereby they are located in 'the production and consumption of images as happening in movement, and [users] consider them as components of configurations of place. Such an approach is not only applicable to digital images' (2011: 4).

Exploring the role of the image as part of a meshwork of movement through a case study of locative media (Google Maps and Google Street View images of Spanish bullfighting), Pink (2011) outlines what she calls a theory for multi-sensoriality and movement. Earlier studies of camera phones failed to study images as not just part of a 'network of connections but an intensity of entangled lines in movement' (Pink 2011: 8). Here Pink's notion of the emplaced provides a more complex understanding of contemporary visual cultures, not as 'an intersection of nodes in networks ... but in terms of a meshwork of moving things' (2011: 8). For Pink, the involvement of images within online contexts means that places become a '"constellation of processes" ... that includes those of moving through localities and those of moving across a screen, and the multi-sensoriality that each of these implies' (2011: 8–9).

In the case of camera phone practices in *Jiepang* we see the multi-sensoriality and movement of the image occurring across various levels. Not only does the genre and content narrate place as part of journey and process, but also the frequency and its link to reinforcing the *guanxi* suggests a complex mapping of place, sociality and visuality. This becomes apparent in case studies of *Jiepang* and its logic of emplaced visualities. With LBS creating new cartographies and connections to place, we see visualities move from first generation notions of the networked visual (Ito and Okabe 2005) to emplaced visualities. In the case studies, the role of camera phone content constructing types of gender performativity – akin to Judith Butler's (1991) notion whereby cultural norms of gender and sexuality are enacted through a series of iterations and regulations – becomes apparent. As we see in the following examples, *Jiepang* not only became a site for gender performativity but also a way in which users could be active in conveying the multi-sensorial movement of the context of the image so that it was not just located, networked or placed but also emplaced.

In the series of *Jiepang* images in Figure 4.3, the female respondent, Ai, has deployed various filters and lenses to her images to create a sense of ambient intimacy (Ito and Okabe 2005). Ai's narrations of place move from humorous and playful self-portraiture to poetic gestures of the everyday. Far

Figure 4.3 Ai's camera phone figures used in *Jiepang*

from taking the 'banal' images that were so characteristic of the first generation of camera phone images, Ai actively works to make 'beautiful' and 'unique' images of places and events. The genres and texture of the images differ from the male respondent Zhong's images (Figure 4.4). There is no reference to people, no portraiture, and instead there are various strategies for creating an ambient intimacy. From images of movies Zhong is watching, to food he is eating, the images not only deploy numerous filters but also paint a picture of the respondent's overlaying of the *guanxi* with cultural capital (i.e. cultivating a 'cultured' sense of self).

Like Zhong, the female respondent Soo is prone to use self-portraiture. Her images also invoke the cultural capital of Zhong's images, although she is more interested in weaving a sense of intimacy through images that evoke taste and smell (i.e. delicious food). They are aesthetically beautiful and attempt to indulge the viewer through documenting beautiful food that looks delicious.

Soo spoke with great enthusiasm about taking and sharing her camera phone photos through *Jiepang*; she noted that she almost always 'checks in' (with image and text) at any restaurant or famous scene (Figure 4.5). Soo noted that food was her dominant genre among the photos taken within *Jiepang*, as she believed it touched the other senses in addition to the visual. Here we see that camera phone picture taking in *Jiepang* is about not just evoking a sense of intimacy with place but also a multi-sensorial experience, using images to invoke the place for her friends.

Figure 4.4 Zhong's camera phone figures for *Jiepang*

An important motivation for taking and sharing photos on *Jiepang* is to tighten the *guanxi* among friends. Soo says: 'I am keen on sharing the memorable experience with my friends through those photos. It is very interested and I feel like that friends and I are always together, even though some of us are miles away apart.' Unlike sharing texts, sharing photos demonstrates a strong sense of maintaining intimacy between users of similar social backgrounds. Such communication can be regarded as part of the construction of 'full-time intimate communities' (Ito and Okabe 2005: 12). The reason why Soo does not like to take and share her self-portraits but prefers portraits of food is that she wants to maintain a sense of privacy. Although Soo admits that many of her friends like to check in at some places just to show off, 'I will not check in at some private dates to protect my privacy', she says. This issue of privacy was clearly gendered as male respondants didn't discuss this element.

Beyond the hype of *Jiepang* as a first-generation commercial mobile LBS game, already we are starting to see some of the ways in which such geosocial applications are being used by respondents as a meaningful part of everyday practice, in which the electronic is overlaid with the social, emotional and geographic in ways that both rehearse older practices of socio-spatial connectivity at the same time as they create new social geographies. Particularly interesting is the way that these cartographies are often gendered in their

Figure 4.5 Female respondent, Soo

deployment, with males and females using *Jiepang* in different ways to map their socio-emotional practices onto everyday coordinates. While being shaped by factors such as gender, age and class, LBS such as *Jiepang* also signal emergent types of connected presence and ambient intimacy. By over-laying the socio-emotional with the geographic and electronic through images that evoke multi-sensorial experiences as images-in-an-event, while, at the same time, creating highly refined and often beautiful images of the everyday, *Jiepang* is illustrating new types of emplaced visuality.

In *Jiepang*, the social asset at play is also geographical or locational knowledge. This echoes Ilkka Arminen's (2006) point that, when it comes to SNS, social context rather than 'pure geographical location' is generally of greatest user interest; what seems to be most at stake in *Jiepang* is new knowledge about particular sites and what these are likely to signify within social network settings. *Jiepang* highlight that the various dimensions around ideas of place as contextualised by the *guanxi*. Thus, many of those surveyed revealed that the higher the perceived level of novelty or uniqueness that is seen to be associated with a place (such as, in the words of one respondent, a 'supreme' restaurant or hotel), the higher the likelihood that their presence in and knowledge of this place will be recorded via *Jiepang*, as 'routine places like home or [their] company are not worth checking in'. In this way, it is geographical (or 'environmental') 'knowing' and an appreciation of the 'capital' that is invested in and carried with this knowledge that is

Figure 4.6 Emplaced placing in Shanghai

paramount, and which forms a vital resource within the participants' wider peer network.

Conclusion: emplaced visuality and geospatial sociality

In *Jiepang* we see new types of emplaced visuality and geospatial sociality that is almost exclusively performed by the *ba ling hou*. Through the locative and microblogging experience of *Jiepang*, users are creating new forms of intimate publics whereby the importance of the network pales into comparison to the significance of the *guanxi* in providing ambient contexts. As part of the smartphone phenomenon, *Jiepang* is accompanied by an accelerated rate of camera phone taking, editing and sharing. Far from banal a-contextualised images, these pictures deploy the newest of filters and photographic tricks in order to give a sense the poetic and the unique that are then overlaid onto places via *Jiepang*. In *Jiepang* camera phone images, images are edited and contextualised so that the *guanxi* clearly overlaid onto place. This is not a mere practice of networked visuality as noted by the first studies into camera phones; rather we see emplaced and multi-sensorial visuality that creates, and reflects, unique forms of geospatial sociality.

A service such as *Jiepang* enables the *ba ling hou* to be part of intimate publics in which the personal practices of the everyday become, on the one hand, commodified and, on the other hand, further tethered to a sense of place that is as much emotional and social as geographic and physical. Social relations are thus played out in public domains in ways that foreground both networked social and place-based settings as they are negotiated in combination. Through *Jiepang*, the public domain becomes a space of multiple localised communities whose members are not wandering *phoneurs* or nodes in information and commercialisation circuits, but are tangling up place and sociality in order to construct and maintain mobile intimacy.

As we have suggested, the deployment of LBS like *Jiepang* illustrates the need to revise the relationship between visuality, sociality and place. Through new types of visuality that are more than just networked but are rather 'emplaced', *Jiepang* users connect the multi-sensorial experience of place with their culturally specific notion of social capital in the form of *guanxi*. The saliency of *guanxi* also highlights that while LBS is creating new forms of ambient, emplaced, social visualities it is also rehearsing and tightening older social ties.

In the next chapter we will continue the exploration of cross-generation media literacy and mobility in the context of Manila in the Philippines. Entitled 'Intimate Distance' we investigate some of the ways in which social and mobile media is being used to negotiate various forms of home and away across numerous intimate publics.

5 Intimate distance

Sociality and identity in the in the face of diaspora (Manila)

When Amelia's parents asked to 'friend' her on Facebook she postponed the inevitable. She had long enjoyed Facebook as a space that she and her friends in Manila and abroad inhabited. Amelia mulled over the fact that, once upon a time, Facebook was for the young, but now everyone was using it. She knew it was only a matter of days before she would have to 'friend' them. Until then, she continued to develop her camera phone images that, when uploaded, always received numerous comments and compliments. She wondered if her parents would understand these images and what they meant to her and her peers.

Makisig is a young man who is very active in student politics at the University of the Philippines. He enjoys using social media to get his message 'out there'. But he is also very critical of the way some people just seemed to wear politics like fashion. Pressing 'Like' on Facebook was not activism in Makisig's view. Everyday Makisig collected pictures via his camera phone and uploaded to Facebook and Twitter as a way to tell a political story.

Sampaguita was heartbroken when Maximillian broke up with her. She was particularly hurt by the way he did it, via Facebook. Sampaguita didn't realise until her best friend called her to see if she was okay. Sampaguita quickly got off the phone and checked her Facebook page to see that Maximillian's relationship status was now single. And what added fuel to the fire was the fact that incriminating pictures of Maximillian with another girl could be found uploaded to Facebook. She felt compelled to look at the girl's Facebook page as her shock turned to anger.

Tala missed her sister so much. Killed in a car accident a week ago, Tala could not accept that her sister was no longer around. From morning to night she clung onto her sister's phone, checking, holding and waiting. Looking through her text messages, call history, photos and Google Maps history, Tala continuously rehearsed the events of her sister's last week. She hoped the phone might help explain how she was feeling. The search for her sister's life through the phone took another twist on the day of her sister's funeral, when the phone inexplicitly began to chime. Tala felt a cold sweat as she looked at the phone. For some reason, her sister had set the alarm for that morning. At that point, Tala knew that her sister was there, watching.

The Philippines has long commanded the attention of global press for its prolific use of SMS – an average of 1.39 billion per day in 2008 – earning it the unofficial title of 'texting capital of the world' (Madianou and Miller 2012: 49). This profligate texting is deployed for social and business communication, of course, but perhaps not surprisingly, in many other contexts as well. For example, in a country with millions of devout Catholics (the third largest after Brazil and Mexico), sending texts to 'God', and receiving texts from 'God' (in reality, commercial and Church text-service providers), is not an uncommon practice (Ellwood-Clayton 2003; Pertierra 2006; Rafael 2003).

In addition to texting, the Philippines have, in some respects, become a global leader in the use of social media (McKay 2010; Universal McCann Report 2009). Friendster and Multiply were the first SNS to gain a significant uptake in the Philippines. Although originating in the US and offering an English-only interface, by 2004 Friendster's growing traffic in South East Asia, particularly in the Philippines, was evident to the company. Chris Lunt, Friendster's director of engineering, tracked the networks of Filipino connections back in time to 'patient zero', Carmen Leilani De Jesus, a 32-year-old Filipina expatriate then living in San Francisco, the 91st person to join Friendster, and the first to provide a link to a Filipino. By 2008 Friendster was the most-visited web site in the Philippines and Filipino Friendster users outnumbered all others (Liu 2008). Acknowledging the significance of the Filipino cultural context (and a localised notion of social capital) in Friendster's popularity in the Philippines, De Jesus wrote:

> I personally think that Friendster took off in the Philippines because that's a culture where friendship and 'who you know' is sometimes a more valuable currency than money. Basically everyone has an 'uncle' or a 'friend' or a 'relative' who can help you get what you need based on nepotism, favoritism, friendship, etc., because not everyone has money. 'But if you do me a favor, I'll owe you a favor.' This is why friendship is important, and why a platform like Friendster, which was a 'friend-collecting' service, took off so rapidly in the Philippine culture.
>
> (Quoted in Maderazo 2007)

Whilst it is still a minority of Filipinos who have internet access (21.5 per cent according to Universal McCann Report 2009) – as one might expect in a largely rural, developing country – those who do would seem to be enthusiastic users, with more than 80 per cent using social media at least monthly (Universal McCann Report 2008), over one million photographs uploaded to Multiply each day (Salazar 2008), and 68 per cent of users uploading video (Universal McCann Report 2009). More recently, the uptake of Facebook and camera phone image sharing has taken on new narratives for identity, intimacy and sociality (McKay 2010).

This enthusiastic deployment of social media is in a sense an extension of earlier modes of civic engagement mediated by text-message services, but it also departs from the previous media by providing various modes of visual and aural communication that provide possibilities for greater affective personalisation. Within the highly networked and intersubjective worlds of social media, the capacity for intertwining different forms of intimate relations and different forms of social engagement among different social and intimate publics is clear. Social media thereby provide networked spaces for *effective* social engagement and *affective* interpersonal engagement, providing a key example of the communicative efficiencies and affective social possibilities of these two different and yet convergent media. As a location renowned for the significant number of female care workers abroad, Manila offers a fascinating context for examining the relationship between intimacy and distance, especially in light of mobile, social and locative media convergence. Does social media, accessed via both the mobile phone and personal computer, affect the performance of intimacy, sociality and identity in the Philippines? What types of social and intimate publics are emerging in the face of diaspora?

Social media in Manila

In the case of Manila, where social media is relatively new for most, one might assume that it would be the province of the young, as it was in the West. But although SNS is very popular among Manila's university students for example, this is not the only significant user demographic. Indeed, uptake has occurred across the generations, and parents and even grandparents are now starting to make use of social media to keep in contact with family and friends, in regional languages (e.g. Cebuano, Ilokano, Hiligaynon) as well as Tagalog, Taglish, English and Spanish. There are also numerous social media services developed specifically for the Filipino and wider South East Asian market – 'Pinoyborn', 'Hikot', 'Eskwela', 'Pinoy', 'Tayotayolang' and 'Pinoy-Kubo' are popular local services, and there are also Filipino takes on Facebook, for example 'Taas Noo Pinoy'.

Mediated communication is particularly important for the 10 million, or 11 per cent of the total population, who are overseas (Madianou and Miller 2012; Philippine Overseas Employment Administration 2007). This very large disaporic community, comprising in the main of women 'care workers' (McKay 2007, 2010), has been an important factor in this rapid uptake of mobile communications and SNS technologies. In the face of this diaspora, intimacy and social media are framed by the phenomena of cascading 'care chains' (Madianou and Miller 2012), where a grandmother in a village looks after her daughter's family, while her daughter is in the capital looking after another woman's children, who is in Singapore looking after another woman's children.

In this context social media plays a double-handed or ambiguous role. On the one hand, contemporary media are implicated in the recruitment and geographic relocation of women from the villages to workforces in the cities and overseas. They are the tools of the professional, and they are part of the women's ostensible but unrecognised social relocation from mother to bread-winner. At the same time, though, these sociotechnologies are used to maintain the semblance of a traditional family structure and the semblance of a maternal role, if not the day-to-day performance of traditional family life. In the Philippines there are not just social networks of 'friends' who are selected and maintained from within the pool of one's peers, there is also the deployment of social media within intimate publics: that is, within extended family structures where traditional family life finds itself reshaped by the socio-economic mobility of youth, by geographic mobility, and by global labour structures and 'transnational motherhood' in particular (Madianou and Miller 2012).

Thus the same communications infrastructure that is used to socialise is now used to afford a sense of stability in a family life that is challenged by the instability associated with geographic dispersal – as students and care workers move from the provinces to the city, and as overseas foreign workers move from the Philippines to other countries. The significance of this diaspora to Filipino society, the strength of traditional Filipino family life, the widespread deployment of mobile SNS technologies and the history of Filipino deployment of technologies in political ways all makes the Philippines an interesting and important context for understanding new ways of maintaining intimate co-presence, intimate publics, social publics more generally, and changing modes of intimate and public engagement. As Deidre McKay notes, the study of Facebook provides insight into changing images of Filipino identity and sociality:

> Facebook is one of several new interactive technologies that shift users towards recognizing a more markedly relational self. The site enables users to deploy digital images in new ways and the images themselves become actors, shaping new modes of interaction and norms for relationships from kinship to romance to friendship to ethnic or national belonging. That new technologies shift users' perceptions of the self suggests that individuality and dividuality are always present, but articulated differently in different cultural contexts and with varying emphasis. My respondents' desire to transfer extended family and collective histories onto Facebook implies a difference between the emphasis and articulation of the dividual and individual aspects of the person between Filipino and non-Filipino users. With Facebook offering such resources to negotiate personhood, relationship and belonging in new ways, it not surprising that post-colonial Filipino users contest understandings of ownership and appropriation of images which they consider follow colonial norms.
>
> (2010: 496)

As McKay observes, while social media 'are inevitably transforming everyday life' (2010: 479), they play a particular role in the historical image and personhood in Filipino uses of Facebook. According to McKay:

Instead of merely re-presenting already familiar forms of personhood and relationship, these sites transform the ways people understand themselves. On them, digital images work to track and shape users' interactions with others in novel ways, revealing these transformations in personhood and norms for relationships.

(2010: 479–80)

In her detailed tracing of the rise of the digital image and social networking, McKay argues that this important union is particularly relevant when thinking about images and personhood that are a reaction to the Filipino diaspora. Moreover, McKay notes 'sites such as Facebook both amplify and complicate the possibilities of exchange and display, juxtaposition and comment, cultural production and self-shaping that give photographic images their varied social meanings' (2010: 481).

As we discuss in detail in Chapter 10, the collaboration between camera phone practices and social and locative media is creating new ways for individuals and groups to redefine a sense of identity and its relationship to place. In particular, these new visualities highlight how complex the overlays of place are – traversing geographic, social, cultural and psychological terrains that are both lived and imagined. As we argue, the convergence between locative, social and mobile media sees place becoming an entanglement of 'placing' and various modes of presence (Richardson and Wilken 2012). This is especially the case with camera phone practices that emphasise the node, travelling and intimate over the network (Pink 2011).

In our case study in Manila, the camera phone was a powerful tool for self-presentation, sociality, placing and presence. Often respondents took pictures they felt were a commentary on the moment, the place and the placing. Shared camera phone pictures, especially through social and locative networks, often represented something significant about the place. Moreover, they often toyed with the 'banality' of camera phones as an always-there eye on the world to reinvent the poetics of the everyday, as well as recontextualising the user's place and presence in that moment. However, in this chapter we focus specifically upon the ways in which respondents spoke about social media as a tool for negotiating self-representation, expression, intimacy and sociality.

The fieldwork was conducted in August 2009, and again in 2010, and was informed by 60 students attending one of Manila's main universities, the University of the Philippines (UP). Our choice of UP was guided by the fact that one of the University's policies is to draw students from predominantly outside of Manila, and from diverse socio-economic backgrounds. Unlike universities that recruit students from the wealthiest families (Ateneo de Manila University for example), diversity at UP is more marked, and it thus represents a better cross-section of young Filipino demographics as a whole. This having been said, the extent of diversity should not be overstated, even at UP. Universities in the Philippines recruit differentially from among the classes, as they do in all countries, and relatively few students are drawn from among the urban or rural poor. 'Diversity at UP' thus refers to its relatively broad spread across the socio-economic middle classes, rather than its reach to the least privileged socio-economic classes.

Intimate publics and social networking: a case study of UP students

Through these themes the realities of convergent social media's undulating landscape appear as multiple narratives, stories, practices and intergenerational politics. We argue that through a revised notion of the personal as public we can gain insights into the emerging and remediated practices that move beyond Manichean paradigms of empowerment versus exploitation around the politics of media practice. Social media blur the efficient and the affective, and proffer great possibilities in understanding the entanglement of the self and its identity with the intimate, the personal and the public. It is argued in Chapter 8 that the potential for collective action is inherent in a public, and in this sense publics are political. Social media entangles intersubjectivities and publics in the performance of social interaction and this entanglement of the personal and the political was made apparent in the words of one male respondent aged 19, Marco:

> I would argue that the personal is political. Everything we do is political. Even if we are talking about a telenovela we are already talking about something that matters ... most of my profile pictures are to promote a cause. It depends upon your personality. If you are an introverted person you might use your pictures to show different sides of yourself. Whereas if you are an extrovert you might just keep the same profile picture and then use other functions and features to express yourself ... I used an image of myself speaking at some political convention because I am shown doing something political. And I'm leaning into my laptop and it had a logo of my organisation. So the image shows that I am someone working for this organisation. As for my other profile pictures, like they all said, it has to be the most aesthetically pleasing image ... But usually they are pictures of me doing something political – like holding a flag of the organisation.

As Marco implies, mediating the expression of self through social media requires a close attention to identity management and impression management through identity, in conditions where many interactions, including those associated with intimate relations, may be public rather than exclusively private. Performing in an intimate public and managing publicness is thus part of the job of doing intimacy. The public interactions that mediate identity and impression were self-consciously monitored and managed by our respondents through profile updates, images, invitations, texts and all the other media social media makes available, a set of behaviours that is complicated by the often diverse range of affective relations that may be present in any given public – lovers, friends, acquaintances, parents, other families, workmates, and so on. In many daily-life circumstances, communicative acts are tailored to the context and to the public, and one presents differently in the exclusive presence of a lover, friends, or parents. On social media, managing identity, self-presentation and the integrity of relations *per se*, while using the same communicative acts across a diverse audience, is no easy feat. It requires either the subdivision of intimates and friends into like publics, some intimate (tightly bound), others social (less tightly bound) and others networks (not tightly bound), and the careful management of communicative acts in these multiple publics, such that each receives appropriate messages and an appropriate impression of the author and the relationship. Miguel's (male, aged 25) strategy is to subdivide his various intimate publics:

INTERVIEWER: So your parents use Facebook?

MIGUEL: My mum.

INTERVIEWER: Do you find that makes you edit or censor the things you say and upload to Facebook?

MIGUEL: I don't let her be my friend. [laughter]

INTERVIEWER: And she's not worried about not being your friend?

MIGUEL: No … Facebook has those privacy settings so you can just select who you want to see things. So it adds to the carefree nature of Facebook. Facebook is quite different from other, older SNS. Because before you might use code names or nicknames [to create multiple identities] but on Facebook people use their own first and last names.

As Miguel highlights, his use of social media constructs multiple intimate publics that often differ from his offline intimate relations. Here, his refusal to befriend his mother on Facebook illustrates how Facebook 'friending' performs differential forms of 'intimacy' and 'sociality' in 'public'. Self-censorship is also a strategy used in parallel with defining and matching identities and publics:

CARISSA (FEMALE, AGED 19):   … when I use SNS I apply self-censorship. I would not write something I think is private.

As do other respondents:

MARIA (FEMALE, AGED 22): I'm not a different person but I do screen everything before I upload to FB. Basically I screen everything. It's to make myself …

INTERVIEWER: Everyone says 'likeable'.

MARIA: No … not likeable, but similar to that.

Here we see that at the local, contingent level of particular intimate and social publics, the aforementioned cartographies of personalisation are mapped out. The emotional labour, the affective behaviour associated with maintaining intimate relations is sub-divided, and boundaries are drawn between family and friends, and among friends. Lines on the map of one's sociality are drawn, and within this personal social cartography, different areas corresponding to different intimate publics are treated differently. Different skill-sets are required to engage in successful emotional labour with each social network, or intimate public. Each intimate public shares its own language, shares tacit and explicit understandings of one another, and shares areas of cognitive alignment. In the case of Marco, national politics is one such source of shared understandings and cognitive alignment, but in a different sense the whole social networking project – involving identity construction, self-censorship, demarking and managing one's intimate publics – is itself an exercise in interpersonal politics. It uses social media as strategic technology for the exercise of power and agency in an interpersonal context.

As noted earlier, Facebook was the most popular SNS for all informants, while Friendster had been their first. These social media provide a common framework, the latitude and longitude as it were, upon which intimate publics are strategically placed, and provide the common infrastructure that shapes their emotional labour. But this common framework and infrastructure does not mean we have a singular group of intimates. As Alicia (female, aged 27) remarks in a conversation recounted later in this chapter, 'People may have the same access, but their context of use is different. It is a venue for different cultures.' The 'context of use' Alicia refers to acknowledges that the cultural context differentiates between one's relations with one's mother, father, siblings, grandparents, closest friends, casual friends and so on, although all may in some sense be regarded as intimates.

In our Chapter 8 discussion of behavioural, affective and contextual aspects of intimacy, we point out that contexts such as privacy and publicness are important to the performance and affects of intimacy, and in the above we see that this is the case. Friends and family are intimates, and many used social media to keep in contact with friends and family. This was especially true of the many respondents who had parents, aunties and even grandparents abroad, who used social media. Like their friends, their family are intimates, and some were happy to befriend their parents online (i.e. add as contacts), and include them (at least potentially) in their social media 'intimate public'. But as we know, others were horrified at the thought of adding parents as contacts, and thus blurring the 'subdivisions' required of emotional labour. The emotional labour required to maintain an intimate relation with one's mother differs from the emotional labour required to maintain an intimate relation with one's girlfriend, and most decide to achieve this division of labour by not including relatives as 'friends'. The cultural context that differentiates familial intimacy and social intimacy is thus reflected in differentiated contexts for the performance of intimacy. In an alternative strategy, those that did include relatives as social media 'friends' set security settings to allow parents access to certain sections of their profile and its stream, but not all sections, and/or self-censored, especially in their uploaded images in order to present a family-friendly identity.

Images would seem to constitute particular powerful landmarks and particularly powerful resources in constructing an emotional topography and locating people strategically within that topography. In a not uncommon example, one female respondent, Marianne, aged 22, had the unfortunate experience of having her account hacked, and pornographic pictures were posted to her site and viewed by her public, including her parents. The presence of peers and parents within the same defined intimate public resulted in an inconsistent, bifurcated response to this uncontrolled posting of images to this non-homogeneous group.

While her peers understood what had occurred – and had perhaps themselves lost control of their own site, their mediated identity and the nature of their relation to their intimates through that site – her parents had not. She tried to explain to her parents that she had been 'hacked' and was not responsible, but she said, 'they had no understanding of what that entails'. So while parents and children might be mingling as one intimate public, is this bridging the generation gap? Or, as one insightful respondent asked, do the generations want the gap bridged? A characteristic of an intimate public is that it is bounded, albeit in a loose and permeable way. As argued in detail in Chapter 8, this boundary is important in distinguishing an intimate public from a social public and from a wider network. Oftentimes, the boundaries constructed by the establishment and performance of these social media publics run parallel to social boundaries that stratify wider society. The issue of whether social media continued to perpetuate generational gaps, gender gaps, class gaps, school gaps, village–urban gaps and so on, or whether the capacity to divide emotional labour among defined intimate publics facilitated the efficient and effective management of intimacy, provoked heated conversation in the focus groups. Following is an example of a discussion related to a generation gap:

ISABEL (FEMALE, AGED 22): I know of parents who have Facebook accounts. Sometimes this can be embarrassing for their children when they say certain things or upload photos.
INTERVIEWER: So parents can leave their children feeling mortified? [laughter]
ISABEL: That is one example. But in general, things like Facebook help the older generation to connect.
INTERVIEWER: So there is an age gap?
ISABEL: I think these SNS bridge the gap between generations. For example, I have a professor who brags about her achievements and interests. And her son was embarrassed by it.
INTERVIEWER: So do you think different generations have various usages?
ALICIA (FEMALE, AGED 20): I don't think it is bridging the gap but providing a venue for the generations. I think the gap could be measured by the frequency or use, etc. The different intended functions can be seen in terms

of generations. People may have the same access but their context of use is different. It is a venue for different cultures.

DIEGO (MALE, AGED 23): But by providing a venue it could provide a way for the generations to understand each other and see how each other perceives stuff.

ISABEL: Yes, but I think that in there is a large discrepancy in usage and so that qualifies as a gap.

ESTELLA (FEMALE, AGED 26): I think the question is whether the different generations want to connect [laughter]. I myself would be mortified if my father accessed Facebook. When I go abroad I use a different SNS because I don't want my mother to see what I'm doing all the time.

In another focus-group discussion, respondents noted that a topography marked out in generational terms may not be as much of an issue as the geographic and class contours that are formed, shaped and performed on a common social platform:

FABIAN (MALE, AGED 22): I think there is much more possible access points today than compared to my parents' generation. People are friendlier now because they are more open to different types of people.

INTERVIEWER: So in terms of cross-generational, how many people see it as bridging gaps? Or class?

JACINTA (FEMALE, AGED 21): I think it is for age gaps, you get to talk to more different ages online.

LOLA (FEMALE, AGED 24): I think it bridges gaps in the city. I could never imagine my mother or father using Facebook or Friendster in the province. But now, in the city, you see your super old prof. [professor] using Facebook, so it does bridge a gap at that point.

The explicit rather than implicit management of identity and impression required by SNS, and the relation between this online presence and one's offline presence, thus becomes an issue in managing relations in public. The issue is played out in instrumental terms (what can one do? What must one do?) and in normative terms (what should one do?). Gerardo (male, aged 23) summed it up well:

The way you know someone online and offline is largely different. You have certain limitations about [understanding what] the person is implying. So you create a different set of values about how relate and define a person. You can't see their expressions or hear their voice. So since there is no delineation between online and offline you often become more judgemental offline if you are well-versed in online SNS.

The effective management of these intimate publics requires strategic thinking:

INTERVIEWER: So do you think it is making people over-analytical?
GERARDO: Yes, spending too much time over-thinking. It's more complicated now.

The question of personal authenticity in relation to one's public identity when online was clearly an issue of concern. Some of our informants pointed out that because one can self-consciously engineer a self-presentation on SNS, one does:

INTERVIEWER: How do you think SNS changed, if at all, the way you present or represent yourself?
MONICA (FEMALE, AGED 25): For me, they know that I can be a bit of a snob. But when I post pictures I try to post images where I look funny or showing myself relaxed because I want people to know that I'm not like that. I have noticed with friends that sometimes they will post pictures, etc. that are controversial, so in this way I think the way you present yourself online is different from what you can do offline.

And that the way one presents politically online may not mirror offline presentation:

LOLA (FEMALE, AGED 23): I think there is a contradiction. I think there are some people who are active online but not offline, and other people who are inactive online are very active offline. Some people are more personable online than offline. There is a contradiction.

Although our respondents are not suggesting dishonesty is at work, rather, it is recognised that the politics of managing intimate publics is a performance that is shaped by the affordances of social media, and this performance in turn shapes the production of identity:

MONICA: Sometimes I have had friends who say that I am deceiving them. But I just think that various sites have specific characteristics which mean that you appear different.

And, as mentioned earlier, an important characteristic is the site's language:

INTERVIEWER: How do you think SNS change, if at all, the way you present yourself?
HECTOR (MALE, AGED 22): The language differs. Most of the status updates, etc. are in English [rather than Tagalog]. And when you talked to them person to person they don't really talk like that. They don't say those things.

Our respondents have moved to university and in so doing are socio-economically mobile and geographically mobile. In a sense they are moving across multiple worlds, and mapping their language use produces overlaying socio-linguistic contours and boundaries, which also map different contexts for the constitution of intimate publics. The mediation of intimacy in English is a characteristic of the world of SNS, whereas the mediation of intimacy in Tagalog is characteristic of their offline sociality. Facebook calls for English and the street calls for Tagalog, producing one set of contours. The city calls for English and their home provinces call for Tagalog, producing an overlay. An educated younger generation calls for English and a less well-educated older generation calls for Tagalog, producing yet another. Professional work calls for English, urban manual work calls for Tagalog, work on a farm may call for a regional language, producing another. So on the one hand we have young, urban, educated peers, all using English on Facebook, at university and in their future professions, but using Tagalog on the street and at home. On the other hand, we have older, regional, less well educated family, some of whom are using Facebook and others not, but all preferring Tagalog. And underneath this complicated, shifting set of contours and boundaries, identity is shaped and displayed, and intimacy is performed.

Surprisingly, considering the experience and expertise our informants have developed in the course of navigating these contours, the issue of online inhibition and impersonalised interactions was still considered a matter of concern. For example, intimacy can be displaced by alienation:

ISABEL: I think with SNS when people don't know each other they tend to say mean things that they wouldn't normally say if you were f2f.

INTERVIEWER: So they forget you are a person?

ISABEL: Yes. Even your friends wouldn't say that f2f but they say and do other things on SNS. When they are online they just say whatever comes to mind.

For Isabel, a relative newcomer to SNS, the experience is also emotionally opaque, even mysterious, and somewhat impersonal:

I started using Facebook in June. I think Facebook and other SNS helps to express yourself because of the interface there is no way to read emotion so people tend to think about what that person really means and thinks. It creates a mystery in a way. So it's a way to express yourself but it is in a way impersonal.

Reflecting the relationship between the contours of the social and intimate on the one hand, and the performance of identity on the other, is the observation that the more calculative distancing effect created by mediations such as the internet could change people's behaviour offline, as well as online. For example, it was argued that communicating through social media didn't challenge people as much as offline interactions. As one male respondent, José, aged 19, noted:

When people are using this SNS it serves as a means for justifying their comfort zones. If you interact in f2f you are left open to other people's values and ideas and so you have your own values challenged. This is opposed to SNS which is a premeditated environment – an environment in which you can control how you interact with people. So it's about their comfort zone because they get used to communicating their way. It models a very individualistic and narcissistic [approach], so if SNS is not used properly it will alienate people from each other. It will create separation. It warps how people relate to each other. They are just communicating online all the time and when they come to meet offline they don't know how to communicate.

Fabián, another male respondent aged 20, clearly prefers the strategic control over communication offered in the online environment:

I consider technology very integrated because it's the primary way to contact people. Especially people who are physically unable to be in contact with you. […] I don't like hearing people's voices too. Being online, like texting, means you can contemplate what you are wanting to say.

As does Immanuel (male, aged 20):

Mobile phones are a big part of my life. I like to text everybody. It's my way of getting in touch with people. I prefer to text rather than call.

Although Rosey (female, aged 24), disagrees:

I think we take for granted traditional ways of communicating like f2f, if its easier to communicate online then you don't think anymore about communicating f2f. I think the f2f is the more human way of communicating – it's more open with all the non-verbal cues and everything. I think that is lost when we communicate online.

And so social media is seen as a controlled environment in which social comfort and personal narcissism act not only to produce intimate publics online, but also to produce alienated publics offline. Some of our informants went so far as to make a clean break between online and offline relations:

DIEGO: I know her [the previous speaker] on cyberspace but I find it strange when she talks to me in person. [laughter]
ISABELLA: Yes, we would talk on Multiply and then we would see each other at school and just walk past each other. If she were to say hello I would think 'but we are only supposed to talk in cyberspace'.

But most were keen to emphasise the strong connection they see between online identity and impression management, and life offline. They are not distinct worlds:

DIEGO: I don't think my image is different in the numerous SNS.
INTERVIEWER: But what about the fact that each SNS has different media tools?
DIEGO: Yes. There are different characters in each one. I try to project the real me through any kind of media.

Loretta (female, aged 22) clearly expresses a normative judgement on identity management and self-presentation, and is prepared to act on that judgement:

> I have some friends who when they use FB post irrelevant stuff or just rant. They forget that even in cyberspace you have contacts who are your friends offline. So the way you relate to them should be similar. What you do online should reflect what you do offline. There are also people that premeditate the material they put on SNS which again is a deviation from who they are offline. Sometimes I will just frankly point that out by saying 'you are being plastic', sometimes I do it privately.

And so Loretta has an expectation of an authenticity that is robust enough and mobile enough to maintain its shape among multiple intimate publics. The norms of identity politics set limits on the extent that online identity presentation can shift from offline identity presentation, and moreover, Loretta is prepared to sanction those seen not to be meeting that expectation.

Important in all of this is the aforementioned Filipino diaspora, separating family and friends along an urban–regional divide, and along a Philippines–abroad divide. When asked to consider how social media has, if at all, changed or impacted upon their lives, respondents commonly noted how important social media were for keeping in contact with people not geographically close – relatives and families overseas or, in the case of many UP students who are not from Manila, keeping in contact with activities at home. For one male respondent aged 19, Gerald, social media was viewed as vital:

> For me, these days it [social media] is a necessity. Everybody is on there using it, the only way to survive is to also use it. As for the mobile phone, if I don't have it I would feel disoriented in regards to schedules and stuff. And in regards to the internet, because it's really important as other people here have said, nowadays people – especially students – really use the internet a lot. The SNS like Friendster, Facebook and Multiply are useful in that they help to communicate more faster and efficiently than before with old friends and long distance relatives.

Here we see that social media are playing an important role in the maintenance of familial and friendship ties in conditions of geographic and socioeconomic mobility, and many stated that the main purpose for using social media was to keep in contact with people not in their physical proximity.

Thus social media play a crucial role, extending the networks and rituals of its precursor, the mobile phone, in catering to the particular forms of mobility – geographic, temporal and spatial – inhabited by Filipino diaspora. For a typical male respondent, aged 22, social media is seen as helpful in coping with mobility and the instability it implies for intimacy and sociality:

> I think that with these online systems – or whatever they are – makes me aware of other people's (pages/lives). I don't really comment that much, I just read what friend's write and say. It's like I can feel what they feel. When I used to have my Multiply account, I think it's the most important thing online to happen to me. Because when I transferred here – I come from outside of Manila – I felt like an outcast because I don't have friends and everything. But through Multiply I can access my friends and classmates accounts and I can read what they are doing. And I feel that life should move on and I should move on. So it basically helped me.

Conclusion: the publicness of intimacy

In the discussion recounted above a rich but complicated picture emerges. This is not just a picture of networked publics, but, rather, an illustration of a picture in which intimacy revises notions of the public and vice versa. The key elements here are a sense of collectivity, and a sense of boundedness.

In Manila we see that intimate publics are often formed across generations, and the performance of intergenerational family roles and intergenerational intimacy are performed and witnessed not so much by ramified dyadic links emanating from a particular node, but by a collective that stands on the common ground of family. The performance of this emotional labour is witnessed by the collective, the intimacy associated with traditional family roles are affirmed through public witness, the intimacy that forms the horizon that bounds this public, which then folds back to shape the performance. The notion of an 'intimate public' captures this collectivity.

We have also seen that issues of identity management and authenticity are entangled with the management of multiple publics. Intimate relations with mother, father, siblings, grandparents, closest friends, less close friends, close workmates and so on, are commonly performed through boundary work; through establishing and managing the boundaries of each of these multiple publics, and through managing the performance of identity and intimacy in the context of each public's character.

Performing intimacy in public through SNS, and social media in general, is quite a juggling act. Personal intimacy mediated by social media addresses multiple publics through multiple modes of self-presentation and applications of self-censorship, but it is also important to be 'oneself' across diverse contexts. Parents must be managed. Friends must be managed. Distance must be managed in the face of collapsing contexts. Intimacy over distance must also be managed in the face of Filipino diaspora. Identity and self-presentation must be explicitly managed. Authentic identity and authentic relationships remain the benchmark for this management, even in conditions where difficulties in maintaining coherency and an authentic human presence across media, across languages and across intimate publics are recognised. Intimacy is tested and stretched in conditions where multiple publics are mapped one over the other, and results are mixed.

We find that our informants negotiate and arbitrate the normative and performative qualities of texting and face-to-face communication; negotiate and arbitrate communications that are paradoxically public and private; negotiate and arbitrate authenticity in the context of online identity and self-presentation. In all of this we see that SNS function both publicly and intimately in a social weave that creates a sense of an intimate public.

6 Generations, mobile intimacy and political affect (Singapore)

Jessie's family was back in Manila, and the years Jessie had been working in Singapore had left their mark. However, her homesickness only surfaced at night, once Jessie had finished housework and childcare for the Lee family. The Lee family were good people and good employers. But just as she would fall asleep after a long day's work, Jessie would think about her young daughter, husband, mother and father back in Manila. During her time in Singapore, costs for 3G mobile phones had dramatically decreased, allowing Jessie more options to try to keep in touch with her family back home. She often used Facebook from her smartphone to send a brief message, or to quickly look at some photos uploaded by her family. Sometimes she used Skype to talk with her daughter, but often found that seeing her daughter on a screen only further reinforced the intimate distance – her daughter seemed so close and yet Jessie was unable to physically hold her. She would try to always sound happy so that her daughter did not worry.

Mr and Mrs Chan were reading the newspaper one Saturday when they came across an advertisement for mobile-phone location disclosure (MPLD). Once used for emergency services, according to the ad, MPLD could also be used as a type of remote parenting tool. Mrs Chan thought it might be a good idea to subscribe so that they could know where their 15-year-old daughter was all the time. But they wondered what their daughter would say ... would she see it as expressing a lack of trust? Would she see it as an invasion of her privacy?

In between university lectures, Kevin can be found playing Facebook *Mafia Wars* with friends. Kevin finds the game a relaxing way to hang out with friends when study commitments mean they can't physically meet up. Often Kevin will flutter between *Mafia Wars*, Twitter and Tumblr, just to catch up on news and gossip. He loves the fact that there are so many social media apps for mobile phones. It means he can discreetly play with others, sometimes even in class when the topic isn't very relevant. It also allows him to keep in constant contact with his girlfriend, Susie, who is currently in London for a semester student exchange. He will often send her a message on Facebook, not saying much in particular, just touching base. He likes the fact that she uses Facebook Places so he can know where she is at any time. He wonders how his parents ever stayed together without a mobile phone and social media.

In Chapter 5 we explored social media use in Manila – a location known for its diaspora of female workers – and how social, mobile media played a role in maintaining a tension that we describe as 'intimate distance'. As a location with high percentages of migrant workers, Singapore also provides an insight into transnational mobility (Thomas and Lim 2011; Thompson 2009). Singapore provides a fascinating case study of forms of mobile intimacy that traverse geographic, temporal, technological and psychological terrains. With mobile-phone penetration rates surpassing 150 per cent, and with 3G customers comprising three-quarters of the total mobile subscriber base (buddecom 2012), Singapore's mobile media landscape reflects its high standard of living, its excellent telecommunications infrastructure, the appeal of new technologies to its consumers and also the high number of migrant workers mostly hailing from the Philippines and India. Sun Sun Lim and Minu Thomas (2011) report that as Singaporean women are entering the workforces in larger numbers, demand for child-care and domestic-service workers has increased, with the result that over 150,000 female workers from Indonesia, Philippines and India are now employed as live-in maids. Eric Thompson observes:

> Mobile phones are constituted as symbol status markers in relationship to foreign workers. Local representations construct foreign workers as users and consumers of mobile telephony, reinscribing ideas of transnational identities as well as foreignness within the context of Singapore.
>
> (2009: 359)

Mobile phones have long played a key role in Singaporean techno-nationalism (Hjorth 2009a) and its post-colonial capitalism (Robison and Goodman 1996). In a country configured by both a complex colonial history and more recent techno-nationalist policies, Singapore presents a particular form of capitalism. As cultural studies scholar Chua Beng Huat (2003) has noted, shopping and consumption play a key role in Singaporean culture. Given that mobile phones have a history as signifiers of lifestyle as much as tools for communication, it is not surprising to see that they are strongly linked to ideas about class and identity within Singapore's multi-cultural social fabric. Like Australia with its National Broadband Network, Singapore has recently launched a nationwide fibre-based broadband network known as the Next Generation Nationwide Broadband Network (NGNBN), in parallel with long-term evolution (LTE) platforms designed to provide faster mobile broadband internet access into the future (IDA Singapore 2012). The provision of this infrastructure, the popularity of smartphones and the mobility of so many of its population are some of the reasons for social media being embraced by young and the old, local and migrant workers in Singapore.

As these smartphones become increasingly a site for multimedia convergence in Singapore, the types of services and brands one uses have become indicative of class, culture and ideologies. For a long time, the mobile phones used by unskilled migrant workers were basic, with little more than talk and SMS capacities. However, with a highly dynamic market in which three key telecommunication providers compete (SingTel, StarHub and MobileOne), Singapore's mobile media consumption has radically expanded, in quantitative terms and in terms of the sophistication of services offered.

Singapore is probably the most important regional economic hub, and with high levels of migration and concomitant cultural diversity, it provides a fascinating example of transnational mobility in the region. In particular, given its high population of Chinese diaspora and Filipino workers, it demonstrates some of the complex and contested ways that mobile intimacy plays out in the region. Noted for its highly paternalistic governmental structures that manifest in a propensity for regulation and in techno-nationalist innovation around technology and creative industries, Singapore's various mobile media practices reflect local cultural, economic and social ideologies. Just as China's migration encompasses the voluntary movement of the *ba ling hou* and the forced movement of its working class 'floating population' migrant workers (Qiu 2009), Singapore's forms of mobility – some chosen, others forced – are reflected in its mobile media practices.

Theorists such as Hannam et al. (2006) have argued that mobility in all of its forms is important in understanding contemporary social media, but so too are various forms of immobilities and 'moorings'. As an evocative keyword for the twenty-first century (Hannam et al. 2006), 'mobilities' draws our attention to the large-scale movements of people, objects, capital and information across the world. Paradoxically, it also draws our attention to the immobile. As Brian S. Turner (2007) has highlighted, though mobility draws our attention to global and regional differences, immobility – or what he calls 'enclave societies' – are perhaps more indicative of cultural and regional boundaries than mobility. Far from nation-state borders being eroded by mobility, mobile social and intimate publics are in fact reinforcing enclaves. According to Turner, 'defending an ethic of cosmopolitanism against the background of an enclave society is highly problematic and uncertain' (2007: 301). Mobility is thus as linked to the local as it is to the global, as mobility transports specific socio-cultural, economic and technological nuances from place to place. In Singapore, with much of its high skilled and unskilled foreign workforce stratified by mobility, we see particular mobile intimacies playing out through mobile media practices.

Social and intimate publics: crossing and merging publics among family and peers

In this region we found various forms of intersubjectivity that reflect and shape the performance of mobility in daily life, the performance of intimacy, and that at the same time highlight immobilities and the distance that mobility and immobility implies. Much like the other case studies in the region, mobile media is being used to maintain cross-generational ties, and like in Shanghai and Manila, respondents in Singapore often included and sometimes resisted parents and grandparents as Facebook friends. Social mobile media was helping alleviate distance between family members. At the same time its use draws attention to the distance created by mobility and immobility.

Filipino migrants in Singapore reported that social technology and its affordances were important to them. For example, they welcomed mobile media as a more intimate and autonomous way to maintain contact with family, as opposed to the use of landlines owned by their employers. But at the same time, multimedia like Skype made 'here' and 'there' more evident, and thus made the distance between the family members more distinct, as noted in the opening vignette of migrant maid Jessie.

As in Shanghai (Chapter 4), Singaporean Generation Y users were, to a certain degree, embracing locative services like Facebook Places and *Foursquare*. In the case of Singapore, though, this deployment was predominantly male, with many female respondents mindful of the 'überveillence' elements of LBS. This gendered difference highlighted the socio-cultural and political currencies of privacy insofar as post-colonial Singaporeans have a more Anglophonic view of privacy than Shanghainese. For 20-year-old female Sasha:

> I think I don't like people to know what I'm doing. I don't use locative media services because I value my privacy quite a bit. I don't mind letting friends know that I'm at an interesting place like Universal Studios [via Facebook Places], but I would not check in regularly. I don't think my friends want to know everywhere I go and vice versa. I don't want my friends to get perpetual notifications of everywhere I go. It's too annoying and doesn't leave space for privacy. I prefer to upload a photo of a special place onto Facebook with a message and so friends get a complex sense of my experience, not just an abstract geographic location.

As Sasha's comment highlights, the co-present sharing of place through location-based services needs to be about creating an ambient, multi-dimensional intimacy that calls upon relationships in place. Here we see the production and consumption of emplaced visualities, that is, visualities that are contextualised in place and in the relationship between creator and viewer, through the choice of ambient visual and textual elements that capture and express something of the place and something of the relationship (see Chapter 10 for details).

Justin is a 22-year-old who enjoyed using *Foursquare* in everyday life. Although his key motivation was the desire to get points from checking in, Justin was also motivated by the fact that he didn't have to tell his friends where he was, as they could just check in and see. However, sometimes when Justin was working he didn't 'check in' as he didn't want to be surveilled by his employers. Here we see fears about surveillance are not so much related to family, friends or other individuals, but to the institutional relations implicit in work.

Mobility, place and distance are problematised by mobile social media, and this includes the problematisation of work and leisure, as well as the problematisation of society based in intimacy, and society based in power. Work and leisure, public and private, here and there, intimate and public, are all hybridised in the often tacit etiquette of social media. And so, the vernacular and colloquial that are in place in this context are out of place in that context. A heat-of-the-moment comment is easily misunderstood once it is recorded, made mobile and recontextualised through social media. Twitter provides another example, as an intimate medium (in so much as it is personalised) and as a public medium (in so much as tweets are broadcast). It also converges interpersonal communication and mainstream journalism. As 19-year-old Clarence notes:

> I love Twitter, it helps me feel connected. I'm always logged in and I often check it hundreds of times a day. I like the fact that I can read a message from a politician or celebrities right next to a posting from my best friend. It layers those worlds in ways that allow me to come and go. I find it works well in my busy schedule. There is no need to respond. And Tweets only take a moment to write. Often, when I write them I think of someone in particular reading it, like my best friend.

Clarence's micronarrative world of Twitter has constructed a particular form of social public in which friends are meshed with news and celebrities. Here the collapsing of contexts (boyd 2011) and the mingling of publics is regarded by Clarence as a positive thing, in which a tapestry of information, sociality and intimacy are woven together in a way that reflects his everyday life. For others, the key aspect of their mobile, social and locative media practices is creating discrete and intimate publics. While many expressed their interest in uploading images and comments as a form of broad social networking, some viewed the ubiquitous nature of the online as requiring compartmentalising. 30-year-old Martin had created two Twitter accounts, one for celebrities, the other for friends. Martin expressed the need to clarify the multiple and discrete intimate publics by clearly demarking certain spaces for particular groups. As Martin stated:

> I find the internet overwhelming at times. So I create different accounts for my different friends, communities and family. This gives me context, something I see missing from much content online. I also don't see everything that I upload as public. In fact I have uploaded a whole lot of images onto Filckr and Facebook and have it on a private setting for viewing. This basically means only I can view them. Sometimes I might show these images to friends on my mobile phone, but I like to keep control over them. I think it's too easy for images to be reappropriated.

Martin's compartmentalisation of mobile intimacy in order to create particular intimate publics highlights one of the key paradoxes of the online, what Chun identified as the control/freedom paradox (2006). For Martin, the network's lack of particular context, or lack of 'place' – the freedom it provides to make communication mobile, means that he needs to deploy strategies of control to prevent the 'collapsing of context' and to clearly align content for specific intimate publics. 32-year-old Mei also performed boundary work to construct intimate publics, and preferred Twitter to Facebook for this purpose. As Mei notes:

> Facebook was becoming too 'blubby' – people pretending to be fun when perhaps they aren't. Also, it is harder to make things private on Facebook. Whereas on Twitter I lock my account so only my friends can see. During the day we will send and read many Tweets. They are very private and intimate messages. When I write a Tweet I know who it's for even though I might not address them or their name. And they will know too. Lots of insider jokes and discussion of feelings. I find it much more meaningful than Facebook acting.

For Mei, Facebook's public and pretentious performativity is contrasted to Twitter's more authentic and intimate affordances. As Mei highlights, Facebook constructs particular types of 'feeling rules' (Hochschild 1983) in which certain types of behaviour, emotions and performativity are rewarded over others. Rather than seeing emotions as individual, private or psychological actions, emotions are an integral part of cultural practice and politics (Ahmed 2004). For Mei, the 'blubby' aspects of Facebook performativity seemed insincere as opposed to the particular economic, compressed and clearly bounded qualities of Twitter. Her Twitter account was intentionally set up to reflect hers and her friends' intimate micronarratives. But as argued throughout the book, the use of a technology is not determined by the affordances of the technology. Mei uses Twitter as the place for the collocation her intimate public in a way that is well bounded. The affordances of the technology do not do this in and of itself. So for example, one's closest friend may not be the most active on Twitter or Facebook. Instead, acquaintances might be much more active, providing copious information on the acquaintance's fleeting thoughts and feelings, and, in a sense, disrupting the agency one expresses in choosing who to be close to.

In another example contrary to Mei's, 25-year-old Cecilia used her Twitter account for following celebrities, not for intimacy. Rather than performing boundary work to define intimate publics, Cecilia used linked forms of social media to create a single broad communicative footprint. As she stated:

> Twitter, I don't exactly update my Twitter but then I connect my Tumblr to both my Twitter and my Facebook so, whatever I post in Tumblr, it

will appear in my Twitter and Facebook. I just go to Twitter to basically just see other people's [celebrity] updates.

Unlike Cecilia, Mei and Martin, who compartmentalise and lock particular forms of social media, 28-year-old David has all his social media accounts open. As he notes:

For me, I open all my social media so I don't really know who follows me on Twitter and who is my friend on Friendster, Facebook. So, I just post on Twitter and regularly update on Facebook so that everybody can see. Or some people, they might be friends with me on Facebook but they may not be following me on Twitter. And so, I just post on both so that everybody can see. I see this media, like the internet, as public. If I post something online, I assume it has gone public and anyone could read it. I don't post everything I think online, I do self-censor. But once its online I do not worry about it.

For 25-year-old Hamsa, Facebook was truly about cross-generational communities, whereas media like Twitter didn't make so much sense to older generations. As she stated:

I think my mum is on Facebook more than me. And one of my friends fathers ask me to be his friend. At first I didn't know who he was. Then when I realised I asked my friend, who answered somewhat embarrassed that her father was trying to 'friend' all of hers and her brother's friends. They couldn't work out whether he was spying or actually trying to just be friendly. Whereas my father doesn't understand social media at all; I signed him up to Twitter at his request and then one day he tweeted 'how'.

As Hamsa's comments highlight, there are great differences in social media literacy among her parent's generation. Moreover, her parents' generation seemed to miss the often tacit nuances of the media, with one mother over-using and one father not understanding the boundaries about whom to friend and who not to. Here we see parallels with the other case study locations, especially Shanghai, where many parents were using social media more often than their children – contradicting the myth that it is only teenagers that are heavy social media users. This observation is also reflected in a study of 1,000 mothers and children conducted by brand-engagement firm GMR Marketing (2012) which noted the increasing role social media played in cross-generational relationships (Laird Mashable 2012).

However, the experiences and associations of intimacy in the social media context still differed markedly between the generations, with mothers more likely to friend their children than vice versa. This reluctance of children to friend parents and bring them into the same intimate public or social public as their peers was general across all of our case studies, though there were also exceptions. A reluctance to 'friend' parents seems to be on the basis that while parents and children are intimate, and may be members of an intimate public mediated by social media, it is a *different* intimate public to that constituted by friends. So we often saw that each occupied its own place – for example, we saw in Shanghai that family is placed on *Happy Farm* and peers are placed on Facebook. The ground shared by the family as a public, and by peers as a public, is different; the shared history is different, the in-jokes are different, the shared language is different, the unstated assumptions are different, and so on.

This situation is not homogeneous though, and others are prepared to draw family and peers into the same intimate public, particularly perhaps when distance is involved. For example, David reported that his father signed up to Facebook when David went to work in Korea so that he could keep in contact with his son. David noted that while his father wasn't active in posting, he knew that his father checked his account regularly and was aware of what David was up to. For David, social media was crucial in maintaining intimate ties when distance was involved:

> There is a difference between when you are geographically close to someone and when you're overseas. When you use the social network more. It's a convenient way to keep in contact. It allows us to keep in closer contact with people who are far away from us. I like the fact that someone close to me who is overseas can have access to my feelings and thoughts. I like using social networks with my parents when I am away. In their day they would have spent a postcard. Now, I can send many postcards in the form of Facebook photos.

The personal as the political: collapsing boundaries of public and intimate media

In the elections of 2011 in Singapore, online media became a battlefield for convergences between the personal and the political. Using examples of the Arab Spring uprising, Goggin points to the economics of mobile media and its capacity to create distinctive forms of news that 'is playing a strategically important role in how contemporary media works' (2011: 101). As an example of what Goggin identifies as the 'intimate' turn in journalism, where broad-casting is also interpersonal (2011: 101), Singaporean media was stratified by tensions between the personal and political, intimate and public.

Along with this distinctive intimate turn in which intersubjectivity and emotion becomes part of the logic and condition of relational media, are the performances of multiple, social, intimate and political publics that Jason Wilson identifies as part of broader 'post-broadcast democracies' (2011). Drawing on Prior's (2006) notion of post-broadcast democracies as increasingly producing a fragmentation of *shared* media experience, Wilson argues that this media fragmentation has led to sharp differences in levels of engagement with political content (2011). As Wilson (2011) notes, 'faking it' on Twitter is part of broader media history of active fan cultures in which 'play' is central to engagement.

However, in the case of the Singaporean elections in 2011, there was little room for mimicry and play. The intimate affordances of Twitter and Facebook soon became fields for misunderstanding and heated debates in clear examples of the political as personal, where no political comment was without personal and passionate affect. Similar to the highly charged emotions around politics in Manila (Chapter 5), which plays out through social and mobile media in intimate ways, Singaporean politics was marked by an onslaught of debate around the young female People's Action Party (PAP) candidate Tin Pei Ling, who attracted much negative attention – especially from young people – during and post 2011 elections. With an image of her playing 'cute' holding a 'Kate Spade'-designed gift from her husband circulated around Facebook, Tin Pei Ling became emblematic of all that was bad in Singaporean society – ignorant, materialistic and privileged, and, as we shall see, her example was used in many contexts. Many of her own generation, Gen Y, were the most critical of her and quickly attached any 'fun' gesture she did on social media as an example of her making a mockery of politics in Singapore. Many used social media to accuse her of not being a worthy candidate – claiming that her political husband performed favours to get her elected. These accusations were fuelled by flippant images of her as superficial and materialistic that seemed to be poking fun of the Singaporean political GRC (Group Representation Constituencies) system. Her backing as a candidate was viewed as responsible for the ousting of popular George Yeo of PAP in a landslide win to the Workers' Party (WP).

The Tin Pei Ling case is just one example of the way in which social media played a key role in the national elections of Singapore in 2011, not only to disseminate news, but also in the use of 'friending' and 'defriending' to define and marshal political allegiances. For 24-year-old male Ryan, a joke went wrong when he humorously stated he would 'like' Singapore's longest-standing, now retired PAP PM, Lee Kuan Yew. As Ryan states:

> Recently during the election, I joked with a classmate – who I often shared a joke with – that I was going to 'like' Lee Kuan Yew's Facebook page. Of course both he and I were not supporters of Lee. But it must have caught him off guard as he actually blocked me from his Facebook profile. And he said I'm still blocked from his Facebook profile.

For Andy, during the 2011 elections, Facebook and Twitter became more interesting places as people used the media to air their opinions about politics. As Andy notes:

Up until the elections I was getting bored with Facebook and not using it much. I was too busy with study to update and didn't feel much need to update. Then the elections came around and Facebook and Twitter exploded with people's comments and opinions. Everyday there were more stories and debates and I found it really fascinating. It was like social media was the perfect model for talking about politics in Singapore. I found what was being said and forwarded by Facebook and Twitter feeds much more interesting than what was being reported in the actual 'official' news. I started to follow comedians on Twitter as some of the jokes they made were fantastic commentary on Singaporean politics today.

As Andy observes, the intimate but public context of Twitter and Facebook afforded types of debate and discussion not usually allowed in the general Singaporean public sphere. The often seriously toned backlash against Tin Pei Ling was a social media phenomenon, not reflected in the mainstream media, and the use of humorous satire was also a social media phenomenon rather than mainstream media. For example, humorous critiques on Twitter by satirist Mr Brown, the self-described 'Blogfather of Singapore', had over 59,000 followers. The tensions between the mass media and interpersonal media were also amplified around various forms of discrimination: racial, sexual and especially anti-foreigner. Justin, an American international student, found himself witnessing racism when political debate erupted in social media terrains:

I originally did not want to get involved in the political debate because I'm a foreigner in this country and I really want to keep my opinions to myself. But another foreigner friend, a Filipino, had posted something after election about how there should be a re-vote because there was only a 78-vote margin to another Singaporean friend. There was a bit of a debate going on about whether there should be a re-vote and then I made a comment that 78 votes majority is still majority and then this friend started to personally attacking me and my Filipino friend saying to one of his friends said in Hokkien [Singaporean dialect], he wrote 'I don't know what the fuck is – I don't know what he's talking about.' I stepped back from that because it was getting very racist. I'm happy to engage with an exchange of ideas but this wasn't what this was. Usually, if you disagree with someone you just hear what their position is. You don't say, 'Fuck you!' I think Singaporeans are very politically naïve. And the discussion on social media really showed how emotional and naïve Singaporeans can be. There was no humour, no dialogue. All Singaporean students seem to hate PAP and I don't think they are that evil. But there is no use trying to get them to understand the complexity, the discussion just becomes directed at anti-foreigner talk.

Whilst there was some debate in Singapore about the influence of social media on the political outcome of the 2011 elections, for male teacher William, social media was not particularly influential. As William states:

> What happened would've happened. I work in a neighbourhood school and this school happens to be in a part of Singapore where there's a lot of working parents. The amount of anger, it's been there for a while. These are not people who are in social media – they had mounting anger at the injustices. On the day of polling I was an election official and I had people screaming and cursing – one had to be escorted by police. I don't think this guy is on any social media, he was pissed off.

In contrast, for Justin, this was a generational difference, and social media was an important political tool for young people. As Justin noted:

> I noticed a lot of young people becoming very active on social media to express their opinion. There was no other space. So Facebook really exploded with young people voicing their views and getting very passionate. I think the big swing happened with people who really didn't have a voice otherwise. I think older generations made their opinion felt offline.

In the events of the 2011 elections, social media was not a homogeneous mono-vocal place, but fragmented along the many fault-lines that exist in Singaporean society. Opinion of social media and its political role was also divided. For some, media like Twitter were a more accurate barometer for political discussion than conventional mainstream news media. For others, Facebook became a space for violent and passionate political engagement that often blurred the personal and political in ways that brought to the surface biases and prejudices, especially around race and foreigners.

Mobile intimacies and intimate distance: diaspora and cross-generational media practices

As noted in previous chapters, the convergence of social and mobile media has afforded new types of cross-generational media practices. Just as we saw in Shanghai (Chapter 4), and in Manila (Chapter 5), social, mobile media was providing a portal for children and their parents to stay perpetually connected and close despite geographic distance. For some, the space of social, mobile media provided new affordances that allowed them to talk about issues they wouldn't normally at home; allowing for different types of performativity and intimate discussion. Moreover, in the case of international students, social, mobile media enabled users to create multiple and discrete intimate publics, some for family, others for friends. For example, Chinese international students in Singapore used the Chinese equivalent of Facebook, Renren, to keep in contact with family at home. In addition to Renren they would also use

Facebook as a type of diary of their time in Singapore, as well as space to collect contacts from their time in Singapore. For Ming, a female Chinese international student, aged 24 years, social media was important as a key medium for keeping in contact with her parents. As Ming observes:

> Social media are quite important for me because now, I'm an international student here and I use QQ, the Chinese version of MSN, to keep in contact with friends and family. I use this medium to communicate with my friend in China and also my parents and sometimes I will do the video call with my parents. And I sometimes feel more intimate with my father by this way.

For Ming, the use of social media to communicate back home means she can talk about some issues she wouldn't necessarily discuss in China. For example, Ming uses Renren to talk with family at home about her study and her supervisor. She then uses Facebook to talk with her classmates and friends here in Singapore. Given Ming has more close friends and family using Renren, she often posts to Renren and then reproduces some of the content (like photos) in Facebook. Ming also sees Facebook as operating as an archive of her time in Singapore. Ming's compartmentalised use of social media for multiple and discrete intimate publics is also structured by techno-affordances of the media – everything in Renren is in Mandarin, and Facebook is banned in China. These particular affordances played out in the types of performativity, especially given that in Renren the owner is notified when someone visits their page. This automated system means that users cannot anonymously observe other's pages, but also creates a compulsion to respond. As Ming notes:

> I like the fact that I can see that my family has visited my Renren page even if they did not make a comment. Whereas with Facebook I don't know if a friend has visited unless they say leave a comment. I like this feature of Renren. Although sometimes when I'm busy and don't have time to make a comment it makes me feel bad, like I have nothing to say to the person or that their page is of no interest.

When Abha moved to Singapore she shifted her social media focus from Orkut (popular in India) to Facebook. As Abha notes:

> When I came to Singapore everyone was talking about Facebook. It seemed as if everybody was using it and that not to use it would mean I would miss out on things. I do find Facebook useful for knowing when events are happening and for knowing interesting and trivial things about friends. I still occasionally sign into Orkut but now some of my friends in India are using Facebook so it makes it easier just to use one.

The development of cross-generational media literacy has been especially afforded through the rise of smartphones. With smartphones now a pervasive feature of mobile media in Singapore, it is no surprise that this has allowed for new users of social media, particularly in the case of older-aged users. Joseph is an older respondent (aged 45) who introduced his wife to Facebook, and he reported that before long she was 'addicted' to using Facebook on her iPhone. According to Joseph:

> It is funny that my wife didn't know how to use a computer when I started a Facebook account for her. But then she got an iPhone and some apps and started using it all the time. She is the most active person on Facebook I know. I don't know how she has the time.

Saniga is an Indian-born Singaporean aged 40, who – like Joseph's wife – was introduced to social media through mobile media. As Saniga said:

> When I got my iPhone, I thought, 'I only have one Facebook account'; that's my experience with the social network. But with iPhone, I'm on Facebook everyday all day because I work from home and I have my computer on all the time because of my work. It has also allowed me to reconnect with old friends left back in India [Saniga married in 1991 and came to Singapore]. I had had no contact with my friends, my college friends, my close friends, but after two decades, this year, I connected with them. All of them suddenly started to contact me. We were like messaging each other so frantically – you wouldn't believe it, I was up two nights because all of them, they were spread all over the world, in the USA, one is in Barcelona, many of them are India, so many of them having different time zones. I had so many messages, my husband was scared that I'm going to run away or something. I was messaging so many people and felt so reconnected. I was so happy. And I'm able to connect with my family too in India because I just go back once a year and my cousins, and my nephews and nieces because that's the best way to connect with them, so that's basically the thing.

As we have already seen in other contexts, some respondents noted a distinction between the generations in terms of understanding the nuances of social media performances, and the consequences of these nuances. In these cases it has more often been the younger generation complaining that the older generation 'didn't get it'. However, in a reversal of this intergenerational positioning, Harry, a 45-year-old father and lecturer, wondered about the impact of social media on his children. Harry used the earlier mentioned Tin Pei Ling case to make his point:

> I really felt for Tin Pei Ling and the backlash against her by her own generation. There is an assumed level of literacy I don't think all young

people have. Tin Pei Ling was an example of someone that didn't realise the negative power of social media. It was an example of the need to have media advisers that understand social media. During this time my wife and I took my daughter aside to talk to her about what was happening. We needed to make sure she was aware of how any post she made could be taken out of context. We did the same for our students explaining that when applying for internships and jobs, their social media would be viewed by potential employers so they had to be mindful of this every time they posted. It's hard because I think young people should have a space to voice their opinion but I don't think places like Facebook are the right spots.

This inconsistency around expectations of social media between the generations was best understood in terms of boundary-making exercises. For 35-year-old Chinese born, Singaporean female Yue:

> I think the confusion about social media boundaries is a generational one. I think my generation [Gen X] is fixated on boundaries post-1960s breaking down of divisions. I think Generation Y is unaware of a lot of the boundaries of the previous generation ... and, at the moment, a lot of that generation are their employers. But that will change.

As discussed in the Manila case study (Chapter 5), mobile media is providing ways to manage and maintain intimacy at a distance. By providing different cartographies of, and for, intimate publics, mobile media offers a variety of co-present spaces that allow users to connect in the face of diaspora. But along with the ability to bring friends and families together across a variety of mobilities, there are costs. Like any act of gift-giving, reciprocity involves obligation. With the assembly of multiple publics and the effect of presence bleed (Gregg 2011) associated with mobile and social media, new lines and spaces are being drawn.

Gifts of presence: social media compulsions and complacencies

Like communities, members of social publics and intimate publics share reciprocal relations. Subjective and material interests are reciprocated, emotional affect is reciprocated, and personal connection is reciprocated. One of the effects of the normative position of reciprocity among these publics is that younger people feel obliged to confirm their parents' request to be Facebook friends, even though they would rather have that space for their own generation. The social and often unspoken tacit understandings around gift giving come into play here in order to negotiate obligation and expectation.

For some, the possibility of places that are messy hybrids of public and private, work and leisure, family and friends, is resisted through the creation of boundaries in their social media cartographies. For example, Ben, a 38-year-old male musician, has three separate Facebook accounts, one for work, one for friends and one for his music-band activities. For Ben these three intimate publics merge public and private in different ways and he works actively to keep them separate:

> For me social media is very, very important because I use it for friends and family. I use it at work to be in touch with my students and I use it for my other activity which is playing in a band. So in all of these ways is a very important way of being in-touch. As a result, I actually have three personas on Facebook. So it's very important. This partitioning of personas happened after an experience I had playing gigs for the Goth community. I was tagged in a photo at one of the Goth events with some of my Goth friends, at which point my mother, as one my Facebook friends, asked my sister, 'Why does Ben have such strange, looking friends?' At this point I said, I decided to partition the identities. I work very hard to keep them separate because not everybody needs to know what I do in the different areas.

Whereas for 35-year-old Sophie, Ben's decision to fragment and 'purify' his identity and his social relations is one to be resisted. For Sophie, a hybridised private–public place is something that should be accepted and embraced by social media users. In an argument for transparency and integration Sophie says:

> If I'm your boss I want to read your Facebook. I want to see both negative and positive comments about their work hours. I think this would help me improve conditions. I want to see my employees having good social lives and that feed back into their positive work attitudes. It also means I can have a sense of how they are feeling and what is going on in their life.

But as was the case in our earlier discussion of children 'friending' their parents, not all are happy about the crossing of boundaries – either generational or work. For 45-year-old male Marcel:

> I hate when I get friend requests from work colleagues. I don't want Facebook for that purpose. I think people have different purposes for social media, and yet they all expect that everyone should have the same as them. I have a colleague who says, 'I sent you a friend request, why won't you friend me?' and I reply that I never use the account, which isn't true. But I just like to have Facebook for my close friends and family.

Monica, a 38-year-old secondary school teacher, has embraced social media with caution. School teachers are in a more ambiguous position than most when it comes to social media, being members of an older generation but mixing on a daily basis with hundreds of people from a younger generation, being on friendly terms with many of these young people, but having legal and institutional responsibilities to them. Monica thought long and hard about whether to friend students or not, and looked for school policy to inform her decision. As Monica notes:

> My students are under 18 years old so if I see them do something like drinking alcohol it is my duty to report it. This creates a problem with media like Facebook where a lot of the rites of passages of teenagers are carried out. I had a student try to friend me and I didn't know what to do, so I asked my principal who then made a school policy that teachers could only friend ex-students. This policy helped me because I no longer had to make a personal choice on my own which I could regret, instead I could just turn to the policies.

For 25-year-old Stephanie, social media usage is about a compulsion. In order to feel in the loop and feel a sense of belonging, Stephanie folded to peer pressure and the network effect by using Friendster initially and, more recently, Facebook:

> I didn't have much interest in social media until I realised that often it was the only way to find out what was happening and to view photos. People used to upload photos to Flickr but now it's all on Facebook so if I don't use it I don't know what's happening and it can be frustrating. It's especially frustrating because it is just assumed that everyone uses it.

As Stephanie identifies, some of the reciprocity of social media involves obligation. Like all acts of gift giving (Mauss 1954; Taylor and Harper 2003), there are often elicit and tacit exercises of power and obligation involved. For Stephanie, as with Abha, the obligation to use Facebook as an integral part of social management in Singapore was high. For Indian female student Darshana, while the content on Facebook and Twitter can be trivial, it's more about providing a space to reflect, listen, share and respond:

> I realised that when a lot of people report just everyday and meaningless bits of information it can be seen as a way of giving. . like social gifts. I kind of felt like it was a way of giving a kind of social approval like, 'Oh, I like this'. Updates can be a way of just letting people know what you are thinking or feeling, if they are interested. But I think some people get addicted to always commenting and they can't stop themselves from saying things, sometimes without thinking. I think frequent updating makes you more [virtually] in someone's face and that can mean they scrutinise you more. Then there are some people who use updates to show how cool they are. That's really boring.

The often-tacit 'feeling rules' of social media also translate into types of taste distinctions about aesthetics and usability that, in turn, feeds into a sense of identity and self-presentation. For early adopter Andy, the move to Facebook was aesthetic, rather than peer driven:

> I originally had a MySpace account in 2005, but I wanted a Facebook account. At that time, you needed a university email address to get a Facebook account. I got a university email address in Autumn [September] 2005. As soon as I got an email address from the university, then I signed up for Facebook and I quickly lost interest in MySpace. I only had a MySpace account for maybe two or three months. I liked Facebook because it seemed more interactive and there was less clutter on the pro-files. I didn't like the profiles in MySpace because people had so much crammed onto their profile from music to hobbies and photos. The clutter was distracting. Whereas Facebook was more minimal.

As is argued in further detail in Chapter 8, the performance of an intimate public and of a social public is shaped by the performance of privacy. These publics are not open, ramified networks; they are bounded and their members engage in the boundary work required to define insiders and outsiders. For 40-year-old Singaporean John, issues about privacy, intimate publics, social publics and networks came to the forefront in a very serious way as a consequence of being stalked. John reports his move from the centre of a ramified network to the safety of an intimate public in this way:

> I think social networking is very important, and has been very important to me for years. I see it as important both personally and professionally. I started using a blog since the mid-1990s. In those days, you don't blog-spots, you don't get press. It was something called the deardiary.net. It was huge for me because I was in the top 20 in the world. But then I had an experience that changed my relationship to the online. I had a stalker follow me for close to three years and I made a police report and then I closed the blog sadly. It was very painful for me because I had lot of pictures. I loved my life contained inside of that blog. I still found that the stalker followed me in whatever I did online so now I can only have a Facebook for my relatives. Not even my friends can see me. The whole experience left me a really, really indelible impression that I should be really careful with myself and now I really value privacy and anonymity online.

For Ling, a 50-year-old female Malay Singaporean, social mobile media is a double edged sword – or what Arnold (2003) has called 'Janus-faced'. She sees distinctive advantages in the immediacy and low costs associated with social media, but also critiques the mediation of intimacy through a text dependent media, and in a further indication of its prominence, also uses the Tin Pei Ling case to make her point:

> I think that one of disadvantages comes with it not being in person. The written word is always open to misinterpretation and there no answers of tone, of volume which are completely lost you know. And so there have been many misunderstandings based on a post or someone else's posts. So that is a distinct disadvantage. Although some people play with that ambiguity in really interesting ways. But that is a rare talent. Tin Pei Ling is an example of someone who, despite being young, had no ability to control the ambiguous nature of social media. It is also a disadvantage because things said in the heat of the moment stay are recorded. It's really important not to just react impulsively despite the 'immediate' feeling of the media. But then there are the benefits. Benefits are that no matter where you are you can contact someone without tremendous phone bills. It has allowed me to keep in constant contact with one of my dearest friends who lives in Malaysia. We share feelings everyday. It's very familiar and intimate. Rather than just thinking of her I can be in contact whenever I like.

When invited to critique social media some respondents worried about the time-wasting associated with its use – especially the time wasting associated with maintaining high-frequency smartphone micro-narratives – so much so that they tried to block in time for social media, and not allow themselves to access it other times. However, male student Roger returned to privacy as the more pertinent issue:

> I will actually say that the time spent is not an issue for me. I think the issue is more about privacy. I don't really know how to manipulate my privacy settings and it just becomes too easy for people to stalk me and for me to stalk other people, and I do of course. But this worries me. How my content could be misunderstood. I would like to use Facebook as a personal diary for my close friends but with the privacy issues I can't.

For Roger, the erosion of boundaries – especially between public and private – that is so prevalent in networked social media, creates tensions about the way in which users want to use social media and actually use social media. For as much as Roger would like to use Facebook as a diary he lacks the confidence in his ability to effectively use privacy settings and other boundary work strategies.

Conclusion: the personal as the political

In this chapter we have explored the role of social media and their intimate and emotional affordances in the context of generation differences, political difference, and personal differences. From the highly emotive personal and political use of social media in the 2011 elections, to the ways in which migrants in Singapore are using social media to construct discrete and multiple intimate publics, Singapore provides yet another example of localised online performances of sociality in the Asia-Pacific. Borrowing from the feminist adage, this chapter, along with Chapter 5 in Manila, has explored the ways in which social media is creating new types of social and political narratives that are also personal micronarratives.

The capacity of social media to assemble multiple publics encouraged many respondents to define and control their social relations through various forms of tailored 'intimate publics'. Sometimes using different social media platforms for different publics, sometimes using different accounts within the same platform and sometimes using different privacy settings within the same account, respondents deployed strategies to align their online sociality with particular social publics and intimate publics. For some respondents, the need to redefine the boundaries of these publics was a generational issue. For other respondents, it is about trying to reflect the multi-faceted nature of life and intimacy personas as it is experienced at work and among different groups of friends.

In this chapter we saw how social media in Singapore is connecting sociality, intimacy and political affect in local ways. In the 2011 elections, the personal and political became interwoven to amplify the intimate and personal. In the case of Tin Pei Ling we see how social media is playing a greater affective role in the connection between personal and political, especially for Generation Y in Singapore. These various forms of online sociality, intimacy and political affect are part of broader 'post-broadcast democracies' that are grappling with the new mobilities and enclaves that help shape social media's intimate publics.

In the next chapter, we further extend this discussion of the cross-generational impact of smartphones to Melbourne. Melbourne, like Singapore, has seen a rapid uptake of smartphones by parents and grandparents, and, not by coincidence, the rapid uptake of social media. In the next chapter we focus upon this phenomenon in the context of gendered use through the study of mothers and smartphones. Do the devices provide new affective forms of co-present intimacy? Or are they but a further extension of the 'wireless leash' possibilities of mobile media? We discuss how mobile media, as a vehicle for domestication (Morley 2003), provide ways in which to reflect upon contemporary forms of 'women's labour' in and outside the home.

7   The place of the domestic
Smartphones, women and labour (Melbourne)

As a single mother, Mary finds herself lost without her smartphone. In under two years since her smartphone purchase, Mary went from a phenomenal 'SMSer' to a prolific social media user. Before having her smartphone, Mary never had the time to access Facebook or Twitter on her desktop. As a mother of a toddler, Mary was always running around, micromanaging work and her child's demands. She often found herself part of the mobile feed of social media when her daughter was asleep. She found it relaxing to keep afloat with her friends' activities, especially as she didn't have the time to catch up with her friends as often as she would like.

Grandmother Amy had never been a key technology person. She grew up in an age when technology was a male domain. On the other hand, her husband was a passionate adopter of new technologies and always had the newest Mac product on hand. But one day Amy's husband brought home an iPad with some of her favourite books uploaded on it. Next minute, Amy was hooked. Before long she had numerous games and social media apps downloaded thanks to her enthusiastic grandchildren. Before long, Amy, like so many grandparents in Melbourne, had joined Facebook. And with that membership, her relationship with her grandchildren took on new forms of intimacy. While Amy was a little unsure about the ways in which her grandchildren seemed to impulsively upload pictures and make comments, she enjoyed seeing this other side to them and their friends. A mobile public if you will.

As a mother of two adult children, Penelope had begun to re-acquaint herself with new media. The first thing she did was buy an iPhone. After a decade of proudly using one of the first-generation 'classic' Nokias which was only capable of SMS and voice calls, Penelope's world quickly expanded. Having never used Facebook prior to the iPhone purchase, Penelope was quick to adopt new social and even locative media practices. She loved catching up with old friends overseas whom she hadn't seen for decades. It created a new world of possibilities and conversations. But her children weren't so keen. Once upon time, Facebook was their social media world. Now, people over 55 are the fastest growing users of Facebook in Australia (SEO Sydney Blog 2009) and parents and grandparents seemed to be dominating the space, causing children and their friends to respond with changed privacy settings and other boundary-defining strategies.

These three stories about three generations of women's mobile media usage in Melbourne signal a few things. First, they highlight, like the previous chapter on Singapore, how smartphones are deployed by a whole new (older) generation of social media users. Second, the stories show how smartphones create a paradox around gendered labour and domesticity. Third, they show the differing notions of mobility, intimacy and public.

As one of the most pervasive examples of domesticated technologies, the smartphone is further blurring contexts, platforms and presences. As we have seen in the previous chapters and their particular localities, various factors inform the uneven uptake of mobile, social and locative media. But what is of particular currency is the way in which smartphones are affording older generations new avenues into social and locative media practices. As Kate Crawford and Gerard Goggin note in their study of young people's mobile media use in Australia, the smartphone has become the key portal for accessing and using social media (2010). However, social media is particularly significant when it comes to cross-generational practices in which notions of mobile, social and intimate publics are assembled and configured in various ways, all influenced by generation and by gender, but also varying from place to place.

In this chapter, the last of our case studies, we explore women's use of smartphones to rethink some of the ways in which mobility, labour, intimacy and the public are transforming one another. These days there seems to be an app for almost everything, and with such a variety of lifestyle and work-related apps on hand, what is the reality for users? After acquisition, our respondents noted how easily using social media everyday became. But just how much do smartphone apps help? Are they, like other domestic technologies, further leashing users to various forms of gendered labour (Cowan 1983)? Are these technologies creating and exploiting more social and emotional labour (Andrejevic 2011; Gregg 2011; Terranova 2004)? In light of these issues, we came to wonder about the relationship between smartphone apps and users' lives, and which apps remain and which ones dissipate after the initial honeymoon period. As an example of technology domestication par excellence, studying app acquisition seemed to good way to make sense of increasingly blurred spaces, places, placings and presences that exist in contemporary society.

Mobile lifestyles: mobile media, home and the family in Australia

Mapping the twenty-first century family has progressively become more complex with the recognition that the home no longer denotes a sense of a bounded and stable place (Silverstone and Haddon 1996). Twentieth-century broadcast media, such as radio and TV, brought the public and global into the home, spurring debates about the ability of life outside the home to influence what occurs behind closed doors. The mobile phone, and mobile media generally, has often been a repository for conflicted feelings around various forms of mobility (Morley 2003). As media continues to become multidirectional, wired and mobile, a number of paradoxes emerge that alter the realities, perception and possibilities of family life. Within this phenomenon, traditional media methods have come under scrutiny.

Australian family media usage is increasingly unbounded and mobile. With the explosion in the use of networked devices – such as smartphones, iPads, tablets and portable gaming systems, as well as older portals like mobile phones with basic features like text – families now have the ability to interact and communicate through a range of platforms, contexts and channels (Hjorth et al. 2012). Although the various mobile media forms – such as iPad, iPhone, Playstation Portable – have convergent uses, their specific histories and affordances lead to different types of practices. Lines between hardcore and casual types of media practice blur (Hjorth and Richardson 2010) and mobile social gaming merges with ambient forms of intimacy. Moreover, multi-tasking within, and between, mobile media devices is also of importance – a factor often overlooked.

Families and households can stay in constant contact throughout the course of their day as they move between work, school, transportation, home and a range of other domains. Yet questions remain as to the impact of mobile media on families and households. Many scholars argue that mobile media and technology are amplifying the erosion of boundaries and distinctions between spaces (e.g. work and home), practices and relationships (Gregg 2011; Wajcman et al. 2009). Other research suggests that mobile media and technology are becoming an increasingly central space for social life in many families (Miller 2011), as well as helping to maintain transnational familial relationships (Hjorth 2012; Madianou and Miller 2011). It is at this crossroads we find mobile media occupying a paradoxical place in the changing social fabric of the contemporary Australian family.

The personalisation and individualisation of mobile media is transforming practices surrounding the reproduction of home and family life (Ito et al. 2005). For example, mobile media and technology have enabled parents to engage in 'flex time' – leaving work early or working from home while managing work, childcare and other domestic responsibilities – that can be viewed as part of broader work/life balance erosions (Gregg 2011; Wajcman et al. 2009). With more working mothers than ever before (ABS 2011) mobile media is not only responding to these changes through practices such as 'mom in the pocket' (Matsuda 2009) but also through amplifying some of the shifts in Australian family. Moreover, we see mobile media use within, and between, the generations operating as a form of constant contact and surveillance. Recent work by danah boyd (2011) and others suggest that avoidance of parental surveillance motivates the ways in which young people edit their privacy settings on social media like Facebook (boyd 2011; boyd and Marwick 2011; Michael and Michael 2010). At the same time, Horst (2010) reveals the influence of parental values through the close continuity between the bedroom spaces and social network profiles of teenage girls. This is echoed in Hjorth's work on Chinese cross-generational literacy in which parents have, in some cases, overtaken their adult children's usage of mobile media such as QQ and social media games – thus undermining stereotypes about youth as prime consumers (Hjorth 2012).

Mobile media and technology have also changed the practices and possibilities of togetherness among different types of families. Recent work by Sherry Turkle (2011) stresses the negative impact of mobile media and technology in family life, highlighting the phenomenon of being 'alone together' to describe practices such as texting under the table during family diner or watching television in the same room while typing on laptops, tablets or mobile phones. Other research suggests that in divorced or separated families parents may use mobile media to maintain relationships with their children, outside of the purview of the other parent (Horst 2006, 2010). In transnational families, mobile media has become a way to create a sense of co-presence, with some families keeping webcams and services such as Skype on throughout the day to create a sense of virtual intimacy (Madianou and Miller 2011; Wilding 2006). Hjorth's previous work on transnational communication by Asian youth highlights the significance of mobile and social media in the study abroad experience. In such instances, mobile media is providing a form of metaphorical tethering and a third space in which to interact (Hjorth 2005, 2012; Horst 2010; Morley 2003; Wilken and Goggin 2012a), raising questions about the very location and meaning of home.

Mobile media has also become embroiled within moral panics around familial practices and family values (Matsuda 2009; Wajcman et al. 2009). As the repository for social and locative media practices, however, mobile media has progressively become a more complex and unruly object and set of practices to analyse. Through the dramatic uptake of smartphones in Australia (ABS 2011), the diversity and complexity of online mobile cultures is intersecting offline spaces in new ways. Adorned with the plethora of apps, smartphones afford new ways in which one can be mobile and social, creating a situation where old co-present binaries around online versus offline, here versus there, may no longer hold (Hjorth et al. 2012). Far from eroding place, smartphones have been important in the uptake of LBS and GPS in which intimacy, proximity, information and geography are overlaid in new ways.

Important mobile media studies in Australia have either expanded discussions around 'youth' (Goggin and Crawford 2008–10; Donald and Spry 2007–9) or urban families (Arnold 2002–5, 2005–7, 2011). As a country with over 100 per cent penetration of mobile-phone registrations and early adopter tendencies that are not confined to youth (ABS 2011), Australia provides a multifaceted model of mobile media practices that migrates across cultural, linguistic, ethnic, age and class divides. Mobile media and technology can provide an insight into the complex intergenerational and cross-cultural dynamics at play in, and around, Australian homes.

With the rise of smartphones and the attendant plethora of apps, parenthood and lifestyle are seeing new forms of personalisation and normalisation. In Julie Frizzo-Barker and Peter Chow-White's discussion of the prolific rise in the number of applications for smartphones, entitled *There's an App for That* (forthcoming), the growing role of smartphone apps in 'mediating' (and perhaps colonialising) 'Mobile Moms' and 'Connected Careerists' in the US is explored. Taking the notion of 'Networked Individualism' explored by Castells (1996) and Wellman et al. (2003), Frizzo-Barker and Chow-White argue that smartphone apps are 'simultaneously empowering and constraining for women's experiences and identities due to their potential to blur the boundaries between public and private spheres' (forthcoming).

Traversing new performances of professionalism and lifestyle, the use of smartphone apps has arguably created just as much work as it has helped to eradicate. But how much of mobile media helps and how much of it hinders professional women who have to 'balance' work with family? In Catherine Middleton and Rachel Crowe's *Women, Smartphones and the Workplace: Pragmatic Realities and Performative Identities* (2012), the authors explore how professional Canadian women strategically deploy the BlackBerry to maintain their professional presence, while erecting boundaries that insulate their personal lives from excessive intrusions. Here we see attempts to reinstate public and private, work and personal life spaces despite the presence bleed of the devices. In order to understand this impact of smartphones (and their apps) on women, this chapter will now explore a case study in Melbourne.

The contemporary caravan: the politics of smartphone apps and mobile labour

In this study we position the phone as a multimedia device akin to a miniature caravan; an artifact that situates and mediates the performance of daily life, much like the function of one's home, as a machine for living, and as a symbol for domesticity, privacy and family. While this 'caravan' affords much mobility, its symbolic weight, and wait (i.e. the temporality), operates as a perpetual reminder of the various tasks and work in need of doing. This phenomenon has been called many things including the 'wireless leash' (Qiu 2007) whereby the mobile sets us free at the same time as it creates more limits, allows one to be 'free' to roam, but also insists that one is available. By thinking about the smartphone as a caravan we are no longer thinking about this technology as new but rather as a 'remediated' version of older domestic technology practices such as using the TV as an electronic baby-sitter, etc. It represents an intensifying of the tethering of domesticity outside the home: a mobile privatisation par excellence (Morley 2003). This miniature caravan also reveals the increasing proclivity towards working at home. Just as the intimate goes public, the public – and especially work – goes private.

The tensions between the pros and cons surrounding mobile intimacy – that is, the overlaying of the physical, geographic and electronic with the social, emotional and cultural – are amplified in the case of working mothers. For working mothers, the tethering of the phone to the domestic is clear – symbolised by the always-on mothering feature that puts 'mum in the pocket' of children (Matsuda 2009) and the children in mum's pocket. As Sun Sun Lim identifies in the case of mainland Chinese parents, many see technologies like mobile media as not only important for their children's education but also a way in which to keep a perpetual eye on them (2006). Indeed the levels and layers of tethering afforded through the so-called mobility of mobile media has its price. Given that many women negotiate mothering along with paid work, there is a tension between mobile media decreasing yet also adding to the daily workload. Not only is the 'miniature caravan' an embodiment of domestic labour and tethering to home, it also represents the home office.

Work, like the domestic, is perpetually carried with us through the mobile phone – summed up by Melissa Gregg's notion of 'work's intimacy', derived from a study in which she followed the lives of some creative workers as they struggled to differentiate between work and leisure time and spaces (2011). Far from helping creative workers, the 'presence bleed' of much of online media means that 'work's intimacy' has many feeling the need to be perpetually online, often sacrificing other personal areas like intimate relationships. In this blurring between work and life, characteristic of ICT's intimate publics, it is women – as often the primary carers – who bear the brunt of the wireless leash's advantages and disadvantages and the tensions between work productivity and leisure in media practices.

Despite many initially downloading many 'cool' apps about creativity (i.e. photo apps like Hipstamatic), play (standard puzzle or simple games like *Angry Birds* and haptic games like *Balloonimals*), socialising (Facebook, Twitter, *Foursquare*) and lifestyle – it was often the basic work tasks like answering and writing emails and surfing the internet that featured in respondents' usage. Many respondents noted that the move to social media on a smartphone (from a PC), that is, a move towards push mobile feed, created what Gregg would call 'presence bleed' – that is, a single sense of self that is located, but 'leaks out' to other places and presences through media. As Gregg notes through work's intimacy, public and private spaces are being perpetually blurred (2011).

Unsurprisingly, one of the key features that emerged in the case study was the difference in personalisation practices between those who had and didn't have children. This quality played out across a variety of personalisation practices – from respondents' creativity and UCC to the types of affordances and applications deployed. For this chapter, we have focused upon a few of the female respondents who were working, some of whom had children and some of whom did not. Given that all respondents either worked or had immense interest in the area of new media, they were happy to discuss their smartphones in relation to other media and work practices. What became apparent in the case study were the respondents' expectations and how this reflected a particular enclave of women grappling with the 'full-timeness' of both public and private elements in their life as they attempted work/life balance.

In this juggling we see that many of the novelties of the smartphone (with the iPhone featuring predominantly) and its overabundance of applications ostensibly dissipate into a basic form of mobile internet. It became apparent that after the frenzied honeymoon of downloading numerous applications, most used their smartphones predominantly for internet searching, email and maps. This meant that work and life were perpetually entangled. For some, this blurring created anxiety in which they felt that others expected them to be 'always on' and thus always responding. Controlling others' expectations, as well as one's own, was a juggling act that smartphones continuously challenged.

For Sophie, a 40-year-old full-time university lecturer and mother of two, the iPhone was an induction to the world of Apple. Having never had an Apple computer or laptop, Sophie's purchase of the iPhone saw her quickly acquire several Apple technologies in order to be compatible. Sophie was an exception in the study as other respondents already had Apple items like iPods or computers when they purchased the iPhone – thus the phone was part of that media personalisation continuum. This factor is not lost on Apple, who actively market their goods as inter-compatible and distinct design artefacts as much as they are technologies. A self-proclaimed frequent new media user, Sophie had previously used her mobile phone for more conventional purposes: SMS, MMS (multimedia messaging service), photos, alarm, calendar, voice calls and games. But like many of the other respondents, the purchase of the iPhone was also an initiation into internet usage from the phone (as opposed the computer). She saw the always-on functionality of the internet via the iPhone as a great way to sandwich work into micro-moments.

As Sophie noted, the haptic screen, QWERTY keyboard and spell check were very useful and enjoyable even though at times she felt that if she had a 'pointy' finger the screen would function better. Many of the iPhone-specific apps were not really 'useful' (as she considered them to be mostly games) 'but they're fun, keep the kids occupied on trips in the car or shopping, etc.'. Sophie continues:

> My most memorable experience is probably related to my son using the iPhone for games the first few times – e.g. when he first played Flick Fishing, where you flick the phone forward to cast the fishing rod, or when he played Pocket God and realised he could cause an earthquake by shaking the phone, he was VERY excited! There's something about the way the phone simulates gravity, movement etc, and the way it contains 'little worlds' that react to the movement of the phone itself, that is very captivating (especially for kids).

For Katherine, a mother of one child working in the creative technology industries and also in her early forties, the iPhone was a part of a broader media ecology, for technology had been an important part of her life for a few decades. Like the first respondent, frequent media and internet usage was a significant part of her life. Katherine viewed her media consumption as a product of her very busy life, which was characterised by multitasking. While Sophie didn't feel the need to curb her high usage, Katherine was the opposite, noting that she even moved to the country in the hope of a sea-change in which the old patterns of technology use would be broken. But part of the challenge of changing her lifestyle and the associated media patterns was the fact that she continued to work for an IT company so that her relocation meant she was doing more work from home. So rather than decreasing the use, Katherine's practices were relocated back into the private domain. As Katherine notes, her intense relationship with technology – thanks to her early adopter tendencies – has been something she struggled with:

> I am an extremely heavy user of which I am not proud. It's a love/ hate thing. My fingers, neck and wrists hurt. I was hoping my move to the country would help curb my overuse of technology, but I seem to be more reliant than ever. I have recently been described in a review as a 'technology pioneer', which makes me feel very old and dusty. I have been directly involved in technology for most of my adult life ... I'm not sure I will ever be able to give up my addiction but I will continue to try.

One of the interesting features of Katherine's practices was how she wove newer and older media together. As she stated, 'I still read a lot of traditional books, but I am reading more and more electronically. I first started reading books on my iPhone because I was co-sleeping with my son and I wanted to continue reading in bed.' Unlike Sophie, Katherine's relationship to the iPhone was part of an Apple genealogy and the role of Apple in making technologies that were more attuned to design and art-related users. For Katherine, her lifestyle was indivisible from her technological practice:

> My tech practice and objects used to reflect this but I now have other priorities and do not have the time or money to keep up with the latest technology. This is something that I wanted to change since having a child. I think being a Mac user vs PC user is becoming more and more obsolete. It's not so much about hardware these days, more about software. However, I am a bit of a snob and still believe that the Mac OS is geared more directly to those users who think intuitively. I am both a Mac and PC user, and would always choose Mac over PC. It's just more beautiful in my eyes.

As Katherine identifies, one of the few differences between a Mac and a PC was visual (the industrial design as well as the system's architecture). One of the key features of respondents who had other Apple products prior to the iPhone was that they first thought of their iPhone as an extension of other, older Apple media. Rather than saying it was an extension of the MP3 player, respondents defined it as a 'glorified iPod'. As Katherine noted, the iPhone represented:

> Creativity and ease of use. Not bogged down in the programmatic, easier to 'make' with. Thoughtful design, in terms of lifestyle choices (e.g. Eco-design). Unfortunately, the 'brand' of Mac and iPhone also now means exploitative labour. Similar to that of *The Simpsons*. What started off as 'independent', creative and a relatively left-of-centre company has been tainted by mass-market priorities. I must admit I am disappointed in the iPhone in terms of apps and some restrictions and bugs.

As an early adopter of new media with experience and expertise in the IT industry, this respondent highlighted one of the key tensions associated with the iPhone in the so-called mobile media revolution. While the increasing popularity of mobile media was accompanied and fostered by the rise of user-created content, the iPhone's highly 'personalised' version of the mobile internet – echoing that of the i-mode in Japan a decade earlier – resists this history and practice (Burgess 2012). Although the iPhone isn't 'gated' as such, one of the ironies about Apple products like the iPod and iPhone has been Apple's resistance to a free and open system, and this is especially true in terms of apps (Goggin 2011, 2012). This controversy around the iPhone as a 'closed' or 'open' device, as discussed by Jean Burgess (2012), was addressed by some of the respondents. For example, Katherine, as an early adopter of technologies for more than two decades, noted that the iPhone's proprietary and semi-closed platform was a great challenge for her as someone that liked to tinker with and personalise media. With strong skills in programming, which was part of her paid work, Katherine found the iPhone system some-what annoying. When asked if there was such thing as an iPhone person or affect, Katherine responded:

> iPhone users are pretty much like Mac users, it's all about design ease and creativity. Not so much into the programming side of technology (PC user/ Blackberry), more into the creative user side. Although you can be both I suppose. Hmmm, there are people who are addicted to 'app chasing' and it's seen as 'cool' to use an iPhone, e.g. people who use apps like 'shake-it' to turn their images into polaroids or old instant film photo-graphs cracks me up. This type of stuff is so cool that it's lame. Is the iPhone a Polaroid? Some says it's close. I don't. These kinds of apps say a lot about nostalgia, history and the past to me – this is a good example of how the speed of technological development causes emotional upheaval and anxiety. Status anxiety too.

Here Katherine identifies one of the key issues surrounding media personali-sation as the extension of identity politics. As Katherine laments, part of her relationship to media, and especially iPhone apps, is not only about a sense of history but also one's role in narrating oneself online and what this reflects about one's identity. Katherine highlights a key paradox in the agency around personalisation – personalisation takes much time and also shapes, at the same time as its shaped by, one's identity. The control of re-creating one's history promised by personalisation also creates much anxiety for the user. So is this (status) anxiety, so prevalent to contemporary media practice, amplified in the case of the iPhone, or do all smartphones signpost this tension? According to Katherine:

> I've never used Android, but it scares me that Google owns it, which is totally paranoid. I don't know much about it, I guess they're more driven towards gamers and people who like to develop their own apps, but I do like the concept behind it, i.e. a more open-ended platform, based on Linux. I'm relatively happy with the iPhone and don't feel like changing interfaces just yet. I love the tactile nature of the iPhone.

Here, while Katherine acknowledges that ideologically she is interested in Android smartphones by way of their open system, she identifies her relationship to the iPhone as one ordered by the haptic nature of its interface. Indeed, the iPhone has been quick to push the possibilities of haptic media especially in terms of games. So has this new appreciation of the haptic through the iPhone changed Katherine's relationship to the internet and communication? Katherine notes:

> I guess the biggest example would be the 'separatist' nature of the 'internet' on the iPhone, e.g. different apps for Facebook, Twitter, YouTube, Browser, Amazon, ABC for Kids, etc. Another example is reading. I read novels on my iPhone via my Kindle app. Also, dialling into my work PC is huge, especially if stuck in a train delay. My laptop is too old and cumbersome to travel with. The battery doesn't charge for very long ... Actually in all honesty, if I didn't have an iPhone, I think I would be making more of an effort to upgrade my laptop. ... I am constantly connected now, and can use it at anytime I need to. Except my kitchen which has no access (thank God). The biggest timewaster (fun) I have is lying on the couch and tweeting at the TV, especially *Q and A* [a political TV show on the ABC] which is GREAT FUN. It's like collective couch-potato goodness, we're all on the couch and we're all bagging Australian politics/personalities, etc.

Here the picture Katherine paints is one in which the iPhone is with her at all times and becomes an active player in all the various activities she does within and outside the home. From work emails to tweeting in response to a TV programme, the iPhone plays a key role in her life. But when we look at her actual activities, apart from the proclivity towards the iPhone's version of the haptic (touch), there isn't anything particularly 'iPhone-ish' about her usage. Another respondent, Kate, in her middle thirties and in a relationship but without children, and also involved in the IT industry, viewed it as part of her work to have both an iPhone and an Android phone in order to test the different phones media and affordances. After a little while she found herself preferring the Android phone over the iPhone due to functionality and hackability. Unlike Sophie, who was a PC user and then was converted to Mac via the iPhone, Kate was a self-professed Mac 'purist' who nevertheless preferred the Android over the iPhone. As Kate noted, her media practices were always 'a combination of creative expression and everyday communication. In fact the two are intrinsically tied for me ... I am a Mac user ... purist ... ordered ... aesthetically pleasing ... just how I like to organise my life'. When asked about the work/life blurring and whether she constructed boundaries between the two, Kate stated:

> Being in a creative field often means that there are no boundaries between work and life. It would be like trying to stop an artist from thinking after 5 p.m. I tend to manage work 'communication' by switching off after a certain time of day.

When asked about what she used the iPhone and Android phone for, as opposed to previous phones, she noted, 'I watch a lot more entertainment – I either access online shows via YouTube or podcast them via iTunes. I spend a lot more using it for leisure rather than just work.' Her main usage was for email, GPS, Faccbook, YouTube and Twitter – all features not particular to the iPhone. Many of the applications she had downloaded she stopped using after a few weeks with only a few still being used if they were practical. She noted great frustration with the iPhone's closed development platform.

Zoe, a new mother, aged 39, and employed in the mental-health sector, was also a self-proclaimed Mac lover. Her personal and professional life played out around the Mac/PC divide – at work she had to use a PC whilst at home she chose to use a Mac. For her, the iPhone allowed her to surf between these two worlds – between the 'clever' and 'intuitive' world of Mac and the 'clumsy' PC. Like Katherine, Zoe loves the iPhone's particular version of the haptic screen and her iPhone accompanies her through a variety of work and leisure activities both in and outside the home. As someone who doesn't work in the IT or creative industries but who is passionate about technology, there was a need to create boundaries between work and the personal. As she noted:

> For me, I have had to create boundaries in my life between the personal and professional. I am now a lot more boundaried about what is work and what is personal than what I used to be. I think when I started working I loved it and saw it as vocational, therefore relating very much to my personal life as well however over the years I have realised that

> I want my work and personal lives to be quite separate, so I don't get swamped by work and potentially burn out.

The need to create clearly defined boundaries between work and life was something that the respondents grappled with as work and intimacy became increasingly mobile and performed both at home and away. On the one hand, the iPhone functioned as a well-designed mobile with internet, allowing them to be connected to work while at home. On the other hand, this flexibility also meant that many felt the pressure to always be 'on' and in work mode whilst also doing domestic work. For Zoe, like other respondents, the main use of the iPhone was emails and internet on the run. Whilst she had initially starting using the calendar she stopped after a few weeks and reverted back to the old mode of writing on paper. As Zoe said:

> I only used the calendar to remind me of things as I found that I missed having a paper diary (which I have since returned to using). I am very visual and the paper diary helps me to plan ahead and comprehend what I have to do in the week or month ahead whereas I found that as I could not see this in the i-calendar I could not really manage my week very well.

As she noted, the multimedia capacity of the iPhone was 'probably wasted on me'. Viewing the iPhone as fun, useful and about connectivity when asked to identify her favourite iPhone experience, she described the iPhone as just a 'glorified iPod' (this was also noted by another respondent). As Zoe stated:

> Hmmm, I would say discovering the joy of the iPod feature (there's something I use that I forgot about!) and downloading zillions of podcasts from radio national which I now listen to every day as I ride to and from work and get myself an education of a different sort!

As stated earlier, one of the key factors separating patterns of use was which respondents had children and which didn't. For those who had children, the role of media such as iPhones clearly helped to forge work/home fusions in what was an already highly multitasking environment. Moreover, many of these women did a lot of their work from home (so that they could effectively do at least two jobs: looking after the children and working), demonstrating the role of personal technologies in not only outsourcing domestication outside the physical home but also bringing work back into the home. The iPhone could be seen to be part of the casualisation of labour whereby work becomes all-pervasive and is squeezed into micro-moments between other activities in the home.

As Gregg notes, with the rise of precarious and casual labour, personal technologies have been integral in not only providing models of freedom to escape the 'oppressive banality' of the home, but also, along with the rise in working hours, has resulted in a difficulty of maintaining a healthy work/life balance. As Gregg identifies in her three-year case study, 'new media technologies encourage and exacerbate an older tendency among salaried professionals to put work at the heart of daily concerns, often to the expense of other sources of intimacy and fulfillment' (2011: 1). This sentiment is clearly reflected in the work conducted by sociologist Judy Wajcman – from her studies into feminism and technology to her work around personal technologies and the work/leisure erosions.

Being a repository for, rather than a cause of, these work/home fusions, the smartphone does highlight how being 'always on' comes at a cost. Just as mobile technologies set us free to roam wherever we wish, they also create new types of restrictions whereby one is always on call – what Jack Qiu calls the 'wireless leash' (2008). They, in turn, impact upon the types of presence (being simultaneously here and there, online and offline) we participate in as the personal and intimate fuses with the public, and work bleeds into the private.

Conclusion: living in a caravan not a home

As spaces and places increasingly become mobile and unbounded across a variety of realms (technological, geographic, psychological) through mobile ICTs, there is a need to rethink the place of domesticity, home and intimate publics. Through the case study of smartphone users, this study has highlighted the need to reconceptualise home and domesticity as concepts no longer tied to a particular bounded place. As a mobile 'home in our hand', smartphones are pushing the unbounded nature of the domestic. If we rethink domesticity (and domestication theory) in terms of the caravan we can consider the node (destination) in the context of the network (journey) and understand some of the complex ways in which familial and domestic patterns are becoming both mobile and entangled. This revision of how we think about mobile media in relation to networks and communities is expanded upon in the next chapter.

In this chapter, as the last of the case studies, we have explored how the increased market share of the smartphone in Australia has resulted in a shift away from social media on the computer to it being part of the mobile feed. In this case study we focused upon the iPhone to see a 'branded' version of the smartphone. As identified by the respondents, after the honeymoon of initial purchase, the iPhone is little more than a glorified, mobile-with-internet iPod. The notion of the caravan, a retro technology of mobility, highlights that smartphones are not necessarily creating new media practices but rather remediating older intimate rituals. In many cases, the smartphone was little more than a glorified iPod or simplified PC. But through the mobile context, media practice is inflexed with different mobile and intimate affects. However, if there is a thing called 'the iPhone affect' (Hjorth 2012) then it is definitely enacted through the deployment and articulation of the haptic screen. Even more significantly, when speaking to respondents about their iPhone, we see how the device represents users' relationship to broader media practices in which the boundaries between 'paid' and 'home' work were perpetually being further blurred. As intimacy goes public, work becomes further privatised and internalised.

On the one hand, the iPhone allowed working mothers to be always available to work demands, especially in terms of the constant emails. On the other hand, this work – in addition to domestic work – meant that many women were feeling perpetually stressed and pressured. While this phenomenon isn't particular to the iPhone, it was the iPhone that, along with simultaneous decreasing mobile internet costs, that has highlighted the increasing demands placed upon women. As a well-designed miniature caravan, the iPhone helps to further make malleable the work–home boundaries as work becomes increasingly casual and private, and intimacy and home becomes increasingly mobile. The iPhone isn't a revolution. Rather, like the i-mode in Japan a decade previously, it represents a Western version of a mobile with internet in which work's intimacy is all-encompassing and whereby the role of personalisation proffers both possibilities and limitations for the user (Burgess 2012). Through its plethora of apps to its haptic screen, the smartphone offers one window onto mobile media personalisation as well as encroaching upon debates about the agency of UCC and the exploitation of user profiles in an age of data-mining (Andrejevic 2011).

In the next chapter we reflect upon the various case studies of converging mobile, social and locative media as reframing how we think and experience mobility, intimacy and a sense of the public. In particular, we try to develop models for intimate, mobile and social publics that reconceptualise metaphors of the network and community.

Part II

Intimate publics and mobile intimacy

8 Intimate publics, communities and networks in an age of mobile social media

In 2008, Bao migrated to Shanghai from a village that lies in the hills some 600 kilometres away. As a consequence, he now occupies a different place in life, not just in terms of geography, but also in terms of his family, his socio-economic position and his sense of self. Arguably, the most significant move for Bao among all of these forms of mobility was his move from the village's well-defined close-knit community – with all that implies – to the city's quite different topographies of intersubjectivity, social and economic structures and social dynamics. According to many who make the argument for the significance of community (e.g. Bauman 2001; Nancy 1991; Nisbet 1953), in taking that train-trip Bao and his mobile generation are both instigating and suffering an important loss – the loss of community. In this argument 'community' is a social good of profound importance, and even if the most romanticised representations of community life don't exist in Bao's village – and have in fact never existed anywhere – then all the more reason to mourn its absence, to reinvent it, and to valorise it as the gold-standard of sociality, for its resistance to the values of both individualism and statism (Nisbet 1953: ix).

In an ideal vision of Bao's village community, Bao has a place in a self-constituted, organically defined group that has taken shape over generations. It is not a group defined on a map by urban planners, demographers or government bureaucracies, or defined according to function in systems of production or consumption, and nor is Bao's community constituted by Bao or, indeed, by anyone else in the community. Rather, a community constitutes itself over time, does its own boundary work, defines its own 'other' just as it defines itself, performs its own social dynamic, and in this sense is a self-constituting, 'bottom-up' rhizomic social construction. A key driver of all this is the extent to which Bao's community recognises that it holds interests in common: material interests – such as a shared interest in good schooling, clean water and honest governance – and immaterial interests – subjective and intersubjective concerns. Moreover, there are shared interests of the more profound immaterial landscapes of language, history, culture, religion and *weltanschauung* (or world-view). These shared material interests in turn give rise to a sense of mutual commitment and obligation signified by the philological conjunction of *com* and *munis* – indicating a 'sense of being bound, obligated or indebted' – a concept of community most clearly represented in Locke's 'social contract' (Van Den Abbeele cited Wilken 2011: 31).

Bao is thus bound, obligated and indebted to his family first and foremost, but also to the community more widely, and Bao fields a steady stream of requests for favours that he can do in Shanghai for people back in the village. Bao is also a communitarian in a second sense, signified by the philological conjunction of *com* and *unis* – indicating 'together as one', or 'an absorption into oneness'(Van Den Abbeele cited Wilken 2011: 31). After all, mobile though he now is, Bao's sensibilities and sense of identity have been formed in significant part from his heritage in this community, and through the same social hermeneutic, Bao's community also derives its identity from Bao and the others who identify as its members. Bao and his mobile companions can't help but to be drawn back to the village on auspicious occasions to participate in culturally significant celebrations and activities, and just as Bao is sensitive to community commitments and obligations, the community reciprocates and fulfils its obligations and commitments to Bao and his family.

In the village Bao has an integrated identity. The Bao who performed so well in high school is the same Bao who runs errands for his uncle, who is the same Bao who gambles at *majong* with his friends, and is the same Bao who as a boy was once in trouble with the police. His teachers, uncle, gambling friends and police are all known to each other, just as Bao knows them, and just as they know him. As an integrated social subject Bao is able to resource his social relations in any given context with social capital earned in other contexts, and similarly, indiscretions committed in one context flow over to other contexts – using a comprehensive social coherence and tight web of inter-connection not available in the more fractured and dispersed world beyond the village community.

This is not to say that Bao is always happy about fulfilling the obligations that identification in and with a small community implies, and like millions of young people before him who have moved from small towns and villages to large cities and now to megacities like Shanghai, Manila and Tokyo, he is pleased to have in some sense escaped to a sociality with broader horizons, and to social expectations that are not as rigid as the ones he has left, though in many ways the expectations of capital are more rigid.

An important implication of these communal interests, obligations, commitments and identities is the implied and sometimes realised capacity for joint action. Although communities like Bao's are importantly constituted in communication, as indicated by 'community's' obvious etymological links to *commune* and *communicate*, and while community members derive considerable benefit from the social capital that weak and bridging communications create, communities also provide the capacity for joint action. Communities communicate, but they don't *just* communicate, they are also capable of political and social action – effective action, even sometimes against the prevailing system of authority (Mills 1956: 303–4 cited in Mejias 2010: 609). From time to time communities like Bao's flex this capacity for action in opposition to exploitation of the community (e.g. taking joint action against corrupt officials), and in this sense community can be a powerful progressive force. In other cases though, for example in the case of the intra-community violence associated with the Cultural Revolution, and the inter-community violence associated with anti-Uighur chauvinism, the claim for social good in community solidarity and the 'Othering' this implies, is harder to make. In either case, 'community' is a social formation that is heavily loaded with political currency. To make a credible claim to speak to power on behalf of a community and its interests is to speak from a position of legitimacy and authority, and to use a position of power to act in communal interests rather than the interests of individuals or the state is to exercise power legitimately.

In this construction of Bao's community we can see a lot to like. A social formation that is self-defining, self-consciously shares material and subjective interests, generates social capital, reciprocates commitment and obligation, is capable of joint action in its own interests, and has political and cultural currency is a social formation that can legitimately have romantic claims made about it.

How then might we characterise Bao's new social situation in Shanghai? In Shanghai, Bao is one of tens of millions of people, one third of whom – like Bao – are internal migrants (Qiu 2008). The citizens of Shanghai initiate billions of communicative acts each day, not simply as a consequence of Shanghai's vastly large population, but also as a consequence of new communicative infrastructure – mobile social media. If we zoom up and aggregate these individual acts of sociotechnical agency, what social formations emerge? Can we still talk of *community* in this situation, as we did in the village, or is this different social topography better understood in terms of *networks* of various kinds, as the popularity of the metaphor over recent decades suggests? And among this dense and extensive weaving of social communication, if community is not able to provide an alternative to atomistic individualism, on the one hand, and totalitarian homogenisation, on the other, what is it to be *public*, to be *private* and what is it to be *intimate*?

Metaphors and tropes like community, network, public, private, social and intimacy tell us a good deal about what we make of the communicative acts in themselves, what we make of the social structures that are emergent in those communicative acts and how we imagine mobile social media to be significant in our lives. We begin a consideration of these questions by positioning publics in relation to networks, and networks in relation to publics. But as we demonstrate in our case studies and detail further in Chapter 9, the convergence of mobile, social and locative media sees place becoming an 'entanglement' (Ingold 2008) of placing (Richardson and Wilken 2012) across a variety of presences which emphasise the intimate node rather than the network (Pink 2011).

The term 'public', like 'social' and 'intimate', is one of those concepts that seems simple enough but turns out to be terribly slippery, and each location demonstrates a different assemblage of mobility, public, sociality and intimacy. Building upon Warner's excellent analysis of public culture (2002), we conceive of a public as existing in three instantiations.

In one instantiation a public is available to us as a phenomenological reality, when we, say, occupy a public place in the company of others. Bao knows full well that he is in public when he walks through his village streets, or takes tea at the closest tea-house, where the recognition factor is high despite a relatively small public presence. In Shanghai, on the other hand, to be in public is to be self-conscious of the co-presence of a great many people, albeit with a far greater anonymity. A public in this sense is ontologically phenomenological, and has a material existence that is experienced in daily life.

Perhaps less available, but no less empirical, are the publics that are dispersed rather than co-present. In this second instantiation, each member of a public may be in their own private place, perhaps never meeting together and certainly not available to one another or to an observer as a phenomenological entity, but nevertheless sharing a common experience – perhaps as newspaper readers, music fans, or voters – and being aware of sharing a common experience. Such a public still has empirical characteristics, but from Bao's point of view this public is more an existential imaginary than a phenomenological experience. He knows he is not alone in playing the game *Nail Household Fighting Against Demolition*. He knows there are many others who also play, together, and yet alone.

Moving still further towards the abstract is the public that is available to us as an analytic concept – when we contemplate what it is for Bao to be 'in public', what it is for a social grouping such as dispersed game-players to be 'a public', and how these 'publics' differ from other social formations such as communities or networks.

In all three of these instantiations – phenomenological reality, existential imaginary and analytic concept – the notion has been crucial to our understanding of our society and our place in it, and continues to be crucial to our electronically mediated society.

Most significantly, 'a public' references people as a collective, and this repositioning of ourselves as members of a collective is a powerful concept. A public is not an individual, and nor is a public simply a plurality of individuals placed in the same category according to a given taxonomy. Rather, a public is a collective that overarches and subsumes its individual constituents to self-construct a new social actor with a sense of collective self. When the Yellow Shirts rallied in Manila they constructed a new social actor – a phenomenological reality – with a sense of collective self. When our Phillipino informants Carlos, Diego and Eva insisted on this form of embodied action – 'It's basically not enough just to post something online, you have to do it in real life' – they were favouring this form of public collective over others. When they voted for Cory Aquino and then mourned her death through distributed displays of yellow ribbons, they constructed a new social actor – an existential imaginary – also with a sense of collective self.

And when our respondents attributed events in Manila to the actions of 'the public', we deploy an analytic concept that emphasises the collective.

In the Western tradition, public stands in contrast to private. In classical Greece, the public sphere was differentiated from the private and the public was privileged as the context for authentic action and self-expression (Arendt undated). In the mid-fifteenth century, the Anglo-Norman public – 'pertaining to the people' [as a whole, or as a community] – implied a contrast to matters pertaining to the private sphere and the individual. Through the enlightenment and modernity we see 'public' contrasted to 'private', and publics acting in the public sphere are invested with responsibilities and duties that transcend private interests and private lives (Rybczynski 1986). Publics constitute nations, bestow rulers with legitimacy, witness facts, and stand for the common good. In further attempts to both clarify and privilege public action, it is contrasted with 'the mob' – a plurality of individuals more than capable of mass action, but lacking the self-constitution and self-organisation of a public, and hence lacking a public's ontological legitimacy. The public may coalesce, but the mob is led. Mobs come to be and to act, not as and of themselves, but by 'group hysteria' or 'moral panic', either 'whipped up' by charismatic demagogues, party leaders, or by the drip-feed of partisan mass media. Of course it must also be said that in Shanghai, Manila, Seoul, Tokyo, Melbourne and Singapore, one person's *public* is another person's *mob*. And these differences offline translate directly onto the online in terms of cultural precepts for what constitutes participation. For example, in China, lurking is viewed as an active part of the online culture (Goggin and Hjorth 2009).

Such a public, then, like a community, has capacities to act and react in ways that individuals in private do not. These different capacities derive from either the phenomenological reality of being in a public (say, at a Yellow Shirt rally), from the experience of being in an imaginary public (say, posting a yellow ribbon to a website), or from the analytic conceptualisation of what public opinion is and what the public can do. A public's capacity to act and react in the way it does is lacking in individuals like Carlos, Diego and Eva as individuals, but nonetheless derives from the acts of individuals as they experience, acknowledge or conceptualise their public position and public action. A public and its members are thus in a hermeneutic relation whereby the individual constituents of a public are folded up and black-boxed by their performance as a collective, and at one and the same time, the shape and demeanour of the public is derived from the collective acts of its members.

Accordingly, the instantiation of a public on the streets of Manila, across Shanghai's computer screens, or as an abstraction in this chapter's analysis, does not exhaust the identities of the members of the public. Bao in Shanghai, Carlos, Diego and Eva in Manila all have identities apart from that shared with their publics – and concomitantly, the identities of all of our informants are only partially deployed to constitute their publics. So, unlike the 'identity politics' of class, gender, race, ethnicity, religion and so on, there is no claim that individual identity is defined by membership of a public. A public has an identity, but the construction of say, a public mourning the death of Cory Aquino does not essentialise its members. They mourn Aquino, but that is not all they do. Many publics exist, one moves from public to public, and membership is contingent rather than inherent in identity.

Also important in the constitution of a public is the idea that it has a notional boundary, an important property shared with community. While *the* public may be thought of as a public of publics, a set of sets, a kind of 'social totality' (Warner 2002: 49), *a* public has limits in time and space. We have seen that throughout history, boundary work has been done to separate public interests, policies, and actions from private interests, policies and actions, and to separate a (legitimate) public from an (illegitimate) mob, but in addition to this analytic differentiation the constitution of boundaries, even if fluid and permeated, also enables us to conceive of phenomenological and imagined 'publics' in the plural, and enables us to differentiate between those who are members of a given public and those who are not.

So at this point in the chapter we can see that a public and a community are social formations that share a number of important properties. Both are self-formed entities emergent in the actions of their members. Both differentiate the individual from a collective and the private from the communal. Both are bounded, and each instantiation stands in relation to other communities and other publics. But they also differ from one another in important respects. A community is a cultural and social entity that only emerges and becomes identifiable over time – often a long period of time – whereas a public lacks institutional being (Warner 2002: 61), has a far shorter gestation, and is far more transient. And not coincidentally, community identification makes an important contribution to long-term identity construction, whereas identification with a public does not.

'Communities' and 'publics' clearly do a lot of work in constituting the sociality of the public sphere, and just as a community and a public are positioned outside of the private sphere, so they are generally positioned apart from intimacy. Perhaps counter-intuitively though, we develop our discussion of social formations in an age of mobile social media by asking the reader to consider the usefulness of the paradox 'intimate publics' – for whilst private and public are binaries, the personal and the public, the intimate and the public are not. Qualifying each of these terms – intimacy and public – with the conjunction of the other, creates a hybrid category of relation that we have found useful in grasping conditions for intersubjectivity created by mobile social media.

Intimate publics

With the 'intimate' turn making an impact upon various facets of cultural practice and politics, notions like emotion are no longer defined individually or psychologically but as an integral part of social life (Ahmed 2004). For Sara Ahmed, emotions are 'the flesh of time' (2004: 10) that get attributed to objects and people in ways that are 'sticky' – that is, full of affective value. As Eva Illouz argues in *Cold Intimacies: The Making of Emotional Capitalism*, rather than capitalism creating boundaries between public and private, emotion and rationality, it fosters an intensely emotional culture that blurs workplace, family, and relationships (2007). Drawing on the growing examples of celebrity and self-help discourses that entwine public and private spheres, Illouz explores the insidious process of blurring the emotional with economic in what she calls 'emotional capitalism'. For Gregg, the role of social and mobile media has helped foster a presence bleed between public and private, work and life, economic and emotional spaces (2011). Increasingly, intimacy and emotion are fuelling many capitalist discourses of the public. Given this phenomenon, how has Berlant's pre-social media notion of intimate publics changed? How have the political practices of mobility formed, and been informed by, localised notions of intimacy and public?

Lauren Berlant observed that intimacy has taken on new geographies and forms of 'publicness' (1998: 281). For although intimacy has its etymological and cultural roots in constructions of privacy – from the Latin *intimus*, innermost, inward – its hybridity has always been evident as these private behaviours are performed in public, for a public, through the establishment of home, family, marriage and all the other institutionalised relationships that are private in the relation, and public in the institutionalisation of the relation. Social media constitute a new sociotechnical institutionalisation of public intimacy, and as intimacy is negotiated within networked social media, the publicness – along with the continuous, multitasking full-timeness – becomes increasingly palpable. Intimate relations are not simply performed privately in pairs or small groups, they are also constructed, maintained, defined and mapped for this intimate public, in visible, institutional, functional and symbolic ways.

With mobile, social and locative media creating new types of intimacy as publicly performed, notions such as privacy – and its relationship to the public and the private – blur. As danah boyd and Alice Marwick observe, social privacy in these contexts involves new types of strategies that reflect newly emergent attitudes to privacy (2011). Newell canvasses these multi-dimensional perspectives across numerous disciples (1995), while Alhaqbani and Fidge provide a pragmatic model of how a multi-dimensional model of privacy might be operationalised (2007). In these accounts, privacy is not as a 'space' to be guarded, and is not an 'asset' that we possess, but is what Dourish and Anderson refer to as a collective informational practice (2006).

In the context of ubiquitous mobile social media, the strategies or informational practices employed by our informants to construct privacy were seen to entail the interplay of four dimensions.

The first is, of course, the nature of the information subject to disclosure. It is not the case that some information is private *per se*, and other information is public *per se*, but the nature of *informational content* is clearly relevant to decision making in respect of that information.

The second dimension is the *identity of the observer* in relation to the informational content, and in relation to the subject of the information. Sensitive content such as indiscreet images taken at a party are not private as a consequence of their content *per se*; they are private only at the intersection of that content and certain observers, such as parents or potential employers, and are not private at the intersection of that content and other observers, such as a social public of peers, or an intimate public of close friends.

The third dimension, the *consequences of disclosure*, flows directly from the first two. The consequences of disclosure (of what, to whom) is strategised in terms of effect and affect: Is this flattering? Is this witty? Is this interesting? In our case studies we saw differing responses to corporate data-mining of the participants' content and interactions. Instead focus lay with patrolling the boundaries of their various intimate publics – not because they see no personal consequences flowing from corporate breaches of boundaries – but because they anticipate significant consequences from interpersonal breaches of boundaries.

The fourth dimension is the trustworthiness of *the systems of disclosure*. Will Facebook do what it promises to do in respect of my profile, my informational content and the permissions I have set, now and into the future, and, if not, what are the consequences? This more nuanced interpretation of what 'privacy' means to users of mobile social media clearly permits intimate publics – publics that are defined and bounded, and are in that sense private – to provide locations for intimacy.

Social media strategies and practices that fuse private acts and intimate publics in the way described do so at an interpersonal level. At a social or cultural level, as opposed to an interpersonal level, intimacy can also be observed, and this is also in a sense public. For Michael Herzfeld, cultural intimacy describes the 'social poetics' of the nation-state and is 'the recognition of those aspects of a cultural identity that are considered a source of external embarrassment but that nevertheless provide insiders with their assurance of common sociality' (1997: 3). The global appropriation of social media provides evidence of this sense of cultural intimacy. In China QQ is not simply a SNS or social media, it is *the* Chinese SNS, *the* Chinese social media. It was the first social media in China and its model is linked into reinforcing national, provincial and vernacular notions. In Korea, Facebook is very popular, but Facebook does not speak to, and of, Korea in the way Cyworld minihompy does. In the Philippines Friendster was being appropriated just as it was being abandoned in the United States. It is through this negotiation between the performance of personal intimacies and the aggregation and identification of public socio-cultural intimacies that we construct a sense of community and, at certain times in certain places, a nation-state.

Moving back to the personal and interpersonal, observers such as Derlega and Margulis (1983), Duck (1988), Giddens (1992) and Sexton and Sexton (1982) have pointed to the difficulty in essentialising and locating intimacy. It is present in *behaviours* such as the reciprocal self-disclosure of privileged knowledge; in *affects* such as empathy, affection, commitment and depth of understanding; and in *contexts* such as privacy, non-dependence and an absence of coercion.

And it is clear that the ubiquity of mobile social media is reshaping the behaviours, affects and contexts associated with intimacy, and that the *mobility* of the social media (in addition to the media content) is an affordance important to this reshaping. When compared to the desktop personal computer, or the wired telephone, mobile media amplifies important properties of intimacy on personal, corporeal, collective and socio-cultural levels. On a personal level, mobile media are intensely personal devices for many people; for Fortunati (2002), the mobile phone is one of *the* most intimate items in everyday life. While the wired telephone is more often than not common property, shared by the family or those who share a flat or an office, mobile social media are not. Though in third-world village contexts mobile phones are commonly loaned and hired, for our young, urban informants, mobile social media devices are very much a personal possession, customised for private use, with a particular collection of games, social applications, albums of personal images and videos, music, contacts, icon-interface settings, caller identification settings, ring tones, clip-on fashion covers, and the like.

The loss of such a device is very much more than the loss of an easily replaceable utilitarian tool – it is more akin to the loss of say, a personal diary, an object with which one has an important affective investment. At this material level, then, the personal nature of a mobile social media device, folding up and materialising a personal history and personal subjectivities as it does, places it in an important position for the performance of the interpersonal as well as the personal.

The mobile device is thus an affective device, but it is also an effective device for the performance of intimacy. Intimacy involves the micro and macro, phatic and tacit gestures – glances, nods, smiles, touches and code-words that reaffirm the existence of a relationship. Using mobile social media, such low-intensity, high-frequency acts of intimacy occur by the billions each day; indeed, for many, these mediated acts of intimacy are far more frequent than those that are embodied. For some, the intensity and frequency have led to a telecocooning between close intimates (Habuchi 2005). For others, the frequency affords new ways in which to weave the micro with the macro among acquaintances. Whereas offline social exchanges punctuate the week and the day, many of our informants tell us that for them, the feed through their various publics is relentless.

Our mobile respondents are never without the opportunity to socialise, are never out of touch, are never alone, and many utilise this capacity to literally and figuratively glance, nod, smile, touch and exchange code-words with intimates more or less constantly. An argument can be made that this hyperfrequency of communicative acts – the sheer aggregated quantity of communicative acts – mediates an authentic and valuable form of intimacy, regardless of the fact that much of the communication content is on the face of it banal

(Koskinen 2007) rather than deeply thoughtful. 'Just being there' in the form of high-frequency low-intensity exchanges, that if nothing else are affectively phatic and affirm a continuous mutual presence, would seem to be important in a relationship (Kjeldskov et al. 2004). The use of mobile social media in the context of intimate publics also enables the 'being there' to be witnessed, and this choice to make 'the interior the new exterior' is often made (Sukhder Sandhi cited in Margaroni and Yiannopoulou 2005: 222). These exteriorised intimacies produce the recursive exchange of intimacies, the witnessing of such exchanges and the sharing of the witnessing of such exchanges as norms.

Of course, important though these exchanges may be, intimacy is also to be found in emotionally charged, high-intensity interactions and, as we saw in the example of Soo-kyung and her best friend He-ran in Seoul (Chapter 2), these too are electronically mediated using the communications system of choice for billions – mobile media that speaks not just to the significant other, but also to the group.

The intimate public that are privy to these low-intensity high-frequency exchanges, and high-intensity low-frequency exchanges, are self-conscious of their collectivity, of their common ground, and are aware of their shared horizon, protected by the boundary of privilege settings, false names and profiles, and in-jokes. Self-disclosure is thus privileged, establishing at least one of the conditions commonly claimed for intimacy. Expressions of friendship, exchanges of kindness, phatic expressions of affection, favours offered, asked and received are all witnessed among this public, and this publicness provides norms for the performance of intimacy, and sets standards of reciprocity among that intimate public, establishing a second condition often claimed for intimacy. It may therefore be claimed that the publics assembled through mobile social media are intimate in that they engage in the reciprocal self-disclosure of privileged knowledge. These intimate publics are instantiated as a phenomenological reality in the feed that streams across the screen, and more so when members get together offline. An intimate public is instantiated as an imaginary as text messages are composed or images uploaded, and of course it is available as an analytic concept as we reflect on all of this.

We recognise, however, that 'intimate' is a powerful term not to be scattered around indiscriminately to describe any and every interpersonal relationship. Intimacy is powerful in part because it is less common than other, less emotionally charged, less tightly bound, forms of sociality. In view of this fact we also use the term 'social public'. A 'social public' like an 'intimate public' is a collective that shares common ground as an affective society, and is brought together by that common ground. Like an intimate public, a social public is bounded as it gels, and this boundary, shifting and permeable though it is, differentiates between those who are members of the affective social public, and those who are not. Also like an intimate public, a social public shares a horizon that demarcates the commonalty that brought it together in the first place, and marks the space beyond which lie other publics and other networks. So, a social public shares emotional affect, but not as intensely as an intimate public; it is bound, but not as tightly as an intimate public; it has a horizon, but at a greater distance than an intimate public.

In view of the above, the terms 'social publics' and 'intimate publics' are used to refer to certain social formations in preference to the more common generic terms 'social networks' and 'networked publics' (e.g. boyd 2007; Langlois et al. 2009). 'Social' and 'intimate' captures the particular nature of the subjectivities and intersubjectivities shared by these publics more accurately than the more generic term 'networked', and 'public' captures the shared or collective nature of the phenomenological experience, existential imaginary and analytic concept. These social and intimate behaviours, affects and contexts *are* networked, as will be explored shortly, but they are more importantly public, a point to be made all the more emphatically at a time when the notion of a public needs defending.

Public expressions of intimacy, where they occur, are as important in their way as public expressions of any other social virtue or vice. Action in public is important to the formation of collective identity, to the body politic, to the achievement of social change, and to our position in the world as people and as subjects. But important though the idea and the reality of a public may be, it has suffered hard times of late.

The continual rise of individualism as a culturally potent resource, and the power of the market as the arbiter of societal relations – now read as relations between individuals – has done terrible damage to 'the public', to the 'social', and to 'the community' as a beneficiary and a claimant of goods, services, duties, interests, policies and decisions (Green 1994; Kumar 1992). The hegemonic ethos over recent decades has been to increasingly demand personal agency and private consumption, mediated through the market, for the satisfaction of private rather than public and social ideals or objectives (McLean and Voskresenskaya 1992). The public institutions and public utilities established in the last half of the nineteenth century to provide education, water, power, health services, transport, communications and opportunities for socialising were informed and legitimised by a modernist discourse which centred on the virtues of public interest decision-making, public duty, public service, public good and public responsibility – now all laughably outmoded tropes. Social relations have thus been reconstituted around a neo-liberal discourse that valorises personal agency, private benefit, individual responsibility and consumer sovereignty. Notwithstanding their role in mediating intimate publics, social media are deeply implicated changes in social infrastructure, symbolised in the discursive shift from 'public' and 'community' to 'network', and, more pointedly, to 'networked individualism' (Wellman et al. 2003).

Networks

The inadequacy of the 'network' metaphor as a signifier of relationships that are social or intimate is evident in the defining structure of a network. As an abstract model a network comprises two elements – *being*, and *relation*, most commonly represented as the node and the link – and from these deceptively simple but elegant elements, structures of great complexity arise. Network theory has devised a number of postulates to account for the performance of networks in terms of generalisable principles. Mejias (2010: 610) draws on Monge and Contractor (2003: 88) to provide a useful summary. Principles of self-interest, collective action, balanced interactions, resource exchange, reciprocal exchange, homophily, proximity and co-evolution are the instrumentalist, functionalist interactions that are said to govern the particular assemblage of nodes and links in any given case, and produce the variety of network structures that are evident in social media, in professions, and elsewhere.

According to Schroeder and Rebelo (2009), the word 'network' can be traced back to at least the 1560s, where one finds it posited as a 'net-like arrangement of threads, wires, etc.'. Network gets its first formal treatment in the work of eighteenth-century mathematician Leonhard Euler who describes the properties of vertices (nodes) and arcs (routes) in the context of the Königsberg Bridges problem. In the 1840s the word tended to refer to 'any complex, interlocking system', and foreshadowing its contemporary use in IT, began to be used in reference to transportation channels such as rivers, railways and canals. Schroeder and Rebelo (2009) point out that roughly sixty years ago, the concept of the network expanded its embrace to include the interconnection of groups of people, and in the early 1990s the term 'network society' was coined by Jan van Dijk (1999).

In their important work *A Thousand Plateaus* Gilles Deleuze and Félix Guattari (1987) entangled the network with the metaphor of the heterarchic rhizome, a term originating in the field of botany where it designates the subterranean horizontal stems of a plant. From these foundations in the natural sciences the concept migrated to management theory (Grabher and Stark 1997), and has since found still wider applications. Rather than a single trunk in a hierarchical tree structure, a heterarchy is rhizomic, and has a number of points that act as centres. Unlike a hierarchic or arboreal system, which rises from a single point of origin, has a single trajectory, or equilibrium, or centre of gravity, (depending on the preferred metaphor), a heterarchic system has many (Grabher 2001; Grabher and Stark 1997). While the internet as a whole is hierarchical rather than heterarchical – with sites like Google, Facebook, Amazon and YouTube sitting on the top of a 'power curve' (Barabási 2002) that dominates a very long tail – *within* a large social media network such as Facebook, we see something more like a rhizomic heterarchy, with 900 million interwoven points of origin, or 900 million interwoven rhizomes, or 900 million interwoven networks with incoming and outgoing links best plotted as a normal curve. In the case of social media, these clusters of circulation (beings or nodes) are generally individual personas or profiles, but may be groups, projects, media objects or issues, for example. Each is at the centre of the whole system for the actors that circulate around it – and there is therefore more than one point of circulation in any given system. This flat, rhizomic structure means that the reach of networked sociality is potentially vast, within and particularly across interlinked networks. Sociality in this new context is broader and flatter than perhaps it has ever been, and this new *structure* for our social *agency* has drawn Manichean responses.

On the one hand, critics of social media argue that networked sociality provides a strong valence for communicative acts that are brief, quick, numerous, relatively indiscriminate and often shallow. Notions like the 'social' have been simplified in social media (Lovink 2012). This amplified and extended reach of disclosure through social media networks democratises communication in a way that is said to occur at the expense of privilege. Social media expert Clay Shirky (2008), for example, takes up this theme to argue that the personal is no longer a space shared between people as a consequence of intimacy (whether in public or private realms) but, rather, it has been hijacked by technologies. That is to say, the self-disclosure associated with intimacy implies a degree of autonomy, a degree of agency and selectivity that gives the connection afforded by self-disclosure its special significance has now become an automated and semi-automated by-product of image construction (see also Amodeo and Wentworth 1986: 15).

Online social networking has established a structure in which hundreds of millions of people are available to us, each in principle as close as the other. We routinely exchange trivialities and banalities but we also disclose our personal history, our autobiography, our emotional state, our bodies, our physical state, our values, goals and ambitions to others, and they disclose to us, and critics argue that by eroding privilege and distance in this way, technologies are eroding closeness as well as distance (Arnold 2003). A conscious decision to self-disclose particular information to particular others is the behaviour associated with intimacy in particular, and sociality more generally – and is not to be confused with surveillance, and is not to be confused with automated feed to all networked contacts. Critics such as Turkle (2011) argue that the sense of trust and mutuality that marks an intimate relationship depends upon revelations that are privileged, special to the relationship and not in the public domain, and that this relationship may only be built in private, though it is often reinforced by being displayed in public. It is argued that rhizomic networks do not provide these preconditions – that ramified online 'Friendship' networks are too extensive, too fluid and too promiscuous.

On the other hand, there are numbers of ways social networks can be defended, without denying that they extend the reach and frequency of communication, and without denying that much of this communication is anything but deep and meaningful. One such argument is in the process of being made here. We argue that *within* these extensive rhizomic networks, social media mediate the construction of intimate publics that do provide the structural preconditions for the expression of sociality and intimacy. We continue the argument by further investigating the contrast between communities, publics and networks in the context of sociality, intimacy and social media.

Communities, publics and networks

We have noted that community is celebrated where it is found and mourned where it is not. It is deployed strategically by ideologues of all stripes, and romanticised to a point where one doubts that it has ever existed but, like the public, it is nevertheless at grave risk of cultural redundancy. We have also noted that the social network is now the preferred metaphor to represent the properties of social connectedness, and ask, are there important differences between communities, publics and networks for our understanding of the use of mobile social media in the Asia-Pacific?

Benedict Anderson's notion of the 'imagined community' has been both useful and limiting in its conceptualisation of the region and its oscillating and contesting localities (1983). For Anderson (1983), 'nation' – as we understand it today – was born through the rise of distribution and printing techniques such as the printing press. Thus a sense of belonging and place, an 'imagining' of community, has never involved just face-to-face (Anderson 1983: 18) and has always deployed some form of virtuality or co-presence. Here intimacy, like place, is seen as a complex web of entangled mediations in which there is no 'unmediated' version. For example, diaspora does not result in an erosion of the nation-state, since 'imagining' is an important part of the sense of belonging (Dirlik 1999). Mechanisms such as the printing press, railway systems and now global mobile technologies operate to further instill notions of intimacy, home and cultural proximity. But unlike the printing press that erodes the local, social and mobile media reinforce the vernacular (Hjorth 2009b). While Anderson's imagined community has been useful in reconceptualising localised notions of community as informed by various dimensions of place – geographic, informational, socio-cultural, psychological – it is also limited in its capacity to understand the complex entanglements between 'placing' and various iterations of presence (Richardson and Wilken 2012).

Clearly, a network is not a community, and nor is the 'network' a value-neutral metaphor for the *structure* of a certain form of sociality, but implicitly embeds a normative argument for a certain form of *functionalist* sociality. This representation of sociality has become the standard model in this space, most clearly presented in Wellman's 'networked individualism' (Wellman et al. 2003), but also to be found to lesser and greater degrees in the work of boyd (2007, 2010), Castells (1996, 2001), Rheingold (1993, 2002, 2008) and other authors prolific in developing, networking, as the trope of choice, a move rarely critiqued (for an exception, see Gurstein 2011).

And yet, the network is a profoundly cynical model of sociality, read as self-serving functionalism. In this model, the social network is an investment in social capital, providing its creator with a net return on social labour. A network is thus constructed as a private and personal asset, different to everyone else's network, painstakingly built and maintained over years of social interaction, now of course called 'networking'. One's network is thus as extensive as possible, with indeterminate boundaries that are in a sense arbitrary. The network is also transient and shape-changing, depending as it does on the social energy and social successes of its owner. Members of the network do not share common ground as such; rather, each node shares connections with connecting nodes. The central node may know the network, and nodes know connecting nodes, but the network is too dynamic and ephemeral to be present to itself as a common entity. There is therefore no sense of solidarity across the network, no sense of tradition, no common identity (in contrast to individual identities) and no common interests (in contrast to individual interests).

In contrast, the notion of a community, and the very thing that has made community obsolete in an age of rampant individualism, at least in the West, is that community is constituted in recognition of a common identity, common interests and common obligations. Community is a model that provides for a shared sociality – in a sense, a normative framework for social interaction and social commitment that stands between the atomism of individuation and the totalitarianism of unification under the state. A social network is not a shared public good held by all in common, but is a private asset; a personal store of social capital actively built and maintained by individuals to suit their own desires, sense of self and self-interests.

For the networked individual, the personal network also substitutes for community in so much as the networked individual *dwells* in the network. That is to say, the network is not just an instrumental device for transmitting signals *between* locations, the network *is* the location, and for the networked individual, dwelling in that location is the preferred mode of being. Our informants don't *use* Facebook or QQ; we have seen that in a sense they dwell in Facebook or QQ. The influential phenomenologist and now post-phenomenologist Don Ihde made a similar point many years ago (1979) when he asked rhetorically, where are we when we are on the (wired) telephone? When truly engaged in a telephone conversation we slip away from the room we are in and enter a different existential space constituted by the conversation. We are *in* conversation; we are not *having* a conversation.

For the denizen of Facebook, for the Cyworld phoneur (Luke 2006), the world is the networked world and the occupants of that world are fellow nodes. Mejias describes this situation when he coins the term 'nodocentrism' which he distinguishes from the 'paranodal' (Mejias 2007, 2010). Nodocentrism refers to an observation that, whilst networks are extremely efficient at establishing links between nodes, and in effect reduce the distance between nodes to near zero, they embody a bias against knowledge of and engagement with anything that is not a node in the same network, in effect making the distance between a node and a non-node infinite. In other words, for the node, only nodes exist, and they exist only by virtue of their links, not by virtue of any properties intrinsic to the node. It is an epistemology based on the logic of the network, which is the exclusive reality of the node and the link. It privileges linked nodes while discriminating against what is not a linked node – the invisible, the other – the paranodal.

Mejias points out that in the network diagrams we are all familiar with, the outsides of the network and the space between the nodes and links are rendered white, as perfect emptiness. The paranodal is Newtonian space – an empty void without existence in itself, serving only to accommodate the existence of beings that do exist. But of course we know (post-Einstein) that this space is not empty and is not without agency. It has its own shape, its own properties, and it is inhabited by multitudes of beings that are not nodes, and do not conform to the organising logic of the network. Mejias suggests that in the face of the network's self-constructed void, an important nodocentric strategy is the assimilation of all beings into networks. Thus, ubiquitous computing seeks to colonise the paranodal and, in principle, connect all people and all artefacts in a single network. The move by some application developers to establish systems of persistent online identity across media and platforms seeks to interconnect all our networks. Search engines are quintessentially nodocentric, and seek in principle to index all informational objects. In this logic, all beings can and should be nodes, and the paranodal is at risk.

To bring this back to social media, we learn from our respondents that Mejias is on to something. To be without Facebook, QQ or Cyworld is to enter the paranodal – to enter a white space where one ceases to exist. Our respondents are nodocentric, and their ontology as nodes is important to the conduct of their lives. This being the case, it becomes all the more vital that we consider intimacy in the context of these new conditions. That is, in conditions where social networking, mobile networking, ubiquitous computing, and universal indexicality continue to colonise the paranodal, and that immerse us more and more deeply in the world of electronically mediated sociality.

Accordingly, and by way of conclusion to this chapter, we contend that 'mobile intimacy' and 'intimate publics' are in a position to borrow some of the qualities attributed to community, and recue social media from the excesses of networks – as a normative ideal for sociality, and as an analytic concept capable of distinguishing forms of phenomenological experience and forms of existential imaginary. Like communities and unlike networks, an intimate public has a collective sense of self, a collective identity as a self-defined group that speaks to the group and speaks of the group, not just to and of individuals. The provision of a boundary, established via multiple accounts on multiple platforms, multiple personas, privacy settings and the like, runs counter to the flat, extensive, infinitely connected, open-ended spirit of the rhizomic network, but provides a precondition for insiders and outsiders; for privilege and for selective, reciprocal disclosure, and therefore for intimacy. And these boundaries are defended against the 'Other'.

In the case of social media, the 'Other' is likely to be a boring acquaintance, a Friend collector, an employer, a mother, or another individual simply 'out of place' in this particular public, rather than a community's more significant enemies, but nevertheless resistance is important to solidarity. Like communities and unlike networks, this intimate public is not nuclear and, rather than being owned by and centred around a particular profile, is centred around and is in a sense owned by, or at least defined by, the shared conditions and interests that give rise to intimacy. This common ground, or shared conditions, transcends the open-ended fluidity of the network's nodes and links by providing for traditions often found in community, more so than networks. An intimate public's sense of self may thus be reinforced as it uses its own dialect, uses obscure personal references, rehearses old stories in their entirety with a single reference, and uses irony and satire confident that misunderstandings will not occur. Like communities and unlike networks, an intimate public has a sense of reciprocal commitment and obligation to the collective, emanating from the public character of interactions, reinforcing the reciprocity emanating from the intimate character of the public interactions – a socially potent combination not found in networks. Like communities and unlike networks, intimate publics recognise the existence of the paranodal, and can gather it up and embrace it. Grandmother can be gathered up and 'made to exist' in the world of social media by being shown how to play *Happy Farm*.

This is not to say that we can or should avoid normative judgements. We are quite prepared to say that social publics and intimate publics have more to offer human sociality than networks, but we say so on the understanding that the norms we are able to bring to bear in the making of this judgement are not standing still in the face of new media. In the next chapter, 'Topographies of the Intimate', we further explore the formation of intimate publics through mobile intimacy.

9 Topographies of the intimate

Mobile publics in the Asia-Pacific

In the last chapter we heard of Bao, a young man who migrated from another province to Shanghai. In one sense Bao's move to university was an unremarkable example of internal migration now common in China. But in another sense, Bao's experience is a remarkable example of mobility. Behind this train trip from place to place were other, more profound forms of mobility that are becoming an integral part of global and local contemporaneity. His was the first generation to migrate from the village to the city, the first to benefit from a university education, the first to move their source of income from agriculture and family businesses to white-collar corporate work, and the first to move from a life structured by layers of localised and national tradition to a life increasingly structured by the demands of globalised modernity. Bao's is a mobile generation indeed.

In *Alone Together: Why We Expect More from Technology and Less from Each Other*, Turkle (2011) presents a description of mobility that is both amusing and troubling. Turkle returns to 1996 when, at the MIT Media Lab, groups of researchers carried keyboards and wore backpacks to carry 'mobile' computers and 'mobile' radio transmitters. From our perspective two decades on, the objective was prosaic – to be mobile while also being online. From their perspective, though, the quest for mobility was more heroic. In Turkle's account they saw themselves as cyborgs, not simply as humans with mobile communications. Turkle notes: 'The cyborgs were a new kind of nomad, wandering in and out of the physical real. For the physical real was only one of the many things in their field of vision' (2011: 151). This 1996 cyborg was nomadic, but always online, always electronically connected – to others, to databases, aurally and visually. The nomadic cyborg self-described as 'more capable', 'more powerful', 'I feel invincible, sociable, better prepared. I am naked without it. With it, I'm a better person.' Turkle adds:

> I saw a bravery, a willingness to sacrifice for a vision of being one with technology. When their burdensome technology cut into their skin, causing lesions and then scars, the cyborgs learned to be indifferent. When their encumbrances caused them to be taken as physically disabled, they learned to be patient and provide explanations.

> (2011: 151)

The technology Bao uses has clearly come a long way, and in an ironic take on Haraway's famous essay (1985), and Hayles's influential book (1999), Turkle points out that 'we are all cyborgs now' (2011). In a dramatic shift from her earlier, positive analysis of online media, Turkle finds herself displaced and suddenly dystopian in her views of media and its impact upon offline. Unlike Turkle, we see the mobility of devices, contexts, platforms and presences creating intimate, social and mobile publics that are not about disconnection. So, what does the turn to mobility enabled by these devices imply, now that they are in Bao's hand, and not on his back?

In this chapter we explore the intersection of mobility and mobile media. As we shall argue, mobility in all its forms is the defining characteristic of contemporary life, and not by coincidence, mobility distinctively marks this century's media practices. One way of conceptualising mobility between co-present worlds is by identifying the localised and vernacular ways in which various forms of *mobility* (across technological, geographic, psychological, physical and temporal terrains) and various forms of *sociality* (in particular intimacy, publics and networks) are spearheaded by the increasing role of mobile media.

As both a symbol and set of practices, mobile media cultures proffer a powerful example of contemporary forms of intimacy and sociality (Fortunati 2002; Lasén 2004). In the last chapter, we contrasted intimate and social publics with the network. Drawing upon Mimi Sheller's notion of publics as an assemblage 'beyond the networked perspective' (2004; Sheller and Urry 2003), and its application through Galloway's (2010) case studies of art locative media projects, and through Mejias's (2007) modelling of the nodocentric and paranodal, we argued for the rubrics 'intimate publics' and 'social publics'. Building upon the work of Berlant (1998) and Warner (2002) in their discussion of counter-publics within the intimate turn, we argued that intimate publics, social publics and networks provided a fluid and socio-culturally specific model to understand case studies of mobile, social and locative media convergence.

We found that deploying a model of intimate and social publics – as part of the emergent mobile intimacies – embraces the contingencies of the local and socio-cultural. As demonstrated through our divergent case studies in the region, the convergence between public and private, personal and political, here and there involves localised notions of sociality and intimacy that occur at the intersection of intimate and social publics and their social technologies. In this chapter we continue the exploration of mobile, social and locative media in the region through a focus on mobility; mobile media certainly, but also social, emotional and socio-economic mobility, and the implication of all of this mobility for social and intimate publics.

Contemporary mobility

By drawing together the ideas of a number of influential social theorists, Sheller (2004: 47) summarises the significance that mobility is thought to have in the contemporary world. She reminds us that the metaphors 'flow', 'the space of flows', 'global fluids' and 'liquidity' have been used by Bauman (2003), Castells (2000 [1996]), Urry (2000) and others to characterise 'the remarkably uneven and fragmented flows of people, information, objects, money, images and risks across regions in strikingly faster and unpredictable shapes' (Urry 2000: 38 cited in Sheller 2004: 47).

Our new forms of increasingly fluid mobility thus operate simultaneously at a number of scales and take a number of forms. At a global scale, mobile media are deeply implicated in the international flows of goods, capital, resources, cultural products and intellectual property; flows that characterise postmodernity. But most importantly, and as we have seen throughout the Asia-Pacific, they are also implicated in the intra-national and transnational flows of people that characterise our era. These forms of global mobility have important implications for the performance of contemporary local and global politics, local and global cultures, and perhaps most prominently, local and global economics. But the global mobility of people cannot be understood simply as an economic equation, stripped of its human dimension.

We have seen in Shanghai, Manila and Singapore that the national and international mobility of people has strong emotional and affective implications for families, friends and communities that are now separated by distance. In this context we have seen that social media plays an effective role (through its efficiencies), and an affective role (through its content), in enabling social publics and intimate publics – enabling people to be here (and in a sense there) doing this (but also doing that) with these people, but also those people.

On a personal scale, mobility also characterises the biographies of billions of people as they move from place to place, from time to time, in the course of a lifetime. Movements of people from country to country and from town to town have never been so frequent for individuals, and have never been so common across populations although, as Castells (2000 [1996]) has shown, this is by no means an option available to all, and has become one of the important foundations of privilege. On the still smaller scale of day-to-day life, mobility is also a key characteristic. Our days and our cities and suburbs are dynamic networks of moving people, goods and data. Again, mobile social media are implicated in this, interpolating peripatetic people through peripatetic communications devices.

Mobility is also closely tied to our sense of place; indeed, a place is constructed by mobility in so much as it is mobility's destination. Places are intersections of mobility, a pause in one form of mobility that creates conditions for other forms of social dynamic. Moving away from geographic mobility, it is clear that we are more mobile today in other important ways. People in the Asia-Pacific are more likely to move from job to job today than in other historical periods, are more likely to move homes and to move schools, and we in the West are also more likely to move from partner to partner and from family to family than in other historical periods.

Our psyches are also mobile, in the sense that our emotions are moved from moment to moment, and through a lifetime, perhaps more often as a concomitant of the above, and in so much as communication with others bears upon the psyche, as it certainly does, mobile social media are implicated in the e-motion of the psyche. Mobility is clearly significant in the contemporary world, and of course in the Asia-Pacific, and in so much as mobile media mediate this mobility, mobile media are also significant. But what exactly do the affordances of mobile media contribute to mobility more generally in these different forms and at these different scales?

The affordances of mobile media can be summed up reasonably simply, but the implications of these affordances are not so easy to tease out. First, a backpack is no longer required. Mobile media can be carried in the hand or about the body, or be attached to the body. It is thus available to us at all times in all places, at least potentially. Second, mobile media are in the possession of individuals, and are not accessed by small or large groups, as is the case with other media. Mobile media are thus personalised media. Third, mobile media provides a single portal to the consumption of multiple mediums – voices, letters, messages, images, maps, videos, music, appointments, contacts and so on – and in many cases, also provides a single portal for the production of these multiple media.

Fourth, mobile media are now social as well as dyadic. Publics of various kinds – in particular, social publics and intimate publics – may be addressed through mobile media, as well as individuals, and as well as networks. These publics and networks may be assembled around voice, text, images, video and so on, at all times and in all places. Fifth, mobile media traverses the offline–online boundary. This is the case in two senses: phenomenologically, one can 'be' online and offline at the same time, and through synchronous and asynchronous communications, one's online and one's offline actions and interactions can be intermeshed. Particularly prominent in this latter case is the use of mobile media for the management and coordination of offline sociality. And sixth, mobile media integrates increasingly sophisticated computational applications that are able to capture data, process data and output data, in ways only previously available to full-scale computers. So how, then, do these mobile affordances mediate sociality, intimacy and social and intimate publics?

Mobility and the changing mediation of sociality

All sociality is mediated, not just the social interactions and publics afforded to us via mobile media. Using a material-semiotic approach adopted from Actor Network Theory and Silverstone's work on 'domestication' (Silverstone and Haddon 1996; Silverstone et al. 1992), Arnold et al. (2006) describe one of the models by which the relationship between mobile media *qua* technologies and the experience of mobile sociality might be understood. In this model, our shaping of technologies and their shaping of us are treated symmetrically.

The model observes first that all artifacts – homes, clothes, cars – or more relevant to our concerns, mobile phones and mobile social media, provide us with semiotic points of self-reference that are ontological markers for constructing ourselves, for recognising ourselves and for presenting ourselves to others. As we have seen in various locations throughout the Asia-Pacific, and as we shall see below, mobile media devices, social media sites and the content made available via these technologies are clearly important in contemporary self-referencing and self-presentation.

Second, it is observed that the psyche is turbulent – constantly fluid or mobile – particularly so when it comes to emotions, and this mobility is reflected in the use of mobile media. For example, mobile media provide material-semiotic markers of changing socio-economic status; mobile media UCC provides markers of emotional status, and so on. These markers are in one sense more obdurate than the psyche, which provides for a sense of continuity and stability through time, but these mobile markers are also fluid, providing the capacity to change and to mark change through time. Again, we see that in various locations in the Asia-Pacific mobile media is important in mediating this ongoing but changing autobiographical presence.

Third, the model goes on to point out that the above-mentioned socio-technologies are not only semiotic objects to be read, but also provide us with a capacity to act materially in the world – through the agency of the above-mentioned affordances. With mobile media, as cyborgs as it were, we can do things the body cannot. We can communicate at a distance, assemble mobile publics around our communications content and in many other ways perform sociality differently.

Fourth, it is recognised that we live in an extant world of 'givens', a world of devices and applications developed and made available by Samsung, QQ, Apple and others, that are appropriated through use, in actions that are 'self-constructing and object constructing, whilst [also] being world-constructing' (Arnold at al. 2006: 98). The personalised acquisition of mobile hardware, the personalised deployment of mobile applications and their particularised use to immerse ourselves in the mobile flow are pre-eminent examples of this world-making process of self-construction and technology construction.

Through the above-mentioned processes that intertwine and overlay self-reference and presentation, ongoing autobiographic presence, a new capacity to act in the world, selective appropriation, customisation and personalisation, our sociality is mediated through mobile media. Our more mobile and fluid social circumstance is, in this model, not a simple social equation in which a) sociality and intimacy are a set of fixed and stable subjectivities and interpersonal performances; b) users of mobile media are the sole agentic subjects in the equation – the instigators of all decisions and social actions; and c) mobile media are merely faithful servants used by b) to achieve a). Rather, society and culture, people and technologies come together to constitute a sociotechnical hybrid in which the performance of sociality is shaped by users and by mobile media, users are shaped by sociality and by mobile media, and mobile media is shaped by users and their social performances. We now link mobility (at the scales and in the forms noted above) to mobile media (and the affordances also noted above).

Mobile media, mobile intimacy and mobile publics

As argued in the previous chapter, convergences of binaries such as public and intimate, social and intimate, online and intimate, networked and intimate are becoming even more contingent, multiple and contested as mobile, social and locative media integrate. For Gerard Raiti, 'mobile technologies are changing personal relationships and intimacy' (2007: n.p.). For Raiti, '"Mobile intimacy", the ability to be intimate across distances of time and space, is a global phenomenon' (2007: n.p.). And yet, as Raiti indicates, it has distinctive features in the Asia-Pacific. In the Asia-Pacific, as in all places, localised notions of mobility and intimacy are not limited to Western or Anglophonic models of the family, of friendship, of social capital, or of individual/group and private/public dichotomies. Indeed, for theorists such as Gregg (2011), Andrejevic (2011) and Matsuda (2005), the affordances of mobile media in the context of contemporary mobile practices mean that no notion of mobility, place or sociality is left unaffected.

As has been argued throughout the book, intimacy is one form of sociality that is affected, and particularly intimacy as it relates to women in the context of developing countries (Ehrenreich and Hochschild 2003). We have shown that the role of the mobile phone in Manila and Singapore as a technology of propinquity (temporal and spatial proximity) is both instrumental in, and symbolic of, the transnational flows of gendered modes of emotional labour and consumption. For Wajcman et al., the association of mobile media with 'affective or emotional work is part of the unequally distributed gender division of labour' (2009: 14). In 'Intimate Connections: The Impact of the Mobile Phone on Work Life Boundaries', Wajcman et al. note that the mobile phone 'characterises modern times and life in the fast lane' and has become iconic of 'work-life balance' – or lack thereof – in contemporary life (2009: 9).

As we see above, and in Manila and Singapore, the hybridisation of intimacy, socio-economic mobility and mobile media emerges clearly in the case of working mothers. For working mothers in the Asia-Pacific, and all over the world, mobile media are essential in the negotiation of paid work, mothering, domestic labour and social interaction. Rather than the home or the workplace being a bounded and defined place with bounded and defined functions, mobile work is now everywhere and nowhere in particular, mobile home-duties are everywhere and nowhere in particular, and so are one's intimates. As related in the Melbourne case study in particular, the material and cultural architecture that sets a boundary, that enables us to perceive a horizon and define a place as a place for work, a place for domesticity, a place for recreation, a place for the public or a private place has been problematised, first by telephones, then by mobile phones and now by mobile media that don't recognise this architecture. Reflecting this implication of mobile affordances is the fact that 'place' is no longer the origin and destination of communications media. Under the regime of mobile media one does not phone 'home' or phone 'work', the mobile individual is now the origin and the destination (Malpas 2012: 27 quoting Wellman), amplifying our status as individual subjects, and reshaping our agency as individuals just as it reshapes the role of places like homes and workplaces.

According to Fortunati (2002), mobile media also reflects particular gendered performativities and intimacies. Indeed, Fortunati clearly identifies the way that practices of intimacy are gendered – and the way that the affordances of mobile media reproduce gendered forms of social labour. For Fortunati:

> the mobile phone might be considered as a *work tool for reproduction*. That is, a tool that supports and facilitates almost all the aspects of immaterial reproductive labour, which are increasingly complex and exponential in influence ... the mobile phone has become also a strategic *tool of social labour*.
>
> (2009: 31)

Intimacy is no longer assumed to be just about the personal or private but rather part of broader global processes in which emotion and social labour get hijacked by capitalism's social factory (Terranova 2000). As we have previously mentioned, Eva Illouz (2007) argues that capitalism is an emotional culture that fosters the bleeding together of workplace, family and intimate relationships. Workers are routinely asked to be 'passionate' about their widgets, while families are asked to be 'objective' about their living conditions; a bureaucratically defined work-section is now a 'team', and bosses are 'team leaders'. Drawing on these growing examples of celebrity and self-help discourses that entwine public and private spheres, Illouz explores the dual, insidious process of blurring the emotional with the economic, in what she calls 'emotional capitalism'.

The social significance of technologies like mobile media is predicated on their role as an *affective* technology through which emotional and affective labour is *effectively* executed. As set out in Chapter 8, technologies and social performances are co-productive, and in this case mobile media and the affordances set out above are a by-product of full-time intimacy as well as tools for full-time intimacy. The tools and the sociality, the effect and the affect, are co-emergent.

In the case of mobile media and intimacy, its technical effect is not so much a product of the *mobility* affordance per se, but of the fact that mobility provides for an 'always connected' affordance that is mobile, and this mobile 'always on' connection mediates the sense in which one is always culturally and psychically connected. As Nancy reminds us, the individual, the 'detached-for-itself', is only an abstract result of the decomposition of relations, and, gloomily, 'can be the origin and certainty of nothing but its own death' (Nancy 1991: 3–4). But when one is always digitally connected, connection with the material world is different (space no longer determines distance), connection with the social world is different (everyone is equally near and equally far) and connection to the world of the psyche is different (independence is weakened as inter-connection is strengthened).

When we are always connected via mobile technologies we dwell in a hybrid space, a phenomenological or existential field comprising corporeality and media, flickering attention back and forth and around and around from a face, to a screen, to a window, to a conversation. When we are always connected there is a sense in which conversation has no beginning and no end. Using mobile media we move into and drop out of conversation at will, using voice or text to move from this person to that, a person who may be here or there, but are present to us nonetheless, through digital coupling, or in the flesh through location services. We cross-fertilise this story with that through tagging, or commentating on status, and we assemble larger gatherings for discursive acts through 'tags', 're-tweets' and 'forwards'. We can escape the conversation at any time, after all, mobile communications can 'drop out' in various ways and we are not at hand to be accountable. But then again, we can never escape in the longer term, because we are never out of reach of the technology, and if we are, someone will want to know why we have made it so. A structure for interpersonal interaction that is 'always on' and is 'open-ended' in this way, resembles the never-ending plot structure of a television soap, more so than the bounded structure of a film or novel, and, like the soap versus the film, different conditions for the performance of intimacy are set.

Mobile media are, of course, digital media, and digital media is in itself fluid, insubstantial, present to us only through what Hayles (1999) called 'flickering signifiers'. The screen refreshes many times per second, the content is transient and flicks from voice to image to map to text to video, the updates of feed are continuous, the intersubjectivity is presentist in its orientation to time. But mobile media are also repositories of important information, materialising (that is digitising) ephemeral and existential properties of our intersubjectivity. Mobile media archives our intimates, our friends and our enemies, and does not discriminate between them, providing on-going and reliable access to all of the above in an equally efficient way, as well as to our appointments, our invitations, our social possibilities and responsibilities, to say nothing of our music, photographs, games, bank accounts, etc. In a sense, we carry our world in our hand, and affordances such as these are, we guess, the reasons why the MIT Media Lab researchers were willing to endure wounds.

One might well think that a world in which we are not always connected is a substantially different world, a world more solid than Hayles's 'flickering signifiers'. After all, when we are offline we are an embodied person, still mobile, but moving and interacting in geographic space, not in the 'space of flows'. In this material world our sense of being – what Hillis refers to as 'a sense of that which ontologically precedes naming and is present to oneself' (1999: xxxi), is a visceral, existential, thing of this world. We are not a profile, or a blog or a stream of tweets, we are flesh and blood materiality – a thing sitting here. But as Arnold argues, this flesh and blood has more in common with our digital presence than appears at first glance (2002). For the body is also a cultured sign – a social, cultural and historical production that identifies my gender, age, class, ethnicity, and so on. In this sense we are not as solid as we may think. As cultured-signs, not just as flesh and blood, we act in the world. As cultured-signs, our bodies are just a place-holder which situates us in the relational conditions through which we read the world, and through which we are read. Such a situation is more fluid, more mobile, than the flesh and blood suggests.

Lasén (2004) suggests that another way mobility has been at the heart of intimacy is demonstrated through the various forms of propinquity that are associated with romance. After all, a romantic relationship is noted for the significance of coming together, parting, chance meetings, the rendezvous and other movements in space that parallel emotional movement. For Ahmed (2004), rather than emotion being 'inside' or 'outside' as proposed by psychological models of emotion, she argues that emotion creates surfaces and boundaries to be traversed. As Ahmed notes: 'emotions are not "in" either the individual or the social, but produce the very surfaces and boundaries that allow all kinds of objects to be delineated. The objects of emotion take shape as effects of circulation' (Ahmed 2004: 10). And staying at this more conceptual level for a moment, we note that the concept of mobility has long been attached to emotion:

> Mobility is part of the original sense of the notion of emotion as it refers to agitated motion, mental agitation or feelings of mental agitation. Emotions are those mental states called 'passions' in the past. An important feature of the affects depicted by the category of passions is the idea that they entail ways of being acted upon, of being moved by other beings, objects, events, and situations. Nowadays people are moved and acted upon by their mobile phones. Mobile phone uses are the result of a shared agency.
> (Lasén 2004: n.p.)

One may easily interpret this connection of intimacy and mobility as dystopic, as does Bauman for example (2003). In Bauman's reading, the restless mobility of our emotions and the transience of our relations, reflected in and reinforced by our obsessive-compulsive use of social technologies, agitate us, uproot us, leaving us without the stable sense of self and sense of others required for intimacy. Alternatively, Giddens (1992) interprets this capacity for mobility in utopian terms. In Giddens's interpretation, personal and interpersonal mobility is associated with the 'pure relationship' – a relationship which is answerable only to itself (not to authority and not to power), and is sustained only so long as it satisfies the desires of those in the relationship.

Notwithstanding the relative strengths and weaknesses of either argument, it is clear that neither is developed in the context of the Asia-Pacific, and each view of contemporary intimacy is founded on the peculiar Judeo-Christian cultural heritage of the West, and the West's own moves through modernity and postmodernity. In the Asia-Pacific we see a very different heritage of culture and capital, and a much different context for family, sexuality and friendship. The export of Bauman's 'liquid love' (2003), Giddens's 'pure relationship' (1992) or any other Anglo-centric model to the Asia-Pacific cannot be assumed to be valid (Raiti 2007). The complexities of the Asia-Pacific are different to the complexities of the West, and require their own empirical mapping and theoretical unpacking, such as we attempt here.

To return to Lasén's conflation of mobility and emotion, mobile social media are technologies that not only move with us in a literal sense, but as important mediators of our sociality, also move us, act upon us, in an interpersonal, intimate way (2004). In this way mobile social media reflect the affordances of other social technologies, such as the letter – a media-form long associated with intimacy (Milne 2004). Like the letter, one's interlocutor is absent but is called into presence; content may be composed in a playful spontaneous way, or it may be carefully composed and considered; it may be written and read in private, but may also be shared; it may be carried on the body, to be read and reread. Mobile social media are clearly the tool of choice for those engaged in 'social labour' (Fortunati 2009: 31) and its affordances are clearly consistent with expressions of intimate sociality.

But in one of the many ironies associated with technology in general and mobile media in particular (Arnold 2003), mobile media achieve this because in one important sense mobile media do not move. That is, mobile media have a unique capacity to place us in an accessible position in the 'space of flows' (Castells 2000 [1996]) and fix us there, ready for contact, regardless of time or place. The objectivities of geographic space and real-time, when overlaid with a stable electronic position and a-synchronicity, gives rise to a new cartography in which relational presence and its emotional and social subjectivities are ever present. This too is consistent with the performance of intimacy, in that it affords the sheer volume of communication that is the new norm among the intimate publics of the Asia-Pacific.

The mobility associated with globalised emotional labour, and associated with mobile work patterns, mobile families and mobile careers, is often motivated by a desire for another form of mobility – upward socio-economic mobility. From iPhones in Singapore to *shanzhai* (copy) phones in Shanghai, mobile media technologies have become a potent symbol of, and mechanism for, lifestyle-based consumption and upward mobility. Popular conceptions of the rise of mobile media tend to assume that such technologies signify a type of globalised, privileged lifestyle of conspicuous consumption, often narrowly conceived of in terms of 'Western', 'Anglophonic' notions of capitalism

(Goggin and Hjorth 2009; McLelland and Goggin 2009; Robison and Goodman 1996).

In fact, the uptake of mobile media is so common, even in the Developing World, that it is not in itself an indicator of any particular socio-economic standing. However, the consumption of a particular mobile device is fine-grained enough to be read as a signifier. The particularities of mobile media handsets and services in particular have become a signifier of nationality, ethnicity, age and rurality, in addition to socio-economic status – a phenomenon that is particularly prevalent in the Asia-Pacific region (Donald et al. 2009; Robison and Goodman 1996). The region has experienced rapid economic growth and many millions have experienced rapid socio-economic mobility, each of which play out through mobile media. At the level of national economics, the move in economic strength is epitomised by the region's powerful and profitable high-tech electronic industries, and at the personal level the upwardly mobile use particular mobile media as powerful signifiers of status.

In this technocultural landscape, where socio-economic mobility and geographic mobility go hand in hand, mobile media operates through the whole of the geographic and socio-economic spectrum. On the one hand, mobile media is important for a growing cadre of migrant working-class workers in China (Bell 2005; Qiu 2008; Wallis 2011), for whom mobility from village farm to city factory, and from dire poverty to less dire poverty, is as likely to be experienced as another manifestation of an oppressed position, rather than as a privilege. On the other hand, there is the fast-growing number of Chinese students studying abroad, for whom the use of mobile media indicates a privileged position, and provides a vehicle for negotiating home while away. While some across the region choose forms of socio-economic and technological mobility, others are forced into physical migration, while many involve negotiations between the two. As both a metaphor for, and of, increasingly divergent and aspirational forms of mobility, mobile media can be viewed as representing, and affording, shifting lifestyle paradigms.

The constant flow of social interaction and the constant social presence made available through mobile media means that our respondents are never without their social and intimate publics or their networks. This constant social presence is played out most obviously online, through the feed of mobile media, but it also has important implications for offline sociality and, in particular, for the coordination of offline sociality. As Rich Ling notes, micro-coordination is a key aspect and affect of mobile communication (2004). We are no longer in a position where we need stable reference points in place or time or people in order to socialise. Instead, we can localise a set of bespoke referents that are as mobile as we are. So, we no longer need make arrangements hours, days or weeks in advance to meet up with someone at a particular time at a particular place. And if we do choose to make such an arrangement in advance, there is no longer any need to stick to that arrangement.

Instead, using mobile media and immersed in the stream of feed, we can make a general, in-principle arrangement to meet, and as we approach the rendezvous, we zoom in on one other, shifting times at will, shifting places at will, but still coordinated in time and in space, and getting closer and closer, until we intersect (or not). After all, nothing is certain and a better option may come up for either of us. We can keep our options open, just as we keep open the feed that provides us with options. We don't have to commit to time, place or person. We don't have to prioritise. We don't have to think ahead. We can continually review and reassess coffee options, party options, film options, work options, home options and adjust our actions accordingly.

One might well regard this weakening of time–space–people coordinates, and the dilution of personal commitment it implies, as compromising the preconditions for stable, committed relationships. However, like so many of the implications of sociotechnology, the situation is not so clear. For the same mobile feed that enables this social flexibility, also binds us tighter. In a paradox that has been often remarked (e.g. Arnold 2003; Morley 2003; Qiu 2008), the mobile feed is pulling us in two directions at once. We may be free to renegotiate a time, a place, work commitments, home life, or our companions, but negotiate we must. We can no longer use geography or use time as the undergrowth in which to hide from our social commitments. The mobile feed we have in hand makes us free and flexible, but it inexorably 'leashes us' in time, in place, to friends, work and to home.

Moving now to a seemingly quite different social formation, we continue the discussion begun in the last chapter to examine the implications of mobile media affordances for the constitution of publics, and to discuss the relationship between these affordances, publics and intimacies.

Mobile publics

In 'Mobile publics: beyond the networked perspective', Sheller addresses the sociality of mobile media. Sheller argues that 'the converging technologies of mobility and communication have created new temporalities and spatialities for public participation' (2004: 39). For Sheller:

> Publics are becoming more 'mobile' in two ways: first, there is an increasing tendency to slip between private and public modes of interaction, as a result of the new forms of fluid connectivity enabled by mobile communication technologies; and, second, there are opportunities for new kinds of publics to assemble or gel momentarily (and then just as quickly dissolve) as a result of newly emerging places and arenas for communication.
>
> (Sheller 2004: 39)

With nearly a decade since Sheller's important notion of the 'mobile public', mobility and publics have taken on even more complexity. As Galloway notes:

If we continue to understand 'public' as situational assemblages of people, places, and objects, and ideas, then there is probably no area of technological research and development that better explores and exemplifies these complex relations than do recent activities in mobile and context-aware computing. Given the imperatives to locate and connect that are embedded in otherwise diverse technologies, it should come as no surprise that today's wireless and wearable devices and applications offer unique glimpses into crucial sets of values and expectations surrounding 'the fate of the public'. However, as long as *mobile publics* are only defined in terms of networked publics, we risk oversimplifying complex relations in ways that may actually prevent certain kinds of political action.

(2010: 69)

If we understand a 'public' as a situated but heterogeneous assemblage of people, and also as (public) places, (public) objects and (public) discourse, then mobile affordances for imaging, mapping, locating, blogging, recording, tweeting, media sharing and the like, are all affordances that mediate the mobilisation of a public. As has been argued in Chapter 8 and illustrated in other chapters, the assembly of a public is a highly politicised act (banned by authorities in some countries, and subject to regulation in all countries), and for researchers and theorists the conception of a public is no less ideological. The near ubiquitous deployment of mobile media and the affordances provided for the assembly of a public draws new attention to the old question of how a public that is so assembled might be understood and represented. As we have seen, the most common answer to the question is that mobile media assembles a network, not a public. However, as long as mobile publics are defined in terms of networked publics, 'we risk oversimplifying complex relations in ways that may actually prevent certain kinds of political action' (Galloway 2010: 69). The concept of a mobile public is not reducible to the concept of a mobile network:

The mobilisation of publics, then, is not simply predicated on increasing the density of either face-to-face or online ties (as in a network), but depends instead on the entire context of communication gelling, which enables momentary stabilisations of collective identities as publics. Mobile publics can perhaps best be envisioned as capacitators for moving in and out of different social gels, including the capacity to take on an identity that is able to speak and to participate in specific contexts.

(Sheller 2004: 49–50)

As Galloway notes, mobile publics are more than *just* networked publics (2010). Drawing on the 'mobilities' turn in social, cultural and mobile communication studies, Galloway observes how little of the discussion has focused upon mobile publics. Instead, she argues current literature is limited by perpetually focusing upon how mobile technologies shaped, and are shaped by, intersections between private life and public space (2010: 70). For Galloway, the important work conducted by *Networked Publics* (Annenberg Center for Communication), Castells (2000 [1996]) and Larsen et al. (2006) collapses the political actions of the 'mobile publics' as part of networked publics. Galloway argues, as do we, that 'the network model or metaphor is not well equipped to deal with uncertainty, inconsistency, and instability – conditions outlined as integral to the sense of 'public' put forth by Lippmann, Bakhtin, Canetti, Marres, Latour and Warner' (2010: 70). Reflecting upon public and counter-public debates in relation to case studies of locative media art projects, Galloway considers how emergent and contingent forms of public are being formed, and informed by, mobile media. As Galloway suggests these 'messy' and 'fluid' assemblages of mobile publics are more than just networked. As a politically powerful rubric, Galloway argues that more research needs to be conducted into localised forms of mobile publics.

Publics, rather than networks, provide a useful rubric for us to understand the converging and localised forms of mobile, social and locative media practices in the Asia-Pacific region. In keeping with Galloway's call for more work into socio-cultural and political uses of mobile media in constructing publics beyond the 'private life/public space' trope, our various case studies have illustrated the performance of social and intimate publics in the region. In each of the six case studies we see very different localised models for sociality and intimacy. For example, in Tokyo the relationship between sociality and mobility in public and in private plays out through mobile devices Ito et al. have called 'personal, portable, and pedestrian' (2005). Alternatively, in Seoul, where 'rooms' (*bangs*) are fixed places with fluid functions determined by the will of the occupant, publics gel through shared relational intimacy (*ilchon*) rather than the performance of private interaction. In Shanghai, Western notions of privacy – especially prevalent in discussions of locative media practice – do not translate. Here we see a very different mobile public in the configuration of place. In Singapore and Manila, mobile publics are spaces in which the political and personal converge with very different results. In both Singapore and Manila the flow of students to the cities and the flow of Filipino women to Singapore to work as housemaids and nannies provide conditions for the construction of intimate publics.

So to conclude by returning to our opening vignettes, in a literal and figurative sense, members of these mobile publics are cyborgs. Bao is now a cyborg, as are mothers in Singapore, activists in Manila, students in Shanghai and mothers in Melbourne. These cyborgs carry devices about the body that have come a long way since 1996 to collapse the body–technology boundary. The body and digital information flows are coupled and are mobile. Mobile media are phenomenologically present at hand, at all times and in all places, and their affordances place our friends and intimates, our photos and letters, our family, our work, our emotions, our obligations and all manner of other things present at hand, at all times and in all places. In the next chapter we reflect upon how these new visual cultures through mobile, social and locative media practices are demonstrating differing social, intimate and mobile publics.

10 Emplaced presences

Visual cultures of embodied intimacies

When Ming visited the new café in Shanghai's Yongpu distinct, her first instinct was to photograph it. Ming was aware how her uptake of the location-based service (LBS) game *Jiepang* made her take and share more spontaneous pictures of the places she had visited. Whilst not part of the game play, Ming felt a desire to add photos was motivated by a need to share with friends as well as creating visual journal entries. She had a plethora of choices about the types of lenses and filters she could use on her iPhone. In particular, she had begun to regularly use Instagram. She liked the way it had so many options for her to customise and edit her pictures, often rendering banal and plain images into beautiful photos. Instagram made it easy for her to edit and upload her pictures quickly. She found that her friends would often comment, saying how beautiful the place looked or how delicious the food was. Ming enjoyed these comments and often also commented on her friends' pictures. It was a nice way to stay in perpetual contact when face-to-face wasn't an option.

Ki-sang had never been a great photographer. When he learnt to take pictures in his youth with an analogue camera, his pictures were often unintentionally blurry and lacking composition. But, when his friend introduced him to Hipstamatic, the smartphone app that renders camera phone images into beautiful analogue photographs he was hooked. As part of a daily ritual, Ki-sang often took pictures on the way to and from work. He was amazed how boring and familiar settings on the subway in Seoul could suddenly look romantic and nostalgic. At first he just took the pictures for himself. But then he started to upload to Korean SNS Cyworld minihompy, and was bombarded by comments from friends and family. These comments inspired him to keep photographing and sharing as well as taking up a course in professional photography. Those days of being a bad analogue photographer were behind him.

With the rise of high-quality camera phones, accompanied by the growth in in-phone editing applications and distribution services via social and locative media, new types of co-present visuality are possible. In the first series of studies of camera phones in Japan by the likes of Mizuko Ito and Daisuke Okabe (2003, 2005, 2006), these critics noted the pivotal role played by the three 'Ss' – sharing, storing and saving – in informing the context of what was predominantly 'banal' everyday content (Koskinen 2007). For Ilpo Koskinen (2007), camera phone images were branded by their participation in a new type of banality. While this banality can be seen as extending the conventions and genres of earlier photographic tropes (i.e. Kodak; Gye 2007; Hjorth 2007a), they also significantly depart by being networked and recontextualised. As camera phones become more commonplace as a part of the ever-more-popular smartphones, and as new contexts for image distribution such as microblogging and LBS become more commonly used, emergent types of visual overlays on geography become apparent. In this cartography, images are given ambient, networked contexts in which geographic place is overlaid with social and emotional affect.

While camera phone genres such as self-portraiture have blossomed globally, vernacular visualities that reflect a localised notion of place, sociality and identity making practices (Hjorth 2007b; Lee 2009a) are also flourishing. Smartphone apps like Hipstamatic and Instagram have made taking and sharing photographs easier and more interesting. Many of our respondents noted an increased interest in camera phone image capture and sharing. With LBS like Facebook Places, *Foursquare* and *Jiepang* we see a further extension of overlaying place with the social and personal whereby the electronic is superimposed onto the geographic in new ways. Specifically, by sharing an image and comment about a place through LBS, users can create different ways to experience and record journeys and, in turn, make an impact upon how place is recorded, experienced and thus remembered. This is especially the case with the overlaying of ambient images within moving narratives of place as afforded by LBS.

The rapid uptake of smartphones has enabled new forms of distribution and has provided an overabundance of apps, filters and lenses to help users create 'unique' and artistic camera phones images. Although iPhone has been quick to capitalise on this phenomenon through applications such as Hipstamatic, other operating systems like Android have also had their share of cornering in this expansive market. So too social media, like microblogs and LBS, have acknowledged the growing power of camera phone photography by not only affording easy uploading and sharing of the vernacular (Burgess 2008), but also by providing filters and lenses in order to further enhance the 'professional' and 'artistic' dimensions of the photographic experience (Mørk Petersen 2009). The Asia-Pacific has been noted as one of the early adopters of camera phone practices, especially in Japan (Ito and Okabe 2006) and South Korea (Hjorth 2007b; Lee 2005). With these locations boasting some of the key global mobile camera phone manufacturers such as Samsung, Sony and LG, the uptake was far from surprising and camera phone practices in these locations were quickly adopted as an integral part of everyday life. Having said that, though, we need to acknowledge that behind the so-called media revolutions of smartphones and Web 2.0 is the far from even participation in a broadband society in which various factors – technological, social and cultural – have continued to distinguish between those who have less and those who have more (Goggin and Hjorth 2009).

For Bo Gai (2009) in her study of camera phone practices in Beijing, mobile media practices are part of expansive media tactics that have seen Chinese everyday mobile users granted a public voice. They are, as she observes, both reinforcing and departing from Chinese notions of media participation by providing public, collective commentary but also individual voices. In China, participation can take many forms, including what in the West is seen as non-participation, lurking (Goggin and Hjorth 2009). Mobile media evokes a particular kind of ambient participation that is configured through, and by, place in specific ways (Hjorth 2012). With the convergence of mobile, social and locative media, how we conceptualise camera phone visuality and affect is changing. So how do we frame these new visualities in motion? One way, as this chapter suggests, is through the movement from 'networked' to what Pink (2011) calls 'emplaced' visuality.

Beyond the snapshot: new visualities in motion

In studies of first-generation camera phone studies in Korea, Hjorth (2007b) noted tensions around the camera phone's relationship to place and mobility in what she called 'snapshots of almost contact'. The increasingly quick edit and deletion of images in situ has created a different relationship between recording and the mediated experience. This tension around mediation, reflection and engagement is amplified in second-generation camera phone studies, with the growth of locative and social media that converge the aesthetics of the captured image, with the sociality of the sharing of the image, the communicative power of the accompanying text, and the specificity of place provided by GPS location. As previously noted, these social-visual performances are about mobile intimacy and how these practices get mapped across a variety of intimate and social publics, where the performativity of place becomes a process of perpetually 'placing' various forms of presence (Richardson and Wilken 2012).

For Daniel Palmer (2012), iPhone photography is distinctive in three areas. First, it created an experience between touch and the image in what Palmer calls an 'embodied visual intimacy' (2012: 88). While 'touch has long been an important, but neglected, dimension in the history of photography … the iPhone, held in the palm of the hand, reintroduces a visual intimacy to screen culture that is missing from the larger monitor screen' (Palmer 2012: 88). Second, the proliferation of photo apps for the iPhone has meant that there are countless ways for taking, editing and sharing photos. No longer do camera phone images have to look like the poorer cousin to the professional camera. Third is the role of GPS capability, with the iPhone automatically 'tagging photographs with their location, allowing images to be browsed and arranged geographically' (Palmer 2012: 88).

As Goggin (2011: 48) has noted, the increasing prominence of the citizen journalist has been epitomised by the camera phone revolution, to a point where even some professional photojournalists have opted for camera phones instead of professional cameras (Palmer 2012). As Daniel Rubinstein and Katrina Sluis (2008) note, the rise of the camera phone has been part of a shift from print-based to screen-based photography. As Rubinstein and Sluis further observe, this 'rise of photo sharing sites have created a context', something 'vernacular photographers have always lacked: a broad audience' (2008: 18). For example, moblogging, that is mobile-phone blogging sites like Weibo and Twitter, have enabled the mass distribution of camera phone images, many of which evoke much more than 140 characters or a text blog. In China, Weibo contains millions of camera phone images which are shared each day. The participatory elements of sites like Flickr with what Burgess (2008) has called their 'vernacular' and 'situated' creativity have created new forms of what Søren Mørk Petersen (2009) calls 'common banalities'.

Rubinstein and Sluis also emphasise the multi-layered, multimedia composition of images that are bundled up with text, GPS and a means of social distribution. They point out that the increasing 'reliance on tagging for organisation and retrieval of images is an indication of the importance of textuality for online photographic procedures ... Tagging provides a substantially different way of viewing and interacting with personal photography' (2008: 19). According to them, these networked images get transformed as a part of metadata in which the original context is lost. Photo-sharing sites become

> vast databases of indexed photographs which can be remixed and remapped online as mashups ... In this new context, the currency of the snapshot ceases to lie in its narrative or mnemonic value, in its indexicality, or in its status as a precious object. Instead, these practices illustrate the way in which the networked image is data, that is: visual information to be analysed and remapped to new contexts via algorithms.
>
> (Rubinstein and Sluis 2008: 20–21)

For Chesher (2012), the rise of smartphones like the Samsung and the iPhone – with their attendant software applications like Instagram, Google Goggles and Hipstamatic – have created new ways in which to think about camera phone practices and their engagement with both image and information. For Chesher the iPhone universe of reference disrupts the genealogy of mass amateur photography. Applications like Instagram, which allow users to take, edit and share photos, partake in what could be called a second generation of camera phone and photo-sharing social media. With 'vernacular creativity' (Burgess 2008) sites such as Flickr being the precursor, Instagram heralds a new generation of visuality in which the cult of the amateur is further commercialised. Launched in October 2010, Instagram quickly grew to boast over 150 million uploaded images. The virtual and viral nature of Instagram was illustrated by a graphic-design firm in Italy who recently built a physical digital camera prototype that looks like the Instagram icon, called the Socialmatic. With these new applications, often working in collaboration with social and locative media, camera phone images have been given new contexts.

> The iPhone camera mobilises longstanding subjective impulses for making images, common not only to Kodak, but also to the motivations for cave drawings, oil paintings and daguerreotypes (a long-term, constantly changing abstract machine). However, iPhone users take up these affective forces and aesthetic values in different ways, with different materials, forming different connections.
>
> (Chesher 2012: 100)

As Chesher (2012) notes, Kodak's 'long moment' that spanned most of the twentieth century was disrupted by the iPhone camera. Kodak had long been 'synonymous with the amateur image-making industry for over a century' (Chesher 2012: 102), represented by the invention of the 'Brownie' camera. Through advertising that linked photography with memory, Kodak colonialised the domestic by implying that a holiday or an event without a Kodak wasn't one at all (Gye 2007). The Kodak was on hand to record the cultural changes in the twentieth century, creating particular 'official' discourses of the unofficial place of the domestic. In the 1990s, the birth and rise of digital photography created momentary ruptures in the analogue universe of references.

However, although the digital has displaced the analogue, theorists such as Lev Manovich (2001) observe that the digital remains 'haunted' by spectres of the analogue. The ghosts of analogues genres, content and conventions were all transferred into the digital world. This 'simulation' of nostalgic prints is continued by camera phone apps like Hipstamatic, in which 'auto-nostalgia' comes in an arty and romantic visual package (Chesher 2012: 107). As Chesher notes, while the iPhone's camera 'opens onto similar Universes of reference as the Kodak ... with apps it reconfigures, or even gets rid of images altogether' by mediating a significantly different set of 'practices in making and consuming images' (2012: 107). For Chesher 'many apps take the camera beyond its photographic heritage to use it as a data input device, collecting information instead of making conventional photos' (2012: 107).

With elements such as augmented reality becoming part of camera phone culture, Chesher argues that this 'regime of vision has less connection with Kodak culture and more resemblance to a gun sight or a head-up display in a modern fighter jet. It visually interprets the surrounding space with a view to action' (2012: 112). As Chesher concludes, 'it is not yet clear what the implications of this emerging Universe of imaging will have for individual and collective senses of identity, place and memory' (2012: 144). For Pink (2011), the rise of smartphones' networked visualities requires us to rethink the relationship between the image and its context. Rather than images being viewed as snapshots that seize a moment, these emergent databases of millions of images are about a diversity of moments electronically framed within particular locations in time and space. Taken as a whole, these temporal–spatial visual configurations are no longer isolated and frozen as suggested by a snapshot, but are part of a vast moving set of image–text–metadata media objects, orchestrated by social and locative services.

The place of visual intimacy: mobile, social and locative media visualities

Rubinstein and Sluis's (2008) study of the networked image operates as a precursor to the second generation of camera phone practices in which GPS creates new levels for recording the 'original' context with a geographic coordinate. As Pink (2011) observes in 'Sensory digital photography: re-thinking "moving" and the image', the recent 'sensory turn' in visual cultures scholarship requires an examination of meanings and materialities associated with the image. Calling for a destabilisation of the authority of the image, Pink (2011) argues that visual production and consumption needs to be conceptualised through movement and place. For Pink (2011), the nexus between locative media and the photographic image requires a new paradigm that engages with the multisensoriality of images. Drawing on Tim Ingold's (2008) critique of the anthropology of the senses and of network theory as well as *Doing Sensory Ethnography*, Pink (2011) argues that by exploring the visual in terms of the multisensorial, the importance of movement and place are re-prioritised.

Rather than viewing networked images as part of an acontextualised metadata as suggested by Rubinstein and Sluis (2008), Pink argues that locative media provide new ways in which to frame images with the 'continuities of everyday movement, perceiving and meaning making' (2011: 4). By contrasting 'photographs as mapped points in a network', with 'photographs being outcomes of and inspirations within continuous lines that interweave their way through an environment – that is, in movement and as part of a configuration of place' (Pink 2011: 4–5), Pink argues that we must start to conceive of images as produced and consumed in movement. Here we can think about how images are being transformed in light of various turns – emotional, mobility and sensory. Indeed, of all the areas to be impacted and affected, camera phones – especially with their haptic (touch) screen interface and engagement, along with their locative media possibilities – can be seen as most indicative of Pink's call for a multisensorial conceptualisation of images (2011). As she notes, the particular way in which text, image and GPS overlay, create a multisensorial depiction of a locality.

This shift can be viewed as the movement from camera phone visuality that is networked to camera phone images that are 'emplaced' (Pink 2011). An image that is socially networked, tagged and GPS located is 'emplaced' in a number of ways. It is emplaced as one of many images captured by a particular member of our intimate or social public and is contextualised by our relation to that person. The co-presence of many images arranged by time or place on the one site places each image in the context of others in order to constitute a narrative, and thus another context. The GPS coordinates place the image in geographic space and invite the viewer to *recall* the place in question as well as *view* the image captured in the place in question, thus overlaying another context. The social distribution of the images creates a social public for those images, thus overlaying yet another context, and the image tags entered by the public overlay another context again.

As discussed in Chapter 4, in Shanghai the uptake of LBS mobile game-*Jiepang* – where users can 'check-in' to online spaces and win prizes when they visit offline places – is creating out-of-game visualities. For many of the Generation Y (*ba ling hou*) respondents, the playing of the official *Jiepang* game was secondary to a social motivation. In this social dimension, the use – with accelerated frequency – of sharing camera phone pictures had become a key practice. The popularity of media-rich moblogging sites such as Sina, Weibo and SNS Renren (China's equivalent of Facebook) is evidence that the compulsion to photograph, edit and share is growing, and in each of the different social media spaces, different types of photographic genres could be found. For example, many used Sina for self-portraiture, whilst Weibo was for more political or news-worthy images, and Renren was a space for reflecting inner feelings. In the case of *Jiepang*, visuality was more about new types of place-making. These place-making exercises are like diaries (Ito and Okabe 2005) but with their active use of filters and perspectives, *Jiepang* is demonstrating emergent forms of creative practice for the *ba ling hou*.

In the fieldwork in our six locations we noted the significance of camera phone photography in the place-making exercises of LBS. In LBS photo albums we noted that while respondents used traditional genres such as the photography of food and places, they did so by using filters and lenses to create highly aesthetic images, often using filters that not only made the pictures look analogue but also gave them a sense of nostalgia. Far from being banal and boring, these images were often unique and creative. These images are not only about the vernacular qualities of UCC, they also signal new types of emplaced visualities. While the first generation of camera phone studies emphasised the three 'Ss' – sharing, storing and saving – of the 'networked' images, the second generation sees an embrace of Pink's (2011) aforementioned idea of 'emplaced images'. Here we see camera phones contributing to a 'fastforwarding present/presence' (Hjorth 2006, 2007b) – that is, the accelerated way in which images are taken, edited and shared often during the experience of an event. Through the overlaying of highly edited camera phone images and comments, respondents can narrate place in new ways. For example, in Shanghai, respondents tried to take more poetic pictures of locations in order to provide a unique comment on that location. Often the visuals were deployed in order to present a unique image of the place, whether through the image genre or, more often, using filters and lenses to create a mood.

As noted in the Seoul case study in Chapter 2, LBS camera phone images are indicative of Massey's notion of place as a series of 'stories-so-far' that reflect disjuncture as much as presence. In LBS camera phone images we see that place is a process of perpetual oscillation between 'placing' (that is, actively situating or contextualizing phenomena) and 'presencing' (that is 'being there' through telepresence, co-presence, located presence and net-local presences) (Richardson and Wilken 2012). The rise of 'emplaced' rather than 'networked' visuality apparent with LBS camera phone practices is a manifestation of the changing performance of co-presence, whereby binaries between online and offline experiences don't hold.

Moreover, these images evoke the multisensory experience of place as a process of perpetually placing – reflect an intersection of senses that are not just visual. By overlaying the social with networked GPS, images provide a multisensorial depiction of visual cultures. For example, our respondents noted that they often took pictures of shared food. In one interpretation this is just another example of a virulent consumer ethos, making the private consumption of food into conspicuous consumption through a public statement. In another interpretation it is a response to the need to create multidimensional and ambient experiences of place that are overlaid by intimacy or the need to convey, in the Korean context, a sense of *bang* (space/room) with the *ilchon* (intimate relation). In a location like Seoul, famous for its high use of *sel-ca* (self-portraiture) (Hjorth 2007b; Lee 2005), it was interesting to note that this genre was on the decline in LBS contexts. As we discussed in Chapter 2, this was the impact of governmental and corporate examples of privacy breaches.

Another example of LBS camera phone practices evoking a particular localised form of intimacy and place was in Shanghai (Hjorth and Gu 2012). According to Ai (female, aged 25), *Jiepang* use was in order 'to record where I go to everyday. It's like a diary with location.' The other respondents shared Ai's sentiment – many viewed recording locational information via *Jiepang* as both for their own and other's benefit. For Bai (male, aged 27), *Jiepang* was primarily used to 'record where I had been' and to have this information 'synchronised to social networks such as Weibo to share with my followers'. For others, they didn't record everywhere they went, but, rather, used *Jiepang* only for those occasions when they went to new places.

For Bai, *Jiepang* was important in recording and archiving his activities and journeys. Unlike Ai, Bai didn't record each place he went to everyday, just a few highlights. Here we see the way in which gender inflects how *Jiepang* relates to ongoing endeavours to narrate the everyday as part of movements through spaces. Bai viewed *Jiepang* as a tool for showing where he was when he wanted people to know. Sometimes checking in on *Jiepang* was accompanied by taking pictures of the place, an activity Bai definitely viewed as gendered, stating, 'usually females would spend more time on it than men, and take more photos'. Both these informants noted that recently there had been a growth in different LBS on smartphone and PC platforms, and that groups of friends would use similar ones – in short, the deployment of an LBS reflected the *guanxi*. With the additional dimension of camera phones being interwoven with locative media, *guanxi* and place can take on more complex cartographies that place, emplace and embody visualities.

With camera phones now an essential part of smartphone culture, we have witnessed not only an expansion in the 'professionalisation' of the amateur through a plethora of photo filters and lenses but we are also seeing an explosion in the number of images taken and shared as part of a 'poetic' intervention that emplaces images within a place. In particular, through LBS like the Chinese *Jiepang*, users are taking, editing and designing camera phone images that as part of representing a place in a unique way that is then shared to reinforce social capital (*guanxi*).

Just as *Jiepang* is 'more about the journey', *Jiepang* images are not only akin to what Ito and Okabe (2005) identified as visual diaries, but indicative of an 'individual' experience that is then emplaced. Through images of food and scenery, and through accompanying text, users communicate the experience and subjectivities of a place to their publics, while through metadata, the technology communicates about time and precise GPS place. While respondents noted that they used Renren (Chinese equivalent of Facebook) for albums and archiving, *Jiepang* visual narratives were more about '*where* I am and doing/feeling what'. All respondents noted that *Jiepang* inspired them to take more camera phone pictures; and thanks to smartphones it was easier to take, edit and share images. Moreover, with *Jiepang*, respondents progressively felt the need to make visual and textual comments about places, especially emphasised through the idea that images were part of an event or movement. Thus *Jiepang* images are part of what Pink identifies as the emplacement of images whereby they are located in 'the production and consumption of images as happening in movement, and consider them as components of configurations of place' (2011: 4).

In the case of LBS games, camera phone images are contextualised through both multisensoriality and movement. Not only is the genre and content about narrating place as part of a journey, but also the frequency and its link to reinforcing social capital suggest a complex representation of place (through image, GPS and text tags), publics (through sharing and distribution), self (through choices made in all of the above), sociality (through participating in all of the above) and visuality (through the reading of the image and its aesthetics). In the case studies, the role of camera phone content constructing types of gender performativity – akin to Judith Butler's (1991) notion whereby cultural norms about gender and sexuality are enacted through a series of iterations and regulations – becomes evident. Moreover, many of the LBS games not only became a site for gender performativity but also a way in which users could be active in conveying the multisensorial movement of the context of the image so that it was not just located, networked or placed but also emplaced.

In case studies in Melbourne and Singapore, the impact of smartphone apps, especially those for the iPhone, dramatically increased the number of images taken and shared. Respondents noted that with the rise of photo apps like Instagram and Hipstamatic, camera phone picture taking and sharing has been made more compelling. Some respondents with no interest or experience in photography found themselves becoming compelled to send and share pictures. Often pictures were an easier and a more convenient way to comment on an experience, as they provided ambience and emotion. With the apps providing those lacking photographic skill with quasi-talents, suddenly the 'bad' amateur photographer could become like an artist. With the apps equalising the fact of skill and also affording easy ways to share, these new visualities were impacting upon not only how place is encoded with particular social and emotional vignettes but also how these records affect collective and individual memories.

In Singapore, Shanghai and Manila, camera phone LBS practices often were used to negotiate diaspora and place. Often respondents used camera phone images, overlaid onto place via Facebook Place, to give distant intimates back home a sense of ambient co-presence. In Seoul and Tokyo – the two places with the longest history in camera phone practices – the relationship between image and place was further complicated by LBS. In Seoul, there was a decline of self-portraiture in the face of growing anxieties around trust and the online. Instead, there was a rise in inanimate objects like coffee cups in what our informants said was an attempt to embrace friends and evoke non-visual senses like smell. So too in Tokyo there was a growth in sharing pictures that were often obscured or abstracted in order to create ambient intimacy.

In many of the locative camera phone images, the social dimension of the image is brought to the forefront first in the sharing or distribution, and second in the overlaying of geographical or locational knowledge among social and intimate publics. Echoing Ilkka Arminen's (2006) point that, when it comes to SNS and social media more generally, social context rather than 'pure geographical location' is generally of greatest user interest, what seems to be most at stake in LBS games is new knowledge about particular sites and what these are likely to signify within social network settings. LBS like *Jiepang* highlight that the various dimensions around ideas of place – as imagined and lived, geographic and psychological – are contextualised by social capital/ network. Thus, many of those surveyed revealed that the higher the perceived level of novelty or uniqueness that is seen to be associated with a place (such as, in the words of one respondent, a 'supreme' restaurant or hotel), the higher the likelihood that their presence in and knowledge of this place would be recorded via *Jiepang*, as 'routine places like home or [their] company are not worth checking in'. In this way, it is geographical (or 'environmental') 'knowing' and an appreciation of the 'capital' that is invested in and carried with this knowledge that is paramount, and which forms a vital resource within the participants' wider peer network.

Conclusion: emplaced visuality and geospatial sociality

The use of smartphone apps has transformed the texture of visuality by rendering it no longer only about the visual. Instead, LBS camera phone images and genres are about evoking a sense of localised place as a multisensorial entanglement, or what Pink (2011) has called 'emplaced' visuality. This transformation of visuality is also about enhancing existing intimate rituals and socio-cultural notions of place in new ways. As we discussed in the case studies of Shanghai or Seoul, each location fused the visual with their own forms of place (*bang*) or intimate relation (*guanxi/ilchon*).

While initial studies into camera phone visuality discussed it as part of networked media (Rubinstein and Sluis 2008; Villi 2010), this second generation of visuality is about new types of place-making exercises. These exercises are emotional and electronic, geographic and social – highlighting the complex entanglement that is the ever-evolving of place. In each location, camera phone images are overlaid onto specific places in a way that reflects existing social and cultural intimate relations as well as being demonstrative of new types of emplaced visuality.

Many of the examples of LBS in the different locations were predominantly the preoccupation of the young: Generation Y or X. The exception in this was Seoul, where LBS is deployed by parents, governments and corporations for different forms of friendly and not-so-friendly survellience (Lee 2011; Wallace 2012). In LBS games like *Foursquare, Jiepang* and *flags* new types of emplaced visuality and geospatial sociality are performed almost exclusively by the *ba ling hou*. Through the locative and microblogging experience of *Jiepang,* users are creating new forms of intimate publics whereby the importance of network pales into comparison to the significance of the *guanxi* in providing ambient contexts. As part of the smartphone phenomenon, *Jiepang* is accompanied by an accelerated rate of camera phone image capture, editing and sharing. Far from banal acontextualised images, these pictures deploy the newest of filters and photographic tricks in order to give a sense of the poetic and unique and are then overlaid onto places via *Jiepang*. In *Jiepang* camera phone images, images are edited and contextualised so that the *guanxi* is clearly overlaid onto place. This is not a mere practice of networked visuality as noted by the first studies into camera phones; rather we see emplaced and multisensorial visuality that creates, and reflects, unique forms of geospatial sociality.

LBS games like *Foursquare, Jiepang, flags* and *IN* enable users to be part of intimate publics in which the personal practices of the everyday become, on the one hand, commodified and, on the other hand, further tethered to a sense of place that is as much emotional and social as geographic and physical. Social relations are thus played out in public domains in ways that foreground both networked social and place-based settings as they are negotiated in combination. In these practices, the unofficial play of camera phone images has become a compelling motivation for users. With new photo apps marketed all the time, respondents found that beyond the 'official' play of the LBS games, 'unofficial' camera phone image sharing afforded for richer experiences of place and co-present sharing. These cartographies are overlaying onto the LBS games in ways that rehearse older socio-cultural notions of place and intimacy while also rewriting them.

As we have suggested, the deployment of LBS games illustrates the need to revise the relationship between visuality, sociality and place through new types of visuality that are more than just networked but are rather 'emplaced', with respondents using the images to reflect the multisensorial experience of place with their culturally specific notion of intimacy. The saliency of localised intimacies and practices of place also highlights that while LBS is creating new forms of ambient, emplaced, social visualities, it is also rehearsing and tightening older social ties. We reflect upon in the next, concluding chapter.

11 Conclusion

Intimacies of the mobile, social and local in the Asia-Pacific

A mother in a province near Shanghai uses the free online media QQ from her phone to instant message her daughter, wishing her luck in her university exam. Two close friends meet up in Tokyo's electric city Akihabara, thanks to using the LBS game *Foursquare*. A university student in Singapore takes a picture of her coffee cup with Instagram and edits it to look 'nostalgic', like an analogue photo, and uploads to Facebook. Her boyfriend, studying in Seoul, now knows she is thinking of him. An art student in Melbourne plays around with the augmented reality app Layar on his phone hoping it will inspire him to make a good project for his final-year assignment. Thanks to the notifications on Facebook Places on their mobile phone, two friends realise they are geographically close and organise to meet at a local café in Quezon City, Manila.

A couple, attempting a long-distance relationship between Australia and Singapore, grow apart through tacit misunderstandings about SMS sent and received. A daughter in Manila becomes increasingly resentful of her mother's frequent Skype calls. Her mother is an overseas worker, and her daughter sees the calls as interfering rather than nurturing. A woman unsuccessfully attempts to contact her parents during 3/11 in Tokyo, and becomes increasingly frustrated with the technology's failure to function as it promises. A student in Shanghai is dumped by his girlfriend via a social media (Renren) notification, and is hurt by the rejection and by the choice of media. An overseas student fears racism on Facebook as debates around the 2011 Singaporean elections heat up. A woman cyber-stalked by her ex-boyfriend in Seoul must discontinue all her social media accounts in order to stop his harassment.

In this book, the need to redefine the notions of intimate publics, social publics and social networks in an age of mobile, social and locative media has been integral. As we have demonstrated through the case studies in Part I, the uneven development of these media practices are reflecting localised notions of intimacy, public, politics and place. In Part II, we shifted the focus towards fleshing out some of the key characteristics of this phenomenon: namely, intimate publics (Chapter 8), mobile intimacy (Chapter 9) and emplaced cartographies (Chapter 10). While these features can be found throughout the world, it is within the Asia-Pacific region that we see some very unique examples. Through the lens of mobile, social and locative media, we gain new insight into the region beyond the often inadequate geo-political models.

The social tapestry of the region and its various mobile, social and locative media practices are situated, and are far from uniform. In Tokyo mobile media has for a long time been the key portal for online social practices. In Seoul, where personal computers and PC *bangs* are plentiful, as are mobile devices, people have a choice of how to access the online social stream. In China, where only a small portion of the population has access to a computer or to a landline telephone, the ubiquity of the mobile phone has provided a dominant form of accessibility to the online. In Japan, the mobile device (*keitai*) has always been the key portal for social and locative media convergence, whereas Melbourne and Singapore have only recently become mobile as the rapid uptake of smartphones began to redirect attention (and distraction) to social and locative media. Different cultural expectations, media literacies, generations, infrastructures, regulations, economies, technological affordances, classes and lifestyles all situate and differentiate the multiple forms of mobile sociality experienced across the Asia-Pacific.

As a location known for its production and consumption of mobile media, the Asia-Pacific region provides a key field for a study of contemporary notions of place, mobility and sociality, and their sociotechnical mediation. Drawing on fieldwork conducted over three years (2009–12) in six locations in the region, we have attempted to provide a snapshot of moving and divergent media dynamics, and have demonstrated some of the ways in which online media is impacting and being impacted by the local. As we have demonstrated through the case studies in Part I, the uneven development of these media practices are feeding from and are feeding into localised notions of sociality, public, politics and place. In Part II, we point to the key characteristics of this phenomenon: namely, intimate publics (Chapter 8), mobile intimacy (Chapter 9) and emplaced cartographies (Chapter 10). We have illustrated the ways in which emergent media practices are shaping, and being shaped, by the affordances of the various technologies deployed in that particular place, and are then inter-tangled with the existing social and cultural practices, to produce hybrid sociotechnical performances. *Online@AsiaPacific* has thus taken a particular view of the interactive relationship between media technologies and the particular performances we have observed across the Asia-Pacific.

The book has of course focused on particular technologies (the convergence of mobile, social and locative media) in particular places (the Asia-Pacific), but this particularity is also generalisable in so much as it constitutes one response to a 'key question' that energises all studies of new media and of technologies in general. The guiding question is a quest to understand the relationship between ourselves and our technologies, and how this relationship reflects, or alters, inner subjectivities as well as socio-cultural rituals and traditions. In answer to this question we have argued that mobile sociality is emergent in situated cultural performances, mediated by the technologies deployed in these performances, and we have attended to the interplay of technologies and performances. As the reader has seen, we have argued that the experience of social media in the Asia-Pacific is distinct in important ways. But we do not argue that particular social, cultural or historical circumstances that pertain in particular places across the Asia-Pacific have, in and of themselves, resulted in the deployment of particular technologies in particular ways. Society matters, but does not shape technology unilaterally. Nor have we argued that the deployment of particular technologies in particular locations has resulted in particular social differences across the region. Technologies matter, but do not shape societies unilaterally. Rather, performances that are at once technical and social emerge in the same acts, and variations in performance flow from the situated particularities of the technical and the social.

The descriptions and accounts we have provided of these performances are informed in particular by a 'material-semiotic' approach (e.g. Latour 2005), and by theories of 'domestication' (e.g. Silverstone and Hirsch 1992). Arnold et al. (2006) describe one of the models by which this approach accounts for the relationship between mobile social media qua technologies, and the situated and particular experience of sociality. In this model our shaping of technologies and their shaping of us are treated symmetrically. The model observes first that just as we act in the world, so too do all artifacts act in the world – homes, clothes, cars – as well as QQ, Skype, smartphones, minihompy, Facebook and all the other technologies that have featured in this book. As described by Latour, Callon, Mol, Law and others, a new actor is constituted in the assemblage of people and mobile technologies, an actor that has characteristics and capacities that emerge from the particularities of the assemblage – the particularities of the people of the Asia-Pacific (culture, class, age, gender and so forth), and the particularities of their technologies (QQ, minihompy, Facebook, *Foursquare* and so on). Important among the characteristics and capacities emerging from this assemblage of people and mobile technologies are the provision of new sociotechnologies for self-reference, place-reference, self-presentation and sociality at a distance. Digitally mediated social interaction and digital UCC is assembled, edited and moves through time and space in ways not possible for the face-to-face social moment and its memory. This material ability to construct and re-present presence, interactions, experiences, people and places through phone calls, Renren, *keitai* messages, *Foursquare* and the like clearly provides us with new resources for intimacy, sociality and networking. The material performance of these media provides us with both new capacities to act in the world, and different ways of seeing ourselves. A Facebook profile or a minihompy constructs semiotic points of self-reference that are ontological markers for constructing ourselves, for recognising ourselves and for presenting ourselves to others. As we have seen in various locations throughout the Asia-Pacific, mobile media devices, social media sites and UCC are important in contemporary self-referencing and self-presentation.

Our sociality is mediated through the abovementioned processes that intertwine and overlay self-reference and presentation, ongoing autobiographic presence, new capacities to act in the world, selective appropriation of technologies, and customisation and personalisation of the technologies we do appropriate. Our mediated social circumstance is not a simple equation in which a) sociality is a set of fixed and stable subjectivities and interpersonal performances; b) users of social media are the sole agents in the equation – the instigators of all decisions and social actions; and c) social media are merely faithful servants used by b) to achieve a). Rather, society and culture, people and technologies come together to constitute a sociotechnical hybrid in which the performance of sociality is shaped by users and by mobile social media, users are shaped by sociality and by mobile social media, and mobile social media is shaped by users and their social performances. In all of this intertwining of the social and the technical, the particular nature of social circumstances and the particular characteristics and affordances of the technologies are of course important and, as these vary from situation to situation, from place to place, place matters.

The place of the mobile: rethinking place

So here we take 'place' to signify several things. At the highest and most obvious level *Online@AsiaPacific* situates social technologies in a particular but quite diverse region in the world. Our separate treatment of Manila, Melbourne, Seoul, Shanghai, Singapore and Tokyo also refers to geographic places, but a similarly high level of generality can be used as a shorthand way to signify the characteristics of a given cultural tradition, brand of technonationalism, politics or set of socio-economic conditions. Working at lower levels, though, place is used to refer to very particular locales, to the particular features of people to be found in those locales and to the particular performances that characterise those places.

Through the convergence of mobile, social and locative media we are seeing emergent forms of micro-politics that link place, presence and intimacy in new ways. They highlight the paradoxical relationship place has played in the rise of mobile media and how locative media like GPS are reshaping that terrain. In Wilken's and Goggin's timely *Mobile Technology and Place* (2012), the various authors reflect upon the conceptual currents and controversies facing notions of place in the face of increasingly ubiquitous mobile and location-aware devices. With the 'spatial turn' in media studies (Falkheimer and Jansson 2006) entanglements between space, mobility and sociality have, for good reason, been further complicated. For Wilken and Goggin:

> place is considered fundamental to the construction of our life histories
> and what it means to be human, while mobiles now form an intrinsic part

of the daily lives and habits of billions of people worldwide – and for the manifold ways that they mutually inform and shape each other. Place is a notion that is of enduring relevance – one worth mobilizing – if we are to comprehend fully how we think about and experience who we are, where we are, and the ways we interact and relate with one another. In other words, place is considered a vital notion in that it represents a "weaving together" of social and human–environment interaction in ways that situate place as central to how embodied, technologically mediated mobile social practice is understood.

(2012b: 18)

Older social technologies engaged us and our social relations in different ways in relation to time and place. City squares, balls and festivals, public halls and Agoras are but a few examples of places that mediated collective locations, actions and purposes, and a collective consciousness – in so much as the public was known to itself as sharing a collective location, sharing a collective occasion and engaging in a collective action. When in a public at the festival, the ball or in the town square, the social actor's public interactions were subjugated by locale – that is, sociality is ordered and enabled by the contingencies of place   'a space which is invested with understandings of behavioral appropriateness, cultural expectations, and so forth' (Harrison and Dourish 1996: 69). It was a prerequisite to be there in a place at a time in order to be immersed in a social public. Place had a significance, and not any old place would do. Mobile, locative media reorient place, and rather than a prerequisite that frames sociality and makes it possible, it becomes a personalised social resource, a variable to be called upon to enrich sociality. Key theorists Eric Gordon and Adriana de Souza e Silva have argued that 'net localities' (or networked localities) are transforming places – especially urban public spaces. As they argue:

the use of mobile and location-aware technologies in public spaces transforms our experience of places and spaces, creating conditions for the emergence of new spaces. What we call networked locality (net locality) is the cultural and technological framework through which people manufacture places mediated by location-aware and mobile devices and digital networks.

(Gordon and de Souza e Silva 2012: 89)

For de Souza e Silva and Daniel Sutko, net locality can be understood as the process whereby location-aware technologies create a perpetual, evolving dynamic between information as place and place as information (2011). While urban spaces have always been mediated by technologies, according to Gordon and de Souza e Silva net localities 'produce unique types of networked interactions and, by extension, new contexts for social cohesion' (2012: 91). They continue: 'co-presence is not mutually opposed to networked interaction – and as emerging practices of technology develop, drawing the line in the sand becomes increasingly difficult' (2012: 91).

Through mobile media, the relationship between being online versus offline has shifted, creating new types of engagement and co-presence. Lines that mark out and differentiate the online and the offline, virtual and actual, here and there, are shifting and fading as these zones overlap and bleed into one another and entangle with one another. In this context Richardson and Wilken (2012) call for a post-phenomenology reading of body–technology relations to understand three key mobile media modalities: located presence, co-presence and telepresence (2012: 185). For Richardson and Wilken 'mobile media use occurs across a spectrum of "placing" and "presencing"' (2012: 185). As they continue:

> Mobile devices clearly antagonize any notion of a disembodied telepresence that is seemingly endemic to digital screen media, as we are frequently on-the-move, on-the-street and purposefully situated in local spaces and places when engaged in mobile phone use and mobile gameplay.
>
> (Richardson and Wilken 2012: 184)

For Richardson and Wilken the 'meshing of located place and networked space' creates crucial questions, especially around whether mobile media 'collapse the space–place distinction, or enable "space" and "place" to be simultaneously present' (2012: 185). As they argue, mobile media devices create a different dynamic around perpetually interrupted and distracted body–screen–place relations (2012: 194) in which 'placing' and 'presencing' are entangled. Building on Gordon and de Souza e Silva, Richardson and Wilken argue that mobile media practices involve a series of overlapping 'presents' (telepresence, co-presence, located presence and net-local presences) in the rich tapestry of everyday spaces (2012: 195).

These 'presences' and their intimate, social and networked affects construct a rich fabric of emotional, social, technological, electronic and geographic overlays that inform, and are formed by, existing social and cultural practices. To understand the implications of these presences on notions of place and intimacy, locative media needs to be studied as part of everyday social and mobile media practices. Case studies of educational, creative and experimental projects by researchers such as Humphries, Gordon, de Souza e Silva and Licoppe, are useful, but are limited in that they are not studies of locative media in the context of the everyday.

Over the three years of our study, the convergence between mobile, social and locative media became more marked. While the everyday use of mobile and locative social media was pedestrian in locations like Tokyo and Seoul, its use in places like Singapore and Melbourne was a relatively new and novel experience for most. In Shanghai our respondents used locative media games like *Jiepang* together with camera phone vignettes to overlay and hybridise *guanxi* (a Chinese notion of social network), UCC and a novel sense of geographic place. On the other hand, in Seoul the *bang* and the minihompy are digital, social and material places that both reflect and transform localised notions of *ilchon* and its relational presence.

At another level, taking 'place' to refer to the situated context of social media use, we saw that the compulsion to be online and to be seen to 'participate' was a highly gendered activity. More female respondents than male were active in camera phone picture taking and sharing, and female users also noted how they felt greater compulsion to take and share pictures. As we saw in Chapter 4 (Shanghai), female users of *Jiepang* felt compelled to take more pictures that provided a unique insight into the location. The content of the images was also changing as users attempted to be more poetic and playful. Rather than providing a 'suspended moment' through an image, the editing highlights the 'multisensory' role of the image (Pink 2011) and further 'emplaces' or embeds the image in a place and in a moment.

As Hjorth notes elsewhere, camera phones have changed photography's relationship between presence, place and memory. With the 'fastforwarding presence' of camera phones, photography is no longer about memory, but is a way of performing the presence of the present (Hjorth 2007b). When camera phone practices migrate into locative media, which is also a social media, they entangle place and sociality in new ways.

Mobile lifestyles: entanglements of the mobile, social, intimate and public

The use of locative social media is changing the everyday ways in which geographic place is overlaid with electronic affordances, emotional affect and social presence, a phenomenon which entangles ourselves as embodied beings in new ways, on a scale not previously possible. As Ingold argues:

> The skin, like the land, is not an impermeable boundary but a permeable zone of intermingling and admixture, where traces can reappear as threads and vice versa. It is not, then, that organisms are entangled in relations. Rather, every organism indeed, every thing is itself an entanglement, a tissue of knots whose constituent strands, as they become tied up with other strands, in other bundles, make up the meshwork.
>
> (2008: 1806)

Against the 'embodied' definitions of place outlined by Edward Casey (1993) Ingold argues:

> Now embodied we may be, but that body, I contend, is not confined or bounded but rather extends as it grows along the multiple paths of its entanglement in the textured world. Thus to be, I would say, is not to be in place but to be along paths. The path, not the place, is the primary

condition of being, or rather of becoming. Places are formed through movement, when a movement along turns into a movement around, precisely as happened in our initial experiment of drawing a circle. Such movement around is place-binding, but it is not place-bound. There could be no places were it not for the comings and goings of human beings and other organisms to and from them, from and to places elsewhere. Places, then, do not so much exist as occur, they are topics rather than objects, stations along ways of life. Instead of saying that living beings exist in places, I would thus prefer to say that places occur along the life paths of beings. Life itself, far from being an interior property of animate objects, is an unfolding of the entire meshwork of paths in which beings are entangled.

(2008: 1808)

Thinking about the convergence between mobile, social and locative sees new forms of entanglements within a broader meshwork. For Ingold (2008) place is a dynamic cartography that is always in a process of becoming: a process that the concept 'network' doesn't fully address. Our various case studies have attempted to map the social entanglements of mobile intimacy in, and across, each of the locations in the region as part of broader entanglements of social publics. Here we can think about the region as an entanglement with both 'effects' and 'affect' (Hjorth and Chan 2009). Drawing on the work of Robert Wilson and Arif Dirlik (1995), we sought to explore place in a way that is both situated and fluid; as a meshwork of entanglements that oscillate across various modalities of sociality that are emotional and geographic, electronic and physical, and social and informational. In our case studies, therefore, the region is mapped through entangling lifestyles that are placed in new ways, and are social in new ways, as people, place and sociality becomes increasingly mobile.

Social media as political places

As the reader has seen, use of social media across the region is divergent, dynamic and evolving, and among the differences that place makes, and that feed into and from the use of social media, are the particular characteristics of places and their politics.

So, while the use of mobile media in a place like Singapore has afforded more people more possibilities to explore political discussion across generational and ethnic divides, social media has not eroded those divides, but has amplified tension around them. Likewise in Seoul, social media has become a tool for political expression, and has also become a tool for locating and punishing people for exercising that political expression. Youkyung Lee provides an example:

Google is not just a search engine for 26-year-old South Korean Ma Han-joo. Nor is Twitter merely a fun way to share pics of K-popstars.

For Ma and thousands of other young conservative activists – many of them teenagers – they are crucial weapons in their campaign to scrub the Internet of North Korean sympathizers.

(2012: n.p.)

Not by coincidence there has been a trend in Korea away from the use of social media for left-wing political purposes towards the use of blogs as spaces for the neo-liberal politics of the personal, in the form of cooking blogs, parenting blogs, hobby blogs and lifestyle blogs. The politics implicit in this form of blogging, sometimes called 'powerblogging', takes several forms. On the one hand, their politics is evident in their avoidance of party politics, and in this sense they are a quietist response to the arrest of bloggers for voicing political opinions (Abell 2009; Hjorth 2011; Wallace 2012). Their politics is also evident in their professionalism. Powerblogs have professional production standards, large publics, and through sponsorship and advertising, power-bloggers can earn significant sums of money.

The politics of this is that it manifests a turn full-circle, away from the blog as an amateur, public alternative to professionally run, corporately owned, mass-media, towards the blog as professional, corporate, mass-media. Pow-erblogging is also implicitly political in another sense. Dong-Hoo Lee (2010) reports on another form of the politics of blogging; that in selling images of 'easy' recipes, these often middle-class 'wife bloggers' create further anxiety for women trying to 'do it all'. Various forms of labour become naturalised within a middle-class notions of gendered domestic labour, selling unrealistic dreams for many Korean women who struggle work/life, home/job balances. Here we also see that social media practices are as gendered as they are stratified by class expectations. Mobile, social and locative media convergence in Seoul in this way highlights the changing relationship between the social, personal and political. As we discussed in Chapter 2, traditional notions of place and intimate relations – *bang* and *ilchon* – are being imported by locative media practices to reflect gendered differences that, in turn, echo broader socio-political shifts. Here we saw how traditional Korean concepts about place and intimacy were being redefined through mobile, social and locative media practices that were both gendered and generational in flavour.

In China the tapestry between the personal and the political is exemplified in the case of microblogging. With media rich microblogs like Weibo, the political and the personal can be interwoven in new ways. For many respondents, Weibo was a more trusted form of news than others, given its relationship to *guanxi* (social networks). For many Generation Y users, experimentation with locative and social media can be read as an expression of the ways in which they grapple with their new forms of economic, political and geographic mobility. While the use of camera phone images through LBS is gendered throughout our various locations, we see the starkest contrast between Seoul and Shanghai. In Shanghai, female respondents are creatively exploring new visualities with little concern for privacy or security issues; alternatively, in Seoul female respondents reported an increasingly unease with the LBS and surveillance – especially in light of the examples of corporate and governmental misuse. In both Shanghai and Seoul, mobile media was the main portal for cross-generational literacy, but unlike Shanghai where LBS was predominantly the preoccupation of Generation Y, in Seoul cross-generational usage (with different expectations and uses) was evident.

In Melbourne the widespread uptake of smartphones increased the fluidity of UCC, the speed with which it moved, and the sheer quantity of social interaction to be managed. We saw how smartphones, as vehicles for cross-generational media convergence, provided new ways for negotiating paradoxes around home and away, work and life, in public and private spaces. In Singapore particularly, cross-generational literacy was important for its many migrants, from students to houseworkers. In all six locations smartphones afforded more possible avenues for engaging home and away and mobility across generational, geographic and socio-economic fields. Concurrently, there was also a convergence between the political and the personal as social media sites like Facebook and Twitter became vehicles for voicing political beliefs. In Singapore and Seoul, this phenomenon saw a wave of conservative backlashes, whereas in places like Manila and Shanghai, microblogging afforded new ways to gain news and beliefs that could momentarily deflect the governmental regimes.

The role of social media in problematising distinctions between amateur and professional, public and private is evident, and through our case studies we revisit the feminist adage that 'the personal is political'. That is, intimacy and the personal are not only entangled into the political through the micronarrative economies of social media, but also, with the convergence of social and mobile media becoming increasingly mundane, the political and personal are becoming increasingly infused. For Lasén (2004), part of social media success has been predicated around its role as an 'affective' technology in which emotional labour becomes an important currency. For Ito et al. (2005), it is the affordances of the personal, portable and pedestrian which have ensured mobile media its central role in contemporary everyday life.

In this light, understanding the various technocultures of intimate publics could be conceptualised as 'emotional capitalism' (Illouz 2007), and mapped in topographies of personalisation (Hjorth 2009b), that are as much emotional and socio-political as they are geographic and spatial. These topographies are marked by the interior, intimate and contingent practices that can both challenge and reinforce notions of labour and intimacy, and under the rubric of cartographies of personalisation, labour takes on various affective modes – a phenomenon accelerated by convergent mobile media practices.

According to *Time* magazine, the 2011 person of the year was the 'protester', and from the 'Arab Spring' to the UK 'BlackBerry' riots and the global 'Occupy' movement, social and mobile media have played important roles. Through these portals people could photograph, write, upload and share almost instantaneously, utilising existent – as well as creating new – intimate, social, and mobile publics and networks. In this phenomenon it is important to put social media like Twitter – and its potential 'revolutionary' ability – in the context of the official and unofficial forms of protesting, political advocacy (Christensen 2011; Segerberg and Lance Bennett 2011) and the intimate turn.

As noted in the case of Tokyo post-3/11 (Chapter 3), mobile media had taken two types of 'intimate' turns in relation to early media. First, we saw how more than one decade on from the use of mobile phones for civic engagement in the Philippines and South Korea, social media has provided new *effective* and *affective* models for capturing, sharing and monumentalising events in a way that encapsulated both collective and individual experiences. New types of intimate citizen journalism have emerged. For Goggin, 'this intimate turn in mobile news' needs to be contextualised with the rise of mobile journalism (mojo) and more general Web 2.0 participatory media. As he notes:

> Surprisingly, the intimate turn also offers new possibilities for how media, their audiences and publics are created and connected – in which large commercial media companies (television broadcasters; Internet and mobile phone companies) and small commercial interests (small software companies; mobile media start-ups; freelance journalists; bloggers) interact in dependent ways with public broadcasters, community media and organised and disorganised citizen media. Its futures, however, are also bound up in the fate of global mobile media, and how these develop, beyond the mobile phone – and what cultural centrality and social significance they garner. Thus small-screen, short-text, little video, mobile news is a ductible, inchoate, incomplete yet powerful form still in the mix.
>
> (2010: 11)

In the case of Tokyo 3/11, the mobile phone was not only a collector, transcriber, translator and disseminator of these horrific events; it also shaped the *affective* nature of the event. It fused the real with the reel. Smartphone photos apps and locative media produced new types of affective economies and, at the same time, rehearsed older analogue media forms (Hjorth 2007b). Placing and presencing were part of these new mobile intimacies, socialities, and networks. For some respondents, the affective nature of mobile media made them feel overwhelmed by the relentless images and comments. Rather than finding comfort, some respondents found that their view of social media changed from participatory to bombardment. Others felt that by holding the mobile media they were holding onto their friends, memories and a sense of being. As also noted, one decade on from the first generation of camera phone studies, new networked and emplaced visualities are producing different types of affective micronarratives.

The further entanglement of the personal and political was articulated by many respondents in the various locations, especially in Manila. As noted previously, social media like Facebook and Twitter extend previously mobile media politics like SMS, and at the same time creates new political affordances and mobile intimacies (Hjorth and Arnold 2011a). In the national party politics of the Philippines, during the 'people power' revolution of 1986, it was the mobile phone that helped coordinate and disseminate messages and actions leading to the demise of President Joseph Estrada. The affordances of mobile SMS in particular made for politically *effective* communications media, and in the weeks that followed the death of ex-President Cory Aquino, it was social media that became important *affective* media for the expression of personal grief.

In the case of Typhoon Onday in 2009, both social media and SMS were appropriated for effective and affective purposes. While the SMS 'people power' revolution extends earlier modes of civic engagement and media (Pertierra 2006; Rafael 2003), it also departs from previous media by providing various forms of visual and aural communication with greater affective personalisation. Moreover, within the intimate, social and networked worlds of SNS, the capacity for politics and its relationship to the personal takes on new forms. Social media, especially via the intimate and personal ('personalised') context of mobile media, proffer great possibilities for understanding the relationship between the personal and political, and understanding the power of identity politics. On social media, political participation is not only outward looking, expressing a desire for social and institutional reconstruction through resistance to other people's projects, or the prosecution of one's own projects, it also turns back and reconstructs affective relations and personal identity in political terms.

The particularities of social media provide new forms of personalisation that are directly linked to one's political context and agendas. While extending the affective technologies trajectory of mobile media such as SMS, social media are also strikingly different in the way they perform networked personalisation. Here we see that the forms of personalisation employed by the user take on new multimedia and networked efficiencies, sketching new types of 'the personal as the political' practices.

For Filipino students, social media provided new ways to mediate the reflexive relationship between their own identity-politics and its personal meaning, as well as political meanings at a collective level. Social media practices like posting on to online discussions allowed them to feel the affect of community, and an effective means to relate to one another individually and collectively through intimate publics, social publics and networks (see Chapter 8). In the case of Twitter, the exercise of political action through these publics and networks has been phenomenal (Christensen 2011; Kwak et al. 2010; Segerberg and Lance Bennett 2011). Twitter provides both the compressed micronarratives and textual economies of SMS but with greater networked and personalisation possibilities, creating new types of convergence between the personal and political. While the case study in Manila demonstrates the most obvious example of the importance of mobile, social and locative media in emergent politics, we argue that all case studies are illustrative of new political media practices. Some cases are more tacit and implicit, whilst others like Manila are more overt. In this topography of contesting intimate, social and mobile publics, mobile media can provide a lens onto new forms of performativity around the personal and the political that, in turn, reflect the uneven narratives for political agency within the contested localities. In sum, mobile media practices epitomise emergent forms of new media agency for better or worse (Nugroho and Syarief 2012).

For Crawford, the particular economies of Twitter provide a way in which news and information is personalised, thus creating new forms of address (2010a, 2010b). As we have identified in this book, contested forms of mobile media convergence are both creating new types of intimate publics, social publics and social networks, at the same time as amplifying existing social and cultural rituals around placing and presencing. During the three years of our case study, media convergence and divergence has continued, especially as cross-generational practices get added to the mix. As transnational (chosen and enforced) mobility grows, mobile media help to negotiate the numerous intimate publics both at home and away. These multiple entanglements provide surprising ways for reimaging the region as it moves into new intimacies that are mobile and immobile, public and private, collective and individual, personal and political. These practices also diverge and converge across space and across the generations.

Social media as family places

With smartphones (or in China, *shanzhai* copies) providing new publics with access to social and locative media, mobile media increasingly becomes a site for cross-generational literacies. The mobile intimacy thus created has multiple meanings and forms of practice. For many of the older generations, the smartphone has provided not just online access, but also access to media that is specifically social. At the beginning of our study many younger people reported that the character and performance of social media was changing as more parents, teachers and even grandparents joined. For some respondents, this created anxiety, especially around different generational interpretations of social media performativity. With the tagging of embarrassing photos, many young people worried that their rites of passage through social media rituals would be diminished.

For some respondents, various forms of social media were used to construct different personas, each with their intimate public, social public or social network. For example, in Shanghai, students often communicated with their parents via QQ and *Happy Farm*, and in many cases the students taught their parents and grandparents to use the media so that they could keep in constant contact while away. At the same time, different social media were deployed for work mates and peers. Here social and mobile media played a key role in helping this new post-eighties generation (*ba ling hou*) negotiate their increasingly diverse forms of mobility such as both home and away (Hjorth and Arnold 2011a).

Young people appropriated LBS games like *Foursquare* (Melbourne, Singapore, Manila and Tokyo), *Jiepang* (Shanghai), *IN*, *SeeOn* and *flags* (Seoul), and through camera phone image sharing created not just new ways for imaging place and intimacy but also new ways of deploying place. In the last year of our study, the number of parents using locative media such as Facebook Places to keep a paternal or maternal eye on their child was also increasing, and in Seoul (Chapter 2), Shanghai (Chapter 4) and Melbourne (Chapter 7) parents were using social media via mobile media to keep a constant watchful eye.

The appropriation of smartphones by new generations made these generational differences clear. As noted above, the first difference can be found in terms of camera phone practices. Increasingly, Generation Y and X respondents were using LBS games to create new social tapestries with intimacy and place that expanded upon previous networked ideas of visuality. These emplaced cartographies were allowing for playful ways to socialise and share. Microblogging was also distinctly generational, with many of the younger respondents but fewer of the older generation using media like Twitter as a form of news or co-present conversation. However, in Shanghai media rich microblog Weibo was being used by different generations as a powerful and subversive way to get messages quickly disseminated.

Transferring calls: placing intimate traces

As a technology that mediates new types of place-making (through LBS games and camera phone image sharing for example) as well as being a tool for rehearsing older, localised notions of sociality, intimacy and place, mobile media is implicated in new forms of social, political and cultural practices. In particular, mobile media – as a series of cross-platform frames, screens and contexts – provides new ways for engaging with place and sociality; or what Richardson and Wilken call 'placing' and 'presencing' (2012), and provides new ways for engaging intimate publics (tightly bound by affect), social publics (bound by affect) and networked publics (not bound by affect).

The Asia-Pacific region is unevenly moving towards a convergence between locative, mobile and social media. With the increasingly common deployment of locative media, mobility, like intimacy, has taken on new geo-imaginaries, most notably as a kind of 'publicness' that is also embedded in localised notions of the private. While some have noted the increasing collapse of contexts in social media spaces, others have remarked upon how mobile media amplify localised notions of place, publics, sociality and intimacy that are about instating boundaries.

These new entanglements are mobile across various modes of presence and engagement as well as numerous subjectivities. As cross-generation media practice gets added to the mix, the relationship between mobile intimacy and intimate publics shifts, and it is this dynamic that we have endeavoured to explore through our various case studies. The six case studies in Seoul, Tokyo, Shanghai, Manila, Singapore and Melbourne have attempted to capture emerging practices as mobile, social and locative media converge unevenly. Through these mobile media practices we have explored how intimacy, mobility and notions of the public are being entangled in new ways across social, cultural, geographic, psychological and emotional terrains. We have considered how these mobile media practices are affording new types of performativity around notions of the personal and political as well as how they amplify existing social and political nuances.

Through the various case studies we have attempted to find new ways to conceptualise the regions' contested and multiple localities. Rather than focusing on social networks per se, we have put forth a more *affective* model, using the notions of intimate publics and social publics in order to accentuate the emotional and interpersonal nature of social media use. As we suggested in Part II, through social media practices we need to understand sociality, intimacy and presence in more complex ways than those signified by social networks. Instead we have offered intimate publics and social publics as ways to envisage the multiple and contested relationships between social media and the lifeworld. This is but a (camera phone) snapshot of things and modes of presence to come.

Bibliography

Ahmed, S. (2004) *Cultural Politics of Emotion*, London: Routledge.

Ahonen, T. and O'Reilly, J. (2007) *Digital Korea*, Mayfair: London.

Ai Weiwei (2012) 'China's Censorship can Never Defeat the Internet', *Guardian*, 16 April, www.guardian.co.uk/commentisfree/libertycentral/2012/apr/16/china-censorship-inter net-freedom (accessed 11 July 2012).

Alhaqbani, B.S. and Fidge, C.J. (2007) 'Access Control Requirements for Processing Electronic Health Records', *Business Process Management Workshops*, 4928, 371–382.

Amodeo, J. and Wentworth, K. (1986) *Being Intimate: a Guide to Successful Relationships*, New York: Penguin.

Anderson, B. (1983) *Imagined Communities: Reflections on the Origin and Spread of Nationalism*, New York: Verso.

Andrejevic, M. (2011) 'Social Network Exploitation', in Z. Paparcharissi (ed.) *A Networked Self*, New York: Routledge, 82–101.

Arendt, H. (undated) 'The Human Condition', *Internet Encyclopedia of Philosophy*, www.iep.utm.edu/arendt/#H4 (accessed 25 May 2012).

Arminen, I. (2006) 'Social Functions of Location in Mobile Telephony', *Personal and Ubiquitous Computing*, 10(5), July: 319–23.

Arnold, M. (2002) 'The Glass Screen', *Information, Communication and Society*, 5(2): 225–36.

——(2003) 'On the Phenomenology of Technology: The "Janus-Faces" of Mobile Phones', *Information & Organization*, 13: 231–56.

——(2007) 'The Concept of Community and the Character of Networks'. *Journal of Community Informatics*, 3(2), www.ci-journal.net/index.php/ciej/article/view/327/355 (accessed 11 July 2012).

——(2002–5) ARC Linkage, *Wired Homes: Communication and Information Technologies in a Residential Setting*.

——(2005–7) ARC Discovery, *The Connected Home: Probing the Effects and Affects of Domesticate Information and Communication Technologies*.

——(2011) 'High-Speed Broadband and Household Media Ecologies', ACCAN grant scheme.

Arnold, M., Shepherd, C. and Gibbs, M. (2006) 'Listening to Things', in L. Stillman and J. Johanson (eds) *Proceedings of the 3rd Prato International Community Informatics Conference: Constructing and Sharing Memory: Community Informatics, Identity and Empowerment*, Prato 2006. Clayton, Monash University: 1–14.

Arrighi, G. (1994) *The Long Twentieth Century: Money, Power, and the Origins of Our Times*, New York: Verso.

——(1996) 'The Rise of East Asia and the Withering Away of the Interstate System', *Journal of World Systems Research*, 2(15), http://jwsr.ucr.edu/archive/vol2/v2_nf.php (accessed 5 July 2007).

——(1998) 'Globalization and the Rise of East Asia', *International Sociology*, 13(1): 59–77.

Arrighi, G., Hamashita, T. and Selden, M. (eds) (2003) *The Resurgence of East Asia: 500, 150 and 50 Year Perspectives*, Asia's Transformations Series, London: Routledge.

Australian Bureau of Statistics (ABS) (2011) 'Australian Social Trends', www.ausstats. abs.gov.au/ausstats/subscriber.nsf/LookupAttach/4102.0Publication14.12.111/$File/4 1020_ASTDec2011.pdf (accessed 11 July 2012).

Bakardjieva, M. (2006) 'Domestication Running Wild: from the moral economy of the household to the mores of a culture', in T. Berker, M. Hartmann, Y. Punie and K. Ward (eds) *Domestication of Media and Technology*, Maidenhead, UK: McGraw-Hill International, 62–78.

——(2009) 'Subactivism: Lifeworld and Politics in the Age of the Internet', *The Information Society*, 25(5): 91–104.

Barabási, A.L. (2002) *Linked: the New Science of Networks*. Cambridge, MA: Perseus.

Barlow, J.P. (1996) 'A Declaration of the Independence of Cyberspace', https://projects. eff.org/~barlow/Declaration-Final.html (accessed 25 May 2012).

Bauman, Z. (2001) *Community. Seeking Safety in an Insecure World*, Cambridge: Cambridge University Press.

——(2003) *Liquid Love*, London: Polity Press.

BBC (2011) 'Fake Apple stores found in Kunming City, China', 23 July, *BBC News*, *www.bbc.co.uk/news/technology-14236786?print=true* (accessed 1 August 2011).

Beck, U. (1999) *What Is Globalization?* Cambridge, UK: Polity Press.

Bell, G. (2005) 'The Age of the Thumb: a Cultural Reading of Mobile Technologies from Asia', in P. Glotz and S. Bertschi (eds) *Thumb Culture: Social Trends and Mobile Phone Use*, Bielefeld: Transcript Verlag, 67–87.

Bell, J. (2009) 'South Korean "Prophet of Doom" Blogger Acquitted', *Wired*, www. wired.com/threatlevel/2009/04/south-korean-pr/ (accessed 11 July 2012).

Bennett, W.L. (2008) 'Changing Citizenship in the Digital Age', in W.L. Bennett (ed.), *Civic Life Online: Learning How Digital Media Can Engage Youth*, Cambridge, MA: MIT Press, 1–24.

Bennett, W.L., Wells, C., and Rank, A. (2009) 'Young Citizens And Civic Learning: Two Paradigms Of Citizenship In The Digital Age', *Citizenship Studies*, 13(2): 105–20.

Berlant, L. (1998) 'Intimacy: A Special Issue', in L. Berlant (ed.) Intimacy. Special issue of *Critical Inquiry*, 24/2 (Winter): 281–88.

Bernard Donals, M. (2001) 'History and Disaster: Witness, Trauma, and the Problem of Writing the Holocaust', CLIO: *A Journal of Literature, History, and the Philosophy of History*, 30, 143–68.

Birdabroad (2011) http://birdabroad.wordpress.com/ (accessed 23 July 2011).

Bolter, J. and Grusin, R. (1999) *Remediation: Understanding New Media*, Cambridge, MA: MIT Press.

Borlow, J.P. (1996) 'A Declaration of the Independence of Cyberspace', https://projects. eff.org/~barlow/Declaration-Final.html (accessed 25 May 2012).

Bourdieu, P. (1984 [1979]) *Distinction: A Social Critique of the Judgment of Taste*, trans. R. Nice, Cambridge, MA: Harvard University Press.

boyd, d. (2007) 'Why Youth (Heart) Social Networked Sites: The Role of Networked Publics in Teenage Social Life', in D. Buckingham (ed.) *MacArthur Foundation Series on Digital Learning – Youth, Identity, and Digital Media Volume*, Cambridge, MA: MIT Press, 119–42.

——(2011) 'Social Networked Sites as Networked Publics: Affordances, Dynamics, and Implications', in Z. Papacharissi (ed.) *A Networked Self: Identity, Community, and Culture on Social Network Sites*, London: Routledge, 39–58.

boyd, d. and Ellison, N. (2008) 'Social Network Sites: Definition, History, and Scholarship', *Journal of Computer-Mediated Communication*, 13(1), article 11, http://jcmc.indiana.edu/vol13/issue1/boyd.ellison.html (accessed 11 July 2012).

boyd, d. and Marwick, A. (2011) 'Social Privacy in Networked Publics: Teens' Attitudes, Practices, and Strategies', work-in-progress paper for discussion at the Privacy Law Scholars Conference, Berkeley, CA, 2 June. Retrieved from: www.danah.org/papers/2011/SocialPrivacyPLSC-Draft.pdf.

Bruns, A. (2005) 'Some exploratory Notes on Produsers and Produsage', *Snurblog*, 3 November, http://snurb.info/index.php?q=node/329 (accessed 11 July 2012).

Bruns, A., Burgess, J., Crawford, K. and Shaw, F. (2012) *#qldfloods and @QPSMedia: Crisis Communication on Twitter in the 2011 South East Queensland Floods*, Brisbane: ARC Centre of Excellence for Creative Industries and Innovation.

Bruns, A. and Jacobs, J. (2006) *Uses of Blogs*, New York; Berlin: Lang.

buddecom (2012) www.budde.com.au (accessed 11 July 2012).

Burgess, J.E. (2008) '"All Your Chocolate Rain Are Belong to Us?" Viral Video, YouTube and the Dynamics of Participatory Culture', in G. Lovink and S. Niedere (eds) *The VideoVortex,* Amsterdam: Institute of Network Cultures, 101–11.

——(2012) 'The iPhone Moment, the Apple Brand, and the Creative Consumer: From "Hackability and Usability" to Cultural Generativity', in L. Hjorth, J. Burgess and I. Richardson (eds) *Studying Mobile Media,*London: Routledge, 28–42.

Buss, D.M. (1994) *The Evolution of Desire: Strategies of Human Mating*, New York: Basic Books.

Butler, J. (1991) *Gender Trouble*, London: Routledge.

Campbell, S.W. and Park, Y.J. (2008) 'Social Implications of Mobile Telephony: The Rise of Personal Communication Society', *Sociology Compass*, 2(2): 371–87.

Caruth, C. (1995) *Trauma: Explorations in Memory*, Baltimore, MD: Johns Hopkins University Press.

Casey, E. (1993) *Getting Back Into Place?: Toward a Renewed Understanding of the Place-World*, Indiana: Indiana University Press.

——(2012) 'Going Wireless: Disengaging the Ethical Life', in R. Wilken and G. Goggin (eds) *Mobile Technology and Place*, New York: Routledge, 175–80.

Castells, M. (2000 [1996]) *The Rise of the Network Society*, New York: John Wiley & Sons.

——(2001) *The Internet Galaxy: Reflections on the Internet, Business and Society*, Oxford: Oxford University Press.

Castells, M., Fernandez-Ardevol, M., Qiu, J.L and Sey, A. (2007) *Mobile Communication and Society: A Global Perspective*, Cambridge, MA: MIT Press.

Chan, D. (2009) 'Beyond the "Great Firewall": The Case of In-game Protests in China', in L. Hjorth and D. Chan (eds) *Gaming Cultures and Place in Asia-Pacific*, London/New York: Routledge, 141–57.

Chee, F. (2005) 'Understanding Korean Experiences of Online Game Hype, Identity, and the Menace of the "Wang-tta"', paper presented at DIGRA 2005 Conference: Changing Views-Worlds in Play, Vancouver, Canada, 16–20 June.

Chen, K.H. (1998) (Ed) *Trajectories: Inter-Asia Cultural Studies?*, London/New York: Routledge.

Cheng, Y. (2010) 'Millions Fall in Love with SNS Games', *China Daily*, www.china daily.com.cn/china/2010–02/12/conten&_;9466051.htm (accessed 29 April 2010).

Chesher, C. (2012) 'Between Image and Information: The iPhone Camera in the History of Photography', in L. Hjorth, J. Burgess and I. Richardson (eds) *Studying Mobile Media: Cultural Technologies, Mobile Communication, and the iPhone*, London/New York: Routledge, 98–117.

China Internet Network Information Center (CNNIC) (2011) *The 28th Statistical Report on Internet Development in China*, www.cnnic.cn/dtygg/dtgg/201107/W020110719521725234632.pdf (accessed 1 December 2011).

Ching, L. (2000) 'Globalizing the Regional, Regionalizing the Global: Mass Culture and Asianism in the Age of Late Capital', *Public Culture*, 12(1): 233–57.

Cho, H.-J. (2000) '"You are entrapped in an imaginary well": The Formation of Subjectivity within Compressed Development – a Feminist Critique of Modernity and Korean Culture', *Inter-Asia Cultural Studies*, 1(1): 49–69.

——(2004) 'Youth, Internet, and Alternative Public Space', paper presented at the Urban Imaginaries: An Asia-Pacific Research Symposium, Lingnan University, Hong Kong, 22–24 May.

——(2009) 'Youth and Technology in Seoul', paper presented at the Inter-Asia Cultural Typhoon Conference, June, Tokyo, 3–5 July.

Choi, J.-H. (2009) 'The City, Self, and Connections: Transyouth and Urban Social Networking in Seoul', in S. Hemelryk Donald, T. Anderson and D. Spry (eds) *Youth, Society and Mobile Media in Asia*, London/New York: Routledge, 88–107.

Christensen, C. (2011) Twitter Revolutions? Addressing Social Media and Dissent, *The Communication Review*, 14(3): 155–57.

Chua, B.H. (ed.) (2000) *Consumption in Asia*, London: Routledge.

——(2003) *Life Is Not Complete Without Shopping: Consumption Culture in Singapore*, Singapore: NUS Press.

——(2006) 'East Asian Pop Culture: Consumer Communities and Politics of the National', paper presented at Cultural Space and the Public Sphere: An International Conference, 15–16 March, Seoul, South Korea.

Chun, W. (2006) *Control and Freedom*, Cambridge, MA: MIT Press.

Cincotta, K. Ashford, K. and K. Michael (2011) 'The New Privacy Predators', *Women's Health*, Nov., www.purehacking.com/sites/default/files/uploads/2011_11&_00&_Australian&_Womens&_Health&_November.pdf (accessed 10 January 2012).

Colman, G. (2010) 'Ethnographic Approaches to Digital Media', *Annual Review of Anthropology*, 39: 1–19.

Cowan, R. (1983) *More Work for Mother: The Ironies of Household Technology from the Open Hearth to the Microwave*, New York: Basic Books.

Crawford, K. (2009) 'Following You: Disciplines of Listening in social Media', *Continuum*, 23(4): 523–35.

——(2010a) 'Listening, Not Lurking: The Neglected Form of Participation', in H. Grief, L. Hjorth and A. Lasén (eds) *Cultures of Participation*, Berlin: Peter Lang.

——(2010b) 'News to Me: Twitter and the Personal Networking of News', in G. Meikle and G. Redden (eds) *News Online: Transformations and Continuities*, London: Palgrave, 115–31.

Crawford, K. and Goggin, G. (2010) 'Moveable Types: The Emergence of Mobile Social Media in Australia', *Media Asia Journal*, 37(4): 224–31.

Crowe, R. and Middleton, C. (2013) 'Women, Smartphones and the Workplace: Pragmatic Realities and Performative Identities', *Feminist Media Studies* (forthcoming).

Damm, J. and Thomas, S. (eds) (2006) *Chinese Cyberspaces Technological Changes and Political Effects*, New York: Routledge.

de Gay, P., Hall, S., Lanes, J., Mackay, H. and K. Negus (eds) (1997) *Doing Cultural Studies: the Story of the Sony Walkman*, London: Sage.

de Souza e Silva, A. and Frith, J. (2012) *Mobile Interfaces in Public Spaces: Locational Privacy, Control, and Urban Sociability*, New York: Routledge.

de Souza e Silva, A. and Hjorth, L. (2009) 'Playful Urban Spaces: A Historical Approach to Mobile Games', *Simulation and Gaming*, 40(5): 602–25.

de Souza e Silva, A and Sutko, D. (2011) 'Theorizing Locative Technologies through Philosophies of the Virtual', *Communication Theory*, 21(1): 23–42.

Deleuze, G. and Guattari, F. (1987) *A Thousand Plateaus*, Minneapolis: University of Minnesota Press.

Derlega, V.J. and Margulis, S.T. (1983) 'Loneliness and Intimate Communication', in D. Perlman and P.C. Cozby (eds), *Social Psychology*, New York: Holt, Rinehart & Winsten, 208–26.

Diamond, L. and M. Plattner (eds) (2012) *Liberation Technology: Social Media and the Struggle for Democracy*. Baltimore, MD: Johns Hopkins University Press.

Dirlik, A. (1999) 'Culture against History? The Politics of East Asian Identity', *Development and Society*, 28 (2): 167–90.

——(2005) 'Asia Pacific Studies in an Age of Global Modernity', *Inter-Asia Cultural Studies*, 6(2): 158–70.

——(2007) 'Global South: Predicament and Promise', *The Global South*, Winter, 1(1): 12–23.

Doel, M. (2000) 'Un-glunking Geography: Spatial Science after Dr Seuss and Gilles Deleuze', in M. Crang and N. Thrift (eds) *Thinking Space*, London: Routledge, 117–35.

Donald, S.H., Keane, M. and Hong, Y. (eds) (2002) *Media in China: Consumption, Content And Crisis*, London: Routledge.

Donald, S., Anderson, T. and Spry, D. (eds) (2009) *Youth, Society and Mobile Media in Asia*, London/New York: Routledge.

Donald, S.H and Spry, D. (2007–9) ARC Linkage, *Mobile Me: Young People, Sociality and the Mobile Phone*.

Dourish, P. and Anderson, K. (2006) 'Collective Information Practice: Exploring Privacy and Security as Social and Cultural Phenomena', *Human-Computer Interaction*, 21(3), 319–42.

Duck, S. (1988) *Relating to Others*, London: Open University Press.

Ehrenreich, B. and Hochschild, A. (eds) (2003) *Global Woman: Nannies, Maids and Sex Workers in the New Economy*, New York: Metropolitan Books.

Ellison, N., Lane, C., Steinfeld, C. and Vitak, J. (2011) 'With a Little Help from My Friends: How Social Network Sites Affect Social Capital Processes', in Z. Paparcharissi (ed.) *A Networked Self*, New York: Routledge, 146–68.

Ellwood-Clayton, B. (2003) 'Virtual Strangers: Young Love and Texting in the Filipino Archipelago of Cyberspace', in K. Nyíri (ed.) *Mobile Democracy: Essays on Society, Self and Politics*, Vienna: Passagen Verlag, 35–45.

eMarketer (2012) *South Korea's Unique Social Media Landscape*, 30 May, www.emarketer.com/Article.aspx?R=1009081&ecid=a6506033675d47f881651943c21c5ed4 (accessed 11 July 1012).

Falkheimer, J. and Jansson, A. (eds) (2006) *Geographies of Communication: The Spatial Turn in Media Studies*, Götenberg: Nordicom.

Farman, J. (2011) *Mobile Interface Theory*, London: Routledge.

Ferguson, J. (2012) 'NBN "black spots" to alienate rural users', *The Australian*, 23 January, www.theaustralian.com.au/business/in-depth/nbn-black-spots-to-alienate-rural-users/story-e6frgaif-1226250794256 (accessed 11 July 1012).

Fisher, H. (2004) *Why We Love: The Nature and Chemistry of Romantic Love*, London: Henry Holt & Co.

Fortunati, L. (2002) 'Italy: Stereotypes, True And False', in J.E. Katz and M. Aakhus (eds) *Perpetual Contact: Mobile Communications, Private Talk, Public Performance*, Cambridge: Cambridge University Press, 42–62.

——(2009) 'Gender and the Mobile Phone', in G. Goggin and L. Hjorth (eds) *Mobile Technologies: from Telecommunications to Media*,London: Routledge, 23–34.

Frizzo, J. and Chow-White, P. (2013) 'There's an App for That', *Feminist Media Studies* (forthcoming).

Fujimoto, K. (2005) 'The Third-Stage Paradigm: Territory Machine from the Girls' Pager Revolution To Mobile Aesthetics', in M. Ito, D. Okabe and M. Matsuda (eds) *Personal, Portable, Pedestrian: Mobile Phones In Japanese Life*, Cambridge, MA: MIT Press, 77–102.

Galloway, A. (2010) 'Mobile Publics and Issues-Based Art and Design', in B. Crow, M. Longford and K. Sawchuk (eds) *The Wireless Spectrum*, Toronto: University of Toronto Press, 63–76.

Gai, B. (2009) 'A World Through the Camera Phone Lens: a Case Study of Beijing Camera Phone Use', *Knowledge, Technology and Policy*, 22: 195–204.

Gazzard, A. (2011) 'Location, Location, Location: Collecting Space and Place in Mobile Media', *Convergence: The International Journal of Research into New Media Technologies*, 17(4): 405–17.

Gergen, K.J. (2002) 'The Challenge of Absent Presence', in J. Katz. and M. Aakhus (eds) *Perpetual Contact*, Cambridge: Cambridge University Press, 227–41.

Gibson, C., Luckman, S. and Brennan-Horley, C. (2012) '(Putting) Mobile Technologies in Their Place: A Geographical Perspective', in R. Wilkenand and G. Goggin (eds) *Mobile Technology and Place*, New York: Routledge, 123–39.

Giddens, A. (1992) *Transformation of Intimacy*, Cambridge, UK: Polity Press.

GMR Marketing (2012) www.gmrmarketing.com (accessed 11 July 1012).

Goffman, E. (1966) *Behavior in Public Places: Notes on the Social Organization of Gatherings*, New York: Simon & Schuster.

——(1969) *The Presentation of Self in Everyday Life*, Harnmondsworth: Penguin Books.

Goggin, G. (2006) *Cell Phone Culture: Mobile Technology in Everyday Life*, London: Routledge.

——(2010) 'The intimate turn of mobile news', in G. Meikle and G. Redden (eds) *News Online: Transformations and Continuities*, London: Palgrave, 99–114.

——(2011) *Global Mobile Media*, London: Routledge.

——(2012) 'Google Phone Rising: The Android and the Politics of Open Source', *Continuum: Journal of Media & Cultural Studies*, 26 (5): 741–52.

Goggin, G and Crawford, K. (2008–10) ARC Discovery *Young, Mobile, Networked: Mobile Media and Youth Culture in Australia*.

Goggin, G. and Hjorth, L. (2009) 'Waiting for Participate: An Introduction', *Communication, Politics & Culture*, 42(2): 1–5.

——(eds) (2009) *Mobile Technologies*, London/New York: Routledge.

Gordon, E. and de Souza e Silva, A. (2011) *Net Locality*, Chichester: John Wiley & Sons Ltd.

——(2012) 'The Urban Dynamics of Net Localities', in R. Wilken and G. Goggin (eds) *Mobile Technology and Place*, New York: Routledge, 89–103.

Grabher, G. (2001) 'Ecologies of Creativity: the Village, the Group, and the Heterarchic Organisation of the British Advertising Industry', *Environment and Planning A*, 33(2): 351 – 374.

Grabher, G., and Stark, D. (1997). *Restructuring Networks in Post-socialism: Legacies, Linkages, and Localities*, Oxford: Oxford University Press.

Green, A. (1994) 'Postmodernism and State Education'. *Journal of Educational Policy*, 9(1): 67–83.

Gregg, M. (2011) *Work's Intimacy*, Cambridge, UK: Polity Press.

Gurstein, M. (2011) 'Up from Facebook: #Occupy—(Re)Building and Empowering Communities', http://gurstein.wordpress.com/2011/10/22/up-from-facebook-occupy%E2%80%94rebuilding-and-empowering-communities (accessed 11 July 1012).

Gye, L. (2007) 'Picture This: The Impact of Mobile Camera Phones on Personal Photographic Practices', *Continuum: Journal of Media & Cultural Studies*, 21(2): 279–88.

Habuchi, I. (2005) 'Accelerated Reflexivity', in M. Ito, D. Okabe and M. Matsuda (eds) *Personal, Portable, Pedestrian: Mobile Phones in Japanese Life*, Cambridge, MA: MIT Press, 165–82.

Hannam, K, Sheller, M. and Urry, J. (2006) 'Editorial: Mobilities, Immobilities and Moorings', *Mobilities*, 1(1): 1–22.

Haraway, D. (1985) 'Manifesto for Cyborgs: Science, Technology, and Socialist Feminism in the 1980s', *Socialist Review*, (80): 65–108.

Harrison, S. and Dourish, P. (1996) 'Re-Place-ing Space: The Roles of Place and Space in Collaborative Systems', in *Proceedings of the ACM Conference on Computer Supported Cooperative Work*, New York: ACM. Retrieved from: www.dourish.com/publications/1996/cscw96-place.pdf (accessed 10 December 2011).

Hayles, N.K. (1999) *How We Became Posthuman: Virtual Bodies in Cybernetics*, Chicago: University of Chicago Press.

Herzfeld, M. (1997) *Cultural Intimacy: Social Poetics in the Nation-State*, London: Routledge.

Hillis, K. (1999) *Digital Sensations Space, Identity, and Embodiment in Virtual Reality*, Minneapolis/London: University of Minnesota Press.

Hjorth, L. (2003) 'Kawaii@keitai', in N. Gottlieb and M. McLelland (eds) *Japanese Cybercultures*, New York: Routledge, 50–59.

——(2005) 'Locating Mobility: Practices of Co-Presence and the Persistence of the Postal Metaphor in SMS/MMS Mobile Phone Customization in Melbourne', *Fibreculture Journal*, 6, http://journal.fibreculture.org/issue6/issue6_hjorth.html (accessed 10 December 2006).

——(2006) 'Fast-Forwarding Present: The rise of Personalization and Customization in Mobile Technologies in Japan', *Southern Review*, 38(3): 23–42.

——(2007a) 'Home and Away: A Case Study of the Use of Cyworld Mini-Hompy by Korean Students Studying in Australia'. *Asian Studies Review*, 31: 397–407.

——(2007b) 'Snapshots of Almost Contact', *Continuum*, 21(2): 227–38.

——(2009a) '*Cybercute@korea:* The Role of Cute Customisation and Gender Performativity in a Case Study of South Korean Virtual Community, Cyworld

Mini-hompy', in Y. Kim (ed.) *Media Consumption and Everyday Life in Asia*, London, Routledge, 203–16.

——(2009b) *Mobile Media in the Asia-Pacific: Gender and the Art of Being Mobile*, London/New York: Routledge.

——(2011a) 'Locating the Online: Creativity and User-created Content in Seoul', *Media International Australia*, 141: 118–27.

——(2011b) 'Mobile@Game Cultures: The Place of Urban Mobile Gaming', *Convergence Journal*, 17(3): 357–71.

——(2012) 'Still Mobile: A Case Study on Mobility, Home and Being Away in Shanghai', in R. Wilken and G. Goggin (eds) *Mobile Technologies and Place*, New York: Routledge.

Hjorth, L. and Arnold, M. (2011a) 'The Game of Being Social: A Case Study of Social Media Games in Shanghai, China', Games and Innovation Seminar, University of Tampere, Finland, 5–6 May, http://gamesandinnovationseminar.word press.com/cfp (accessed 5 October 2012).

——(2011b) 'The Personal and the Political: Social Networking in Manila', *International Journal for Learning and Media*, http://dx.doi.org/10.1162/IJLM_a&_00059 (accessed 11 July 2012).

——(2012) 'Home and Away: A Case Study of Students and Social Media in Shanghai' in P. Law (ed.) *New Connectivities in China: Virtual, Actual and Local Interactions*, Dordrecht: Springer, 171–83.

Hjorth, L., and Chan, D. (2009) *Gaming Cultures and Place in Asia-Pacific*, New York: Routledge, 273–88.

Hjorth, L. and Gu, K. (2012) 'Placing, Emplacing and Embodied Visualities: A Case Study of Smartphone Visuality and Location-based Social Media in Shanghai, China'. *Continuum*, 26(5): 699–713.

Hjorth, L. and Kim, H. (2005) 'Being There and Being Here Gendered Customising of Mobile 3G Practices through a Case Study in Seoul', *Convergence*, 11(2): 49–55.

Hjorth, L. and Kim, K.H.Y. (2011) 'The Mourning After: A Case Study of Social Media in the 3.11 Earthquake Disaster in Japan', *Television & New Media*, 12(6): 552–59.

——(2011b) 'Good Grief: A Case Study of Social Media in Japan Post 3.11', *Digital Creativity Journal*, 22(3): 187–99.

Hjorth, L., Na, B. and Huhh, J.-S. (2009) 'Games of Gender: A Case Study on Females who Play Games in the Seoul, South Korea', in L. Hjorth and D. Chan (eds) *Gaming Cultures and Place in the Asia-Pacific region*, London: Routledge, 273–88.

Hjorth, L. and I. Richardson (2010) 'Playing the Waiting Game: Complicated Notions of (Tele)Presence and Gendered Distraction in Casual Mobile Gaming', in H. Greif, L. Hjorth, A. Lasén and C. Lobet-Maris (eds) *Cultures of Participation: Media Practices, Politics and Literacy*, Berlin: Peter Lang, 111–25.

Hjorth, L., Wilken, R. and Gu, K. (2012) 'Ambient Intimacy: A Case Study of the iPhone, Presence, and Location-based Social Networking in Shanghai, China', in L. Hjorth, J. Burgess and I. Richardson (eds) *Studying Mobile Media: Cultural Technologies, Mobile Communication, and the iPhone*, London/New York: Routledge, 43–62.

Ho, K.C., Kluver, R. and Yang, K.C.C. (2003) *Asia@Com*, London: Routledge.

Hochschild, A.R. (1983) *The Managed Heart: Commercialization of Human Feeling*, Berkeley, CA: University of California Press.

——(2000) 'Global Care Chains and Emotional Surplus Value', in W. Hutton and A. Giddens (eds) *On the Edge: Living with Global Capitalism*, London: Jonathan Cape, 130–46.

——(2001) *The Time Bind: When Work Becomes Home and Home Becomes Work*, Los Angeles, CA: Holt Press.

——(2003) *The Commercialization of Intimate Life: Notes from Home and Work*, Los Angeles, CA: University of California Press.

Horst, H. (2006) 'The Blessings and Burdens of Communication: The Cell Phone in Jamaican Transnational Social Fields', *Global Networks: A Journal of Transnational Affairs*, 6(2): 143–59.

——(2010) 'Aesthetics of the Self: Digital Mediations', in D. Miller (ed.) *Anthropology and Individuals: A Material Culture Approach*, New York/Oxford: Berg Publications, 99–114.

——(2012a) 'Grandmothers, Girlfriends and Big Men: The Gendered Geographies of Jamaican Transnational Communication', in L. Fortunati, R. Pertierra and J. Vincent (eds) *Migration, Diaspora and Information Technology in Global Societies*, London: Routledge, 65–76.

——(2012b) 'New Media Technologies in Everyday Life', in H. Horst and D. Miller (eds) *Digital Anthropology*, New York: Berg Publications, 61–79.

Horst, H. and Miller, D. (2006) *The Cell Phone: An Anthropology of Communication*, New York: Berg Publications.

——(2012) *Digital Anthropology*. Oxford: Berg Publications.

Hughes, C.R. and Wacker, G. (eds) (2003) *China And The Internet: Politics of the Digital Leap Forward*, London: Routledge.

Huhh, J.-S. (2008) 'Culture and business of PC bangs in Korea', *Games & Culture*, 3(1): 26–37.

IDA Singapore (2012) www.ida.gov.sg/Infocomm%20Industry/20060406160952.aspx (accessed 11 July 1012).

Ihde, D. (1979) *Technics and Praxis*, Dordrecht, Holland: D. Reidel Publishing Company.

Illouz, E. (2007) *Cold Intimacies: The Making of Emotional Capitalism*, Cambridge, UK: Polity Press.

Ingold, T. (2008) 'Bindings against Boundaries: Entanglements of Life in an Open World', *Environment and Planning A*, 40: 1796–1810.

Ingram, M. (2010) 'Average Social Gamer is a 43-Year-Old Woman', *GIGAOM*, 17 February. Retrieved from http://gigaom.com/2010/02/17/average-social-gamer-is-a-43-year-old-woman/ (accessed 11 July 1012).

International Labour Office (ILO) (2008) 'Global Employment Trends for Women', www.ilo.org/public/english/employment/strat/global.htm (accessed 2 March 2008).

Ito, M. (2002) 'Mobiles and the Appropriation of Place'. *Receiver* 8, http://academic. evergreen.edu/curricular/evs/readings/itoShort.pdf (accessed 10 December 2010).

——(2005) 'Introduction: Personal, Portable, Pedestrian', in M. Ito, D. Okabe and M. Matsuda (eds) *Personal, Portable, Pedestrian: Mobile Phones in Japanese Life*, Cambridge, MA: MIT Press, 1–16.

Ito, M., Baumer, S., Bittanti, M., boyd, d., Cody, R., Herr-Stephenson, R. and Horst, H. (2010) *Hanging Out, Messing Around, and Geeking Out: Kids Living and Learning with New Media*, Cambridge, MA: MIT Press.

Ito. M., boyd, D. and Horst, H. (2008) *Digital Youth Research*, http://digitalyouth. ischool.berkeley.edu/files/report/digitalyouth-WhitePaper.pdf (accessed 5 January 2012).

Ito, M., and Okabe, D. (2003) 'Camera Phones Changing the Definition Of Picture-Worthy', *Japan Media Review*, www.ojr.org/japan/wireless/1062208524.php (accessed 12 August 2011).

——(2005) 'Intimate Visual Co-Presence', paper presented at Ubicomp, Takanawa Prince Hotel, Tokyo, Japan, 11–14 September, www.ojr.org/japan (accessed 10 December 2011).

——(2006) 'Everyday Contexts of Camera Phone Use: Steps Towards Technosocial Ethnographic Frameworks', in J. Höflich and M. Hartmann (eds) *Mobile Communication in Everyday Life: An Ethnographic View*, Berlin: Frank & Timme, 79–102.

Ito, M., Okabe, D. and Matsuda, M. (eds) (2005) *Personal, Portable, Pedestrian: Mobile Phones in Japanese Life*, Cambridge, MA: MIT Press.

Jamieson, L. (1998) *Intimacy: Personal Relationships in Modern Societies*, Cambridge, UK: Polity Press.

——(1999) 'Intimacy Transformed: A Critical Look at the "Pure Relationship"'. *Sociology*, 33: 477–94.

Katz, J.E. and Aakhus, M. (eds) (2002) *Perpetual Contact: Mobile Communication, Private Talk, Public Performance*, Cambridge: Cambridge University Press.

Kennedy, H.W. (2002) 'Lara Croft: Feminist Icon or Cyberbimbo? On the Limits of Textual Analysis', *Game Studies*, 2(2) www.gamestudies.org/0202/kennedy (accessed 14 January 2011).

Kidder, T. (1989) *The Soul of a New Machine*, New York: Random House.

Kim, D.H. (2005) 'KOREA: Future is Now for Korean Info-tech', *The Korea Herald*, AsiaMedia Archives, www.asiamedia.ucla.edu/article.asp?parentid=25697 (accessed 14 June 2005).

Kim, S.D. (2003) 'The Shaping of New Politics in the Era of Mobile and Cyber Communication', in K. Nyiri (ed.) *Mobile Democracy*, Vienna: Passagen Verlag, 317–26.

Kim, Y. Y.-H. (2012) 'The Landscape of *Keitai Shōsetsu*: Mobile Phones as a Literary Medium among Japanese Youth', *Continuum: Journal of Media & Cultural Studies*, 26(3): 1–11.

Kinsella, S. (1995) 'Cuties in Japan', in L. Skov and B. Moeran (eds) *Women, Media and Consumption in Japan*, Richmond: Curzon Press, 220–54.

Kjeldskov, J., Gibbs, M.R., Vetere, F., Howard, S., Pedell, S., Mecoles, K. and Bunyan, M. (2004) 'Using Cultural Probes to Explore Mediated Intimacy', *Proceedings of OzCHI 2004: Supporting Community Interaction: Possibilities and Challenges*, University of Wollongong, 22–24 November.

Koch, P., Koch, B., Huang, K. and Chen. W. (2009) 'Beauty in the Eye of the QQ Beholder', in G. Goggin and M. McLelland (eds) *Internationalizing Internet Studies*, London: Routledge, 265–284.

Kogawa, T. (1984) 'Beyond Electronic Individualism', *Canadian Journal of Political and Social Theory/Revue Canadienne de Thetorie Politique et Sociale*, 8(3), http://anarchy.translocal.jp/non-japanese/electro.html (accessed 11 July 2012).

Kopomaa, T. (2000) *The City in Your Pocket: Birth of the Mobile Information Society*, Helsinki: Gaudemus.

Kopytoff, I. (1986) 'The Cultural Biography of Things: Commoditization as Process', in A. Appadurai (ed.) *The Social Life of Things. Commodities in Cultural Perspective*, Cambridge: Cambridge University Press, 64–91.

Korean Communications Commission (KCC) (2010) *Statistics of Subscribers of Wired/Wireless Communication Service in Korea*, www.kcc.go.kr/user.do?mode=viewand

page=P02060400anddc=K02060400andboardId=1030andcp=1andboardSeq=29191 (accessed 11 July 2012).

Korea Internet & Security Agency (KISA) (2012) *January Report*, www.kisa.or.kr/eng/main.jsp (accessed 5 November 2011).

Korean Government Website (not dated), http://english.seoul.go.kr/gtk/about/fact.php (accessed 25 May 2012).

Koskinen, I. (2007) 'Managing Banality in Mobile Multimedia', in R. Pertierra (ed.) *The Social Construction and Usage of Communication Technologies: European and Asian Experiences*, Singapore: Singapore University Press, 48–60.

Kumar, K. (1992) 'New Theories of Industrial Society', in P. Brown and H. Lauser (eds) *Education for Economic Survival: From Fordism to post-Fordism?* London/New York: Routledge, 45–75.

——(1995) *From Post-Industrial to Post-Modern Society: New Theories of the Contemporary World*, London: Blackwell Publishing.

Kwak, H.W, C.H Lee and S. Moon (2010) 'What is Twitter, a Social Network or a News Media?', Proceedings of the 19th International World Wide Web (WWW) Conference, Raleigh, NC. 26–30 April.

Lacapra, D. (2001) *Writing History, Writing Trauma*, Baltimore, MD: Johns Hopkins University Press.

Laird, S. (2012) 'This Is Your Mum on Social Media', *Mashable Lifestyle*, http://mashable.com/2012/05/14/mom-social-media (accessed 8 November 2012).

Lally, E. (2002) *At Home with Computers*, New York/Oxford: Berg.

Langlois, G., Elmer, G., McKelvey, F. and Devereaux, Z. (2009) 'Networked Publics: The Double Articulation of Code and Politics on Facebook', *Canadian Journal of Communication*, 34: 415–34.

Larsen, J., Urry, J. and Axhausen, K. (eds) (2006) *Mobilities, Networks and Geographies*, Aldershot: Ashgate.

Lasén, A. (2004) 'Affective Technologies – Emotions and Mobile Phones', *Receiver*, 11, www.receiver.vodafone.com (accessed 11 July 2012).

Lasswell, H.D. (1971) *Propaganda Technique in World War I*, Cambridge, MA: MIT Press.

Latour, B. (1993) *We Have Never Been Modern*, Cambridge, MA: Harvard University Press.

——(2005) *Reassembling the Social: An Introduction to Actor-Network Theory*, New York/Oxford: University Press.

Law, J. (1991) *A Sociology of Monsters: Essays on Power, Technology, and Domination*, London/New York: Routledge.

——(1999) 'Materialities, Spatialities, Globalities', www.lancs.ac.uk/fass/sociology/papers/law-hetherington-materialities-spatialities-globalities.pdf (accessed 11 July 2012).

Law, P.L and Peng, Y. (2006) 'The Use of Mobile Phones Among Migrant Workers in Southern China', in P.-L. Law, L. Fortunati and S. Yang (eds) *New Technologies in Global Societies*, Singapore: World Scientific, 245–58.

Lee, D.-H. (2005) 'Women's Creation of Camera Phone Culture'. *Fibreculture Journal*, 6, www.fibreculture.org/journal/issue6/issue6_donghoo&_;print.html (accessed 3 February 2006).

——(2009a) 'Mobile Snapshots and Private/Public Boundaries', *Knowledge, Technology & Policy*, 22(3): 161–71.

——(2009b) 'Re-imaging urban space: mobility, connectivity, and a sense of place', in G. Goggin and L. Hjorth (eds) *Mobile Technologies*, London/New York: Routledge, 235–51.

——(2010) 'Wife-bloggers', paper presented at Crossroads Conference, Lingnan University, Hong Kong, 17–21 June.

Lee, D.K. (2009) 'Catch the Digital New Tribes, "Chal-na-jok"', *Yonhap News*, http://app.yonhapnews.co.kr/YNA/Basic/article/new_search/YIBW&_showSearchArticle.aspx?searchpart=articleandsearchtext=찰나족andcontents_id=AKR20100417073700003 (accessed 8 December 2009).

Lee, K.S. (2011) 'Interrogating "Digital Korea": Mobile Phone Tracking and the Spatial Expansion of Labour Control', *Media International Australia*, 141: 107–17.

Lee, Y.K. (2012) 'SKorea Teens Flock Online, Snitch Pro-North Posts', *The Age*, 30 May, http://news.theage.com.au/breaking-news-technology/skorea-teens-flock-online-snitch-pronorth-posts-20120530-1zj8t.html (accessed 7 June 2012).

Licoppe, C. (2004) '"Connected" Presence: The Emergence of a New Repertoire for Managing Social Relationships in a Changing Communication Technoscape', *Environment and Planning Design: Society and Space*, 22(1): 135–56.

Lim, S.S. (2006) 'From Cultural to Information Revolution. ICT Domestication by Middle-Class Chinese Families', in T. Berker, M. Hartmann, Y. Punie and K. Ward (eds) *Domestication of Media and Technology*, Maidenhead: McGraw-Hill International, 185–201.

Ling, R. (2004) *The Mobile Connection*, San Francisco: Morgan Kaufmann Publishers.

Ling, R. and Horst, H. (2011) 'Mobile Communication in the Global South', *New Media & Society*, 13: 363–74.

Liu, L.W. (2008) 'Friendster Moves to Asia', *TIME*, www.time.com/time/business/article/0,8599,1707760,00.html. (accessed 11 July 2012).

Lovink, G. (2007) *Zero Comments*, New York: Routledge.

——(2012) *Networks Without a Cause: A Critique of Social Media*, Cambridge, UK: Polity Press.

Lowe, A. (2012) 'There's Ads on Social Media?' *The Age*, 29 May, www.theage.com.au/technology/technology-news/theres-ads-on-social-media-20120528-1zff2.html#ixzz1x6PCSZZj (accessed 11 July 2012).

Luke, R. (2006) 'The Phoneur: Mobile Commerce and the Digital Pedagogies of the Wireless Web', in P. Trifonas (ed.) *Communities of Difference: Culture, Language, Technology*, London: Palgrave, 185–204.

Lumby, C., Green L. and Hartley, J. (2009) CCI report, 'Untangling the Net: The Scope of Content Caught By Mandatory Internet Filtering', www.saferinternetgroup.org/pdfs/lumby.pdf (accessed 11 July 2012).

McKay, D. (2007) 'Sending Dollars Shows Feeling—Emotions and Economies in Filipino Migration', *Mobilities*, 2(2): 175–94.

——(2010) 'On the Face of Facebook: Historical Images and Personhood in Filipino Social Networking', *History and Anthropology*, 21(4): 479–98.

McLean, M. and Voskresenskaya, N. (1992) 'Education Revolution from Above: Thatcher's Britain and Gorbachev's Soviet Union'. *Comparative Education Review*, 36(1): 71–90.

McLelland, M. (2007) 'Socio-Cultural Aspects of Mobile Communication Technologies in Asia and the Pacific: A Discussion of the Recent Literature'. *Continuum*, 21(2): 267–77.

McLelland, M. and Goggin, G. (eds) (2009) *Internationalizing the Internet*, London: Routledge.

McVeigh, B. (2000) 'How Hello Kitty Commodifies the Cute, Cool and Camp: "Consumutopia" Versus "Control" in Japan', *Journal of Material Culture*, 5(2): 291–312.

——(2003) *Nationalisms of Japan: Managing and Mystifying Identity*, Oxford/New York: Rowman & Littlefield.

Maderazo, J.W. (2007) 'Orkut, Friendster Get Second Chance Overseas', *Media Shift*, 15 June, www.pbs.org/mediashift/2007/06/orkut-friendster-get-second-chance-overseas166.html (accessed 11 July 2012).

Madianou, M. and Miller, D. (2011) *Migration and New Media: Transnational Families and Polymedia*, London: Routledge.

Malpas, J. (2012) 'The Place of Mobility: Technology, Connectivity, and Individualization', in R. Wilken and G. Goggin (eds) *Mobile Technology and Place*, New York: Routledge, 26–38.

Mantovani, G. and Riva, G. (1998) '"Real" Presence: How Different Ontologies Generate Different Criteria for Presence, Telepresence and Virtual Presence'. *Presence: Teleoperators and Virtual Environments*, 1(1): 540–50.

Manovich, L. (2001) *The Language of New Media*, Cambridge, MA: MIT Press.

Margaroni, M. and Yiannopoulou, E. (2005) 'Intimate transfers: Introduction', *European Journal of English Studies*, 9(3): 221–28.

Marvin, C. (1988) *When Old Technologies Were New: Thinking About Electric Communication in the Late Nineteenth Century*, Oxford/New York/Toronto: Oxford University Press.

Massey, D. (1993a) 'Power-Geometry and a Progressive Sense of Place', in J. Bird, B. Curtis, T. Putnam, G, Robertson and L. Tickner (eds) *Mapping the Future: Local Cultures, Global Change*, London: Routledge, 59–69.

——(1993b) 'Questions of Locality', *Geography,* 78: 142–49.

Matsuda, M. (2005) 'Discourses of Keitai in Japan', in M. Ito, Okabe, D. and M. Matsuda (eds) *Personal, Portable, Pedestrian: Mobile Phones in Japanese Life*, Cambridge, MA: MIT Press, 19–40.

——(2009) 'Mobile Media and the Transformation of the Family', in G. Goggin and L. Hjorth (eds) *Mobile Technologies*, London/New York: Routledge, 62–72.

Mauss, M. (1954) *The Gift*, London: Kegan Paul.

Mejias, U.A. (2007) 'Networked Proximity: ICTs and the Mediation of Nearness', www.citeulike.org/group/1738/article/1280635 (accessed 30 October 2012).

——(2010) 'The Limits of Networks as Models for Organizing the Social', *New Media and Society*, 12 (4): 603–17.

Michael, M.G. and Michael, K. (2010) 'Towards a State of Überveillence', *IEEE Technology and Society Magazine*, 29(2): 9–16.

Middleton, C. and R. Crowe (2012) 'Women, Smartphones and the Workplace: Pragmatic Realities and Performative Identities', *Feminist Media Studies*, 12(4), 560–569.

Miller, D. (2011) *Tales from Facebook*, Cambridge, UK: Polity Press.

Miller, D. and Slater, D. (2001) *The Internet: An Ethnographic Approach*, London: Berg Publications.

Mills, C.W. (1956) *The Power Elite*, New York: Oxford University Press.

Milne, E. (2004) 'Magic Bits of Paste-board', *M/C Journal,* 7(1), http://journal.media-culture.org.au (accessed 12 October 2008).

——(2011) 'Technologies of Presence: Intimate Absence and Public Privacy', Seminar Series presentation, The Winchester Centre for Global Futures in Art, Design & Media, 3 November, Winchester, UK.

Mitra, A. (1997) 'Virtual Commonality: Looking for India on the Internet', in S. Jones (ed.) *Virtual Culture: Identity and Communication in Cybersociety,* Thousand Oaks, CA: Sage, 55–79.

Monge, P.R. and Contractor, N. S. (2003) *Theories of Communication Networks*, Oxford: Oxford University Press.

Mørk Petersen, S. (2009) 'Common Banality: The Affective Character of Photo Sharing, Everyday Life and Produsage Cultures', PhD thesis, ITU Copenhagen.

Morley, D. (2003) 'What's "Home" Got To So with It?', *European Journal of Cultural Studies*, 6(4): 435–58.

Morris, M. (1988) 'Banality in Cultural Studies', *Discourse*, 10(2): 3–29.

Murphie, A. (2007) 'Mobility, Work and Love', http://researchhub.cofa.unsw.edu.au/ccap/2007/07/10/mobility-work-and-love/ (accessed 30 August 2007).

Nancy, J.L. (1991) *The Inoperative Community*, Minneapolis: University of Minnesota Press.

Newell, P.B. (1995) 'Perspectives on Privacy', *Journal of Environmental Psychology*, 15: 87–104.

Nielsen KoreanClick (2012) *May Report*, www.koreanclick.com (accessed 11 July 2012).

Nisbet, R. (1953) *The Quest for Community: A Study in the Ethics of Order and Freedom*, New York: Oxford University Press.

Nugroho, Y. (2011) 'Citizens in @ction: Social Media in the Contemporary Civic Activism in Indonesia', paper presented to Social Media Cultures: Political Economic Social and Journalistic Challenges Conference, Atma Jaya University Yogyakarta, 22 September.

Nugroho, Y and S. S. Syarief (2012) *Beyond Click-activism? New Media and Political Processes in Contemporary INDONESIA*. Jakarta: Friedrich-Ebert-Stiftung, fesmedia Asia series, www.fes.de/cgi-bin/gbv.cgi?id=09240&ty=pdf (accessed 10 July 2012).

Nye, D. (1994) *American Technological Sublime*, Cambridge, MA: MIT Press.

O, Y.H. (2004) 'KOREA: Prosecution Probes Alleged Tracking of Samsung Workers', *Korean Herald*, 11 August, www.international.ucla.edu/article.asp?parentid=13451 (accessed 25 May 2012).

Okabe, D., and Ito, M. (2003) 'Camera Phones Changing the Definition of Picture-Worthy'. *Japan Media Review*, 28 August, www.ojr.org/japan/wireless/1062208524.php (accessed 7 January 2006).

Olson, P. (2008) 'The World's Hardest-Working Countries', *Forbes*, www.forbes.com/2008/05/21/labor-market-workforce-lead-citizen-cx_po&_0521countries.html (accessed 25 May 2012).

Organisation for Economic Co-operation and Development (OECD) (2012) *Broadband Portal: Press Release*, www.oecd.org/document/4/0,3746,en_2649_34225_4280 0196_1_1_1,00.html (accessed 11 April 2012).

Palmer, D. (2012) 'iPhone Photography: Mediating Visions of Social Space', in L. Hjorth, J. Burgess and I. Richardson (eds) *Studying Mobile Media: Cultural Technologies, Mobile Communication, and the iPhone*, London/New York: Routledge, 85–97.

Papacharissi, Z. (ed.) (2011) *A Networked Self: Identity, Community and Culture on Social Network Sites*, New York: Routledge.

Parreñas, R. (2001) *Servants of Globalization: Women, Migration, and Domestic Work*, Stanford, CA: Stanford University Press.

——(2005) *Children of Global Migration: Transnational Families and Gendered Woes*, Stanford, CA: Stanford University Press.

Pearce, C. (2009) (with Artemesia) *Communities of Play: Emergent Cultures in Multiplayer Games and Virtual Worlds*, Cambridge, MA: MIT Press.

Pertierra, R. (2006) *Transforming Technologies: Altered Selves*, Philippines: De La Salle University Press.

Pfanner, E. (2011) 'Naming Names on the Internet', *New York Times*, 4 September, www.nytimes.com/2011/09/05/technology/naming-names-on-the-internet.html?_r=1 (accessed 25 May 2012).

Philippine Overseas Employment Administration (2007) 'Table 30. Stock Estimate of Overseas Filipinos As of December 2007', www.poea.gov.ph/stats/stats2007.pdf (accessed 11 July 2012).

PhysOrg (2011) http://phys.org/news/2011-06-seoul-free-wifi-areas.html (accessed 25 May 2012).

Pink, S. (2011) 'Sensory Digital Photography: Re-thinking "Moving" and the Image', *Visual Studies*, 26(1): 4–13.

Prior, M. (2006) *Post-Broadcast Democracy: How Media Choice Increases Inequality in Political Involvement and Polarizes Elections*, Cambridge: Cambridge University Press.

Qiu, J.L. (2007) 'The Wireless Leash: Mobile Messaging Service as a Means of Control', *International Journal of Communication*, 1: 74–91.

——(2008) 'Wireless Working-Class ICTs and the Chinese Informational City', *Journal of Urban Technology*, 15(3): 57–77.

——(2009) *Working-Class Network Society: Communication Technology and the Information Have-Less in Urban China*, Cambridge, MA: MIT Press.

——(2012) 'Network Labor: Beyond the Shadow of Foxconn', in L. Hjorth, J. Burgess and I. Richardson (eds) *Studying Mobile Media Cultural Technologies, Mobile Communication, and the iPhone*, London/New York: Routledge, 173–89.

Rafael, V. (2003) 'The Cell Phone and the Crowd: Messianic Politics in the Contemporary Philippines', *Popular Culture*, 15(3): 399–425.

Raiti, G. (2007) 'Mobile Intimacy: Theories on the Economics of Emotion with Examples from Asia', *M/C Journal*, 10(1), http://journal.media-culture.org.au/0703/02-raiti.php (accessed 11 July 2012).

Rheingold, H. (1993 [2000]) *The Virtual Community: Homesteading on the Electronic Frontier*, rev. edn, Cambridge, MA: MIT Press.

——(2002) *Smart Mobs: The Next Social Revolution*, Cambridge, MA: Perseus Books.

——(2008) 'Using Participatory Media and Public Voice to Encourage Civic Engagement', in W.L. Bennett (ed.) *Civic Life Online: Learning How Digital Media Can Engage Youth*, Cambridge, MA: The MIT Press, 97–118.

Richardson, I. (2011) 'The Hybrid Ontology of Mobile Gaming', *Convergence: The International Journal of Research into New Media Technologies*, 17(4): 419–30.

Richardson, I. and R. Wilken (2012) 'Parerga of the Third Screen: Mobile Media, Place, and Presence', in R. Wilken and G. Goggin (eds) *Mobile Technology and Place*, New York: Routledge, 198–212.

Robison, R. and Goodman, D.S.G. (eds) (1996) *The New Rich in Asia: Mobile Phones, McDonalds and Middle-Class Revolution*, London: Routledge.

Rubenstein, D. (2005) 'Cameraphone Photography: The Death of the Camera and the Arrival of Visible Speech', *The Issues in Contemporary Culture and Aesthetics*, 1: 113–18.

Rubinstein, D and Sluis, K. (2008) 'A Life More Photographic: Mapping the Networked Image', *Photographies*, 1(1): 9–28.

Rybczynski, W. (1986) *Home: A Short History of an Idea*, New York: Viking.

Salazar, T. (2008) 'Filipinos Are Prolific, Go and Multiply', *Philippine Daily Inquirer*, A1, A10, 22 June. http://newsinfo.inquirer.net/inquirerheadlines/nation/view/20080622-144061/Filipinos-are-prolific-go-and-Multiply (accessed 11 July 2012).

Sato, K.(1994) *Fûke no seisan, fûke no kaihou: media no arkeoloji. [Production of landscape, emancipation of landscape: Archaeology of media]*, Tokyo: Kodansha.

Sawhney, H. (2004) 'Mobile Communication: New Technologies and Old Archetypes', in A. Lin (ed.) *Proceedings of the Mobile Communication and Asian Modernities I Conference*, City University of Hong Kong, 7–8 June, http://com.cityu.edu.hk/mobile_comm/programme.html (accessed 10 October 2010).

——(2005) 'Wi-Fi Networks and the Reorganisation of Wireline–Wireless Relationship', in R. Ling and P.E. Pederson (eds) *Mobile Communications: Re-Negotiation of the Social Sphere*, London: Springer, 45–61.

Schroeder, F. and Rebelo, P. (2009), 'Sounding the Network', *Leonardo Electronic Almanac*, 16(4–5): 1–10.

Sconce, J. (2000) *Haunted Media: Electronic Presence from Telegraphy to Television*, Durham, NC/London: Duke University Press.

Segerberg, A and W.L. Bennett (2011) 'Social Media and the Organization of Collective Action: Using Twitter to Explore the Ecologies of Two Climate Change Protests', *The Communication Review*, 14 (3): 197–215.

SEO Sydney Blog (2009) 'Facebook Australia: User Statistics & Demographics', www.seosydneyblog.com/2009/08/facebook-australia-user-statistics.html (accessed 11 July 2012).

Sexton, R.E. and Sexton, V.S. (1982) 'Intimacy: a historical perspective', in M. Fisher and G. Stricker (eds) *Intimacy*, New York: Plenum Press, 1–20.

Sheller, M. (2004) 'Mobile Publics: Beyond the Networked Perspective', *Environment and Planning D: Society and Space*, 22: 39–52.

Sheller, M. and Urry, J. (2003) Mobile Transformations of the 'Public' and 'Private' Life, *Theory, Culture & Society*, 20(3): 107–25.

Shirky, C. (2008) 'Here Comes Everybody', The Aspen Ideas Festival, Aspen, CO, 30 June–8 July, www.channels.com/episodes/show/12772338/Clay-Shirky-Here-Comes-Everybody?page=5.

Silverstone, R. (1994) *Television and Everyday Life*, London/New York: Routledge.

Silverstone, R. and L. Haddon (1996) 'Design and Domestication of Information and Communication Technologies: Technical Change and Everyday life', in R. Silverstone and R. Mansell (eds) *Communication by Design: The Politics of Information and Communication Technologies*, Oxford: Oxford University Press, 44–74.

Silverstone, R. and Hirsch, E. (eds) (1992) *Consuming Technologies*, London: Routledge.

Silverstone, R., Hirsch, E. and Morley, D. (1992) 'Information and Communication Technologies and the Moral Economy of the Household', in R. Silverstone and E. Hirsch (eds) *Consuming Technologies: Media and Information in Domestic Spaces*, London: Routledge, 15–31.

Tai, Z. (2012 [2006]) *The Internet in China: Cyberspace and Civil Society*, New York: Routledge.

Takano, H. (1995) *GO EQUAKE – Pasokon netoga tsutaeta hanshin daishinsai no sinsou. [GO EQUAKE: The reality of Hanshin earthquake from PC net]*, Tokyo: Shodensya.

Taylor, A. and Harper, R. (2002) 'Age-Old Practices in the "New World": A Study of Gift-Giving Between Teenage Mobile Phone Users', in *Changing Our World, Changing Ourselves*, Proceedings of the *SIGCHI* Conference on Human Factors in Computing Systems, Minneapolis, MN: 439–46.

——(2003) 'The Gift Of Gab? A Design Oriented Sociology of Young People's Use of Mobiles', *Journal of Computer Supported Cooperative Work*, 12: 267–96.

Terranova, T. (2000) 'Free Labour: Producing Culture for the Digital Economy', *Social Text*, 63(18): 33–57.

——(2004) *Network Culture: Politics for the Information Age*, London: Pluto Press.

Thomas, M. and Lim, S.S. (2011) 'On Maids and Mobile Phones: ICT Use by Female Migrant Workers in Singapore and Its Policy Implications', in J. Katz (ed.) *Mobile Communication: Dimensions of Social Policy*, New Brunswick, NJ: Transaction, 175–90.

Thompson, E. (2009) 'Mobile Phones, Communities and Social Networks Among Foreign Workers in Singapore', *Global Networks*, 9(3): 359–80.

Turkle, S. (2008) (eds) *The Inner History of Devices*, Cambridge, MA: MIT Press.

——(2011) *Alone Together: Why We Expect More from Technology and Less from Each Other*, New York: Basic Books.

Turner, B. (2007) 'The Enclave Society: Towards a Sociology of Immobility', *European Journal of Social Theory*, 10(2): 287–303.

Universal McCann Report (2008) www.krishnade.com/blog/2008/universal-mccann-power-to-the-people-wave-3-report (accessed 11 July 2012).

——(2009)   www.viralblog.com/research/universal-mccann-launches-wave-4-report/ (accessed 11 July 2012).

Urry, J. (2000) *Sociology Beyond Societies: Mobilities for the Twenty-First Century*, London: Routledge.

——(2002) 'Mobility and Proximity', *Sociology*, 36(2): 255–74.

Van Den Abbeele, G. (1991) 'Introduction', in Miami Theory Collective (ed.) *Community at Loose Ends*, Minneapolis, MN: University of Minnesota Press, ix–xxvi.

Van Dijk, J. (1999) *The Network Society: Social Aspects of New Media*, London: Sage

Villi, M. (2010) 'Visual Mobile Communication: Camera Phone Photo Messages as Ritual Communication and Mediated Presence', academic dissertation, Aalto University School of Art and Design, Helsinki.

Wajcman, J., Bittman, M. and Brown, J. (2009) 'Intimate Connections: The Impact of the Mobile phone on Work Life Boundaries', in G. Goggin and L. Hjorth (eds) *Mobile Technologies*, London/New York: Routledge, 9–22.

Wallace, R. (2012) 'Free Speech Fight over Arrest of Seoul Satirist', *The Weekend Australian*, 7–8 April, 9.

Wallis, C. (2011) '(Im)Mobile Mobility: Marginal Youth and Mobile Phones in Beijing', in R. Ling and S.W. Campbell (eds) *Mobile Communication: Bringing Us Together and Tearing Us Apart*, New Brunswick, NJ: Transaction Books, 61–81.

Warner, M. (2002) 'Publics and Counterpublics'. *Public Culture*, 14(1): 49–90.

Wellman, B., and Haythornthwaite, C.A. (eds) (2002) *The Internet in Everyday Life*, Oxford: Blackwell.

Wellman, B., Quan-Haase, A., Boase, J., Chen, W., Hampton, K., de Diaz, I. and Miyata, K. (2003) 'The Social Affordances of the Internet for Networked Individualism', *Journal of Computer Mediated Communication*, 8(3), http://jcmc.indiana.edu/vol8/issue3/wellman.html.

West, D.M. (2006). *Global e-government*, Providence, RI: Center for Public Policy, Brown University.

Wilding, R (2006) '"Virtual" Intimacies? Families Communicating across Transnational Contexts', *Global Networks: A Journal of Transnational Affairs*, 6(2): 125–42.

Wilken, R. (2011) *Teletechnologies, Place, and Community*, New York/London: Routledge.

Wilken, R. and Goggin, G. (eds) (2012a) *Mobile Technology and Place*, New York: Routledge.

——(2012b) 'Mobilizing Place: Conceptual Currents and Controversies', in R. Wilken and G. Goggin (eds) *Mobile Technology and Place*, New York: Routledge, 3–25.

Wilson, J. (2011). 'Playing with Politics: Political fans and Twitter Faking in Post-broadcast Democracy', *Convergence*, 17(4), 445–61.

Wilson, R. (2000) 'Imagining 'Asia-Pacific': Forgetting Politics and Colonialism in the Magical Waters of the Pacific. An Americanist Critique', *Cultural Studies*, 14(3/4): 562–92.

Wilson, R. and Dirlik, A. (eds) (1995) *Asia/Pacific As Space Of Cultural Production*, Durham, NC: Duke University Press.

Wolfreys, J. (2002) 'Trauma, Testimony, Criticism: Witnessing, Memory and Responsibility', in J. Wolfreys (ed.) *Introducing Criticism at the 21st century*, Edinburgh: Edinburgh University Press.

Yoon, K. (2006) 'The Making of Neo-Confucian Cyberkids: Representations of Young Mobile Phone Users in South Korea', *New Media & Society*, 8(5): 753–71.

Yu, H. (2007) 'Blogging Everyday Life in Chinese Internet Culture', *Asian Studies Review,* 31(4): 423–33.

Zittrain, J. (2008) *The Future of the Internet – and How to Stop It*, New Haven, CT: Yale University Press.

Zumbrun, J. (2008) 'In Pictures: World's Most Economically Powerful Cities'. *Forbes.*, www.forbes.com/2008/07/15/economic-growth-gdp-biz-cx_jz_0715powercities_slide_7.html?thisSpeed=15000 (accessed 25 May 2012).

Index

2ch (*ni channeru*) 15, 39
3/11: demonstrations after 3; and
   locative media 1; and mobile intimacy
   18; new media in 40, 45, 173;
   vignettes of 38–39

Actor Network Theory 139
affect, textures of 51
affective behaviour, in intimate relations
   75
affective cultures 43–46, 51
affective engagement 70
affective personalization 13
affective power 49
affective technologies 9, 142–43
affective value 125
agency, personal 129
Ai Weiwei 56–57
almost contact 153
alone together 106
Amazon 112, 130
analogue genres 155
Anderson, Benedict 132
Android phones 59, 112–13, 152
Angry Birds 108
Anomalous Female Teenage
   Handwriting 42
anonymity, eradication of 27
anti-Uighur chauvinism 121
Apple products 57, 109–11, 140
appropriation, selective 140, 166
Aquino, Cory 122, 124, 174
Arab Spring 3, 6, 13, 91, 172
Asia, consuming 14
Asia-Pacific region: being online in
   12–13; media convergence in 176;
   media practices in 152, 163–65;
   mobile intimacy in 141, 145; multiple
   localities in 177; social mobility in 146;

social performances in 4–5; use of
   new media in 2–3, 6, 8, 16; use of
   term 14–15
Australia: family media usage in 105;
   mobile media in 104, 106;
   smartphones in 18, 106, 115
authenticity: and multiple publics 82;
   personal 78; and social media 81,
   83
authority, and community 120–21
auto-nostalgia 155

Bahrain 6
ba ling hou: characteristics of 53–54; and
   Jiepang 18, 53, 55–56, 60, 66–67, 157;
   and locative media 2, 18, 161;
   mobility of 86, 176; online media use
   of 53
Balloonimals 108
banality: aesthetic of 32; and camera
   phone images 152; common 32, 154
bang: conveying sense of 34; and *ilchon*
   28–30, 32, 37, 158, 171; and intimacy
   30; and LBS 34–35; use of term 18
behaviours, intimate 129
Beijing 59, 153
being, sense of 144
binaries: convergences 141; co-present
   106
BlackBerry 107, 111, 172
Blast Theory 59
blogging, and politics 6, 171
body: coupled to digital information
   149; as cultured sign 144
body–technology relations 168
boundaries: breaches of 126; cultural
   architecture of 141; erosion of 101,
   105
boundary-making exercises 97, 104, 107

Milton Keynes UK
Ingram Content Group UK Ltd.
UKHW020324111024
449327UK00036B/123